Pictorial History of

THE MAFIA

DON MACLEAN

PYRAMID BOOKS ▲ NEW YORK

PICTORIAL HISTORY OF THE MAFIA
A PYRAMID BOOK

Photos courtesy of UPI.

Pyramid edition published December 1974

ISBN 0-515-03472-X

Library of Congress Catalog Card Number: 74-24655

Printed in the United States of America

Pyramid Books are published by Pyramid Communications, Inc. Its trademarks, consisting of the word "Pyramid" and the portrayal of a pyramid, are registered in the United States Patent Office.

Pyramid Communications, Inc., 919 Third Avenue, New York, N.Y. 10022

(graphic design by anthony basile)

AMONG GANGLAND'S ELITE:

ALBERT ANASTASIA. Smuggled into the United States in 1917, Anaştasia became the big boss of Murder, Inc. Strangely enough, he was always acquitted of murder, but finally went to his reward while sitting in a barber chair in 1957.

JOSEPH COLUMBO. Boss of a New York family, Joe ran into trouble over his income tax in 1970, but the charges were conveniently dropped. He was very outspoken about "slurs" being cast on Italian-Americans and even aired his righteous indignation on a TV show. Possibly all that publicity was the reason for his being shot in 1971.

MIKE GENNA. One of the "Terrible Gennas," Mike was a power in Chicago where his family ran a $5 million business in tenement distilleries. Unfortunately, he was shot in a fight with police, but he managed to give a parting kick in the face to the ambulance attendant before dying.

LUCKY LUCIANO. One of the organizers of the National Crime Syndicate in 1929, Lucky was jailed by Thomas E. Dewey. But Lucky was a great American patriot. From his jail cell during World War II, he helped out the United States by preventing sabotage on the New York docks. Another notable achievement—he died in his bed of natural causes.

DION O'BANNION. Youthful altar boy and choir boy, O'Bannion graduated to a bootleg career with honors. Although he was accused of 25 murders, he was never convicted. After the Genna gang gunned him down, O'Bannion was planted in a $10,000 coffin, with $50,000 in flowers, including a basket of roses with a card, "From Al."

JOHN SCALISE. Chicago gangster and triggerman, Scalise managed to get out of a murder rap even though two policemen had been killed. However, as a dinner guest of Al Capone, he didn't fare so well. Along with two other guests, he was permanently retired from this world after an excellent meal.

TABLE OF CONTENTS

Pictorial History of

THE MAFIA

INTRODUCTION

In a biography of Al Capone, written in 1930, F.D. Pasley tells the story of Amato Gasperi, a barber whose shop was a favorite hangout for Chicago's leading hoodlums. Each had his own private shaving mug there, with his name in gilt Spencerian lettering. Whenever one of his clients would suffer the fate so common to that peculiar profession, Mr. Gasperi would sigh and take the victim's mug down from the shelf, paint a black cross beside the name and place the mug back with the others. There were black crosses on 19 shaving mugs when Pasley's book was written; many more were to follow.

It was all rather bewildering to Mr. Gasperi and his old-country intellect. Why were his best customers always killing each other here in the land of opportunity?

"Such nize boys," he would lament, sadly indicating the mugs with a sweep of his hand. "Such nize boys."

This book is a history of "such nize boys." It begins in ancient Sicily and it ends in a New Jersey dump. And the bodies of "such nize boys," shot, garrotted, stabbed, drowned, poisoned and burned alive litter the path. As well as in Chicago, there have been and are "such nize boys" in New York, Detroit, Los Angeles, Miami—in fact, in every big American city.

Mr. Gasperi's barbershop was in Chicago, but imagine, if you can, that it could have served a national criminal clientele, between 1920 and today. It would have needed some 10,000 shaving mugs, of which 3,500 would have borne black crosses after the names of so many customers, all "such nize boys."

--- Don Maclean ---

Joe Adonis, of Brooklyn, is being led into a New Jersey court-room to answer gambling charges.

The same man, now smiling broadly, has just been released from prison after serving 26 months.

A snarling Johnny Dio is photographed outside of a New York Federal courthouse in 1958 while standing trial on tax charges.

Dio in a more friendly mood.

Joe Adonis, a New York mobster, as he learns that he is to be deported to his native Italy. In 1953, the then—Attorney General, Herbert Brownell, Jr., had ordered a hearing on the Government's charge that Adonis had entered the country illegally.

Johnny Dio is shown being sworn in before his testimony at the Senate Labor Rackets Committee. Administering the oath is Sen. John L. McClellan. Seated, to the immediate right of the Senator, are Committee Counsel Robert Kennedy, and his brother, Sen. John F. Kennedy. On April 5, 1956, the labor

newspaper columnist, Victor Riesel, was blinded for life when someone threw acid in his face as he emerged from a New York restaurant. Police later said that Johnny Dio was the "mastermind" of the attack, as Riesel had been exposing New York labor rackets in his column.

In 1957, New York racketeer Johnny Dio testified before the Senate Labor Rackets Committee. He invoked the Fifth Amendment 140 times.

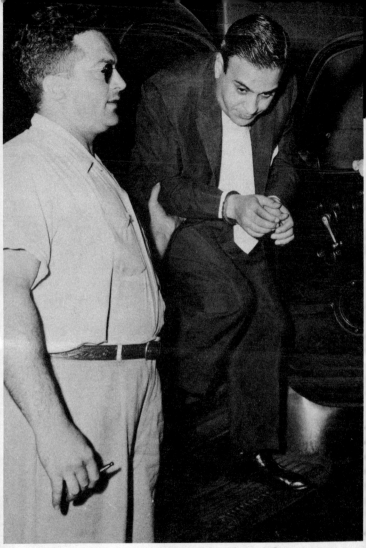

Dio, handcuffed, is being hauled into a Federal Court on conspiracy charges.

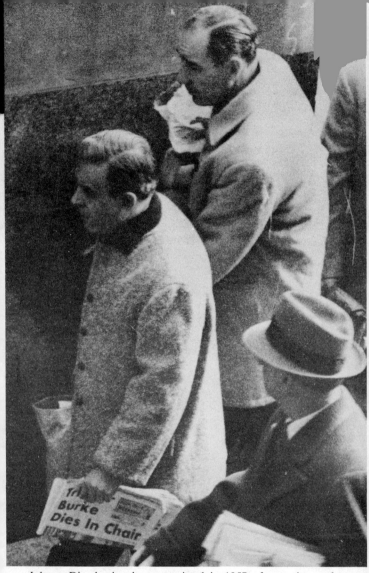

Johnny Dio, having been convicted in 1957 of extortion and conspiracy in the New York labor rackets, is marched off to begin a 15 to 30 year prison sentence.

New Jersey boss Abner (Longy) Zwillman seems to be contemplating his future. In 1956, Zwillman was charged with tax evasion, but the trial ended in a hung jury. Federal authorities remained after him, though, until 1959, when Zwillman was found, an apparent suicide, hanging from a rafter in the basement of his stately West Orange, N.J. home.

Police think he may have been despondent over his legal problems. In any case, Zwillman had a long run, having started as a bootlegger during Prohibition.

Over the years, police and the FBI have found that weddings often provide rare opportunities to photograph certain Mafia figures. At left, Anthony "Big Tuna" Accardo, reportedly the gang boss of Chicago, arrives at a Chicago church in 1961 to attend the wedding of his son.

This is the man from whom Accardo may have inherited his position and the man who helped organize crime in the first place—Al Capone. Here, Capone is shown after attending his son's wedding in Miami.

The smiling face of notorious Chicago hoodlum Charles (Cherry Nose) Gioe, an old Capone associate, following his release from prison after doing a 10-year stretch for practicing extortion on the movie industry. While still on parole, in 1950, Gioe was questioned by Chicago police in connection with the murder of Police Lieutenant William Drury.

A Gioe associate, Hyman Weisman, 39, turned up two days after Gioe's assassination, saying that he was with Gioe, getting into Gioe's car, when shooting began. Weisman said he ran away, and didn't see who shot Gioe.

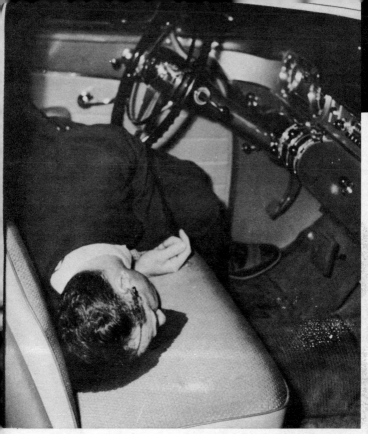

Cherry Nose Gioe lies slumped dead behind the wheel of his car, shot through the head. The car was parked in front of the restaurant he owned with two partners.

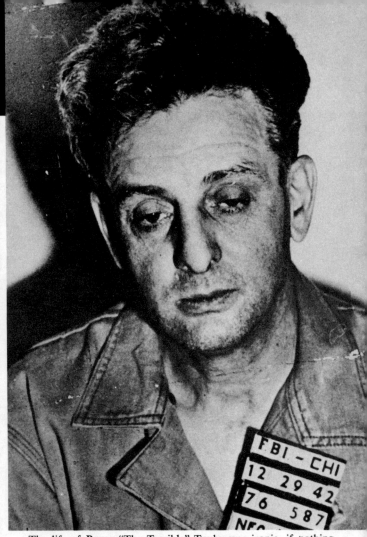

The life of Roger "The Terrible" Touhy was ironic, if nothing else. Touhy, seen here in his prison garb, ran a gang during Prohibition that operated in the Mid-West. In 1934, he was sentenced to life imprisonment for the kidnapping of John "Jake the Barber" Factor, a crime for which he maintained he'd been framed by his underworld rivals.

Eight years later, Touhy and Basil Banghart made headlines in a sensational prison break. Freedom lasted but a few days, as Touhy and Banghart were recaptured by the FBI in the Chicago apartment building pictured here.

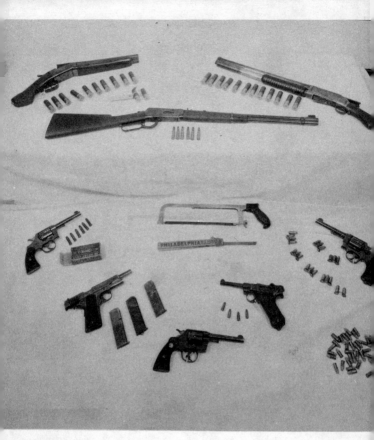

When Touhy and Banghart were taken, they were found with this arsenal in their room.

Touhy's next bid for freedom came 12 years later, in 1954, when he was briefly released pending an appeal of his sentence. However, he was turned down and spent only two days outside the walls.

Roger "The Terrible" Touhy's final release from prison came in 1959, after he'd served 25 years for a kidnapping he'd always claimed was a phony rap. He's greeted by his wife, Clara, on Nov. 24, 1959, the day the prison dors opened. The same day, Touhy plugs his book, "The Stolen Years."

33

On Dec. 17, 1959, Touhy, age 61, is found bleeding to death on a Chicago sidewalk after he and a companion had been

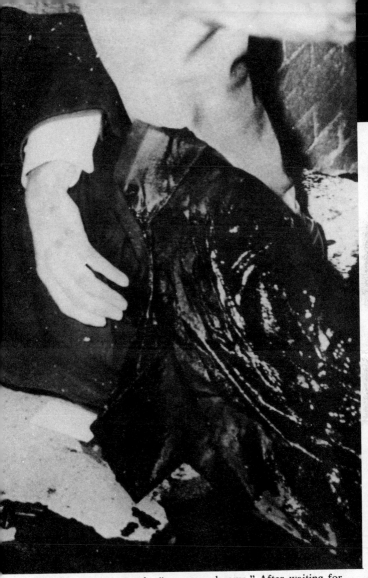

blasted with shotguns by "persons unknown." After waiting for 25 years, Touhy's taste of freedom lasted but 24 days.

Big Jim Colosimo, the Chicago gambling club operator who brought his nephew, Johnny Torrio, to Chicago from New York, is shown with his bride, Dale Winter, in 1920. He is to live but three years longer, when Torrio and Al Capone have him killed.

The facade of the Everleigh Sisters Club, the fanciest brothel in Chicago.

A view of the fantastic Moorish Music Room of the Everleigh Sisters Club, of Chicago's early 1900's.

Johnny Torrio, late of New York, who took over one of Chicago's largest gangs upon the slaying of his mentor, Big Jim Colosimo.

Torrio's arch rival, the gangster Dion O'Bannion, who was soon to be assassinated in his flower shop.

The closely-knit Genna family, at dinner. The Gennas had Chicago's largest moonshine liquor business and one that was much envied by the Torrio-Capone and O'Bannion gangs. Police suspect that it was the Gennas who got O'Bannion. The men seated around the table, left to right, are brothers Sam, Angelo, Peter, Tony and Jim Genna.

At top, left, is Vincent "The Schemer" Drucci, one of the top guns of the Bugs Moran gang, in Chicago. Upper right: Hymie Weiss, Dion O'Bannion's second in command and his chief avenger. The Capone gang eventually cut Weiss down in a hail of bullets. Lower left: An early photograph of Al Capone, when he was still in partnership with Torrio. Lower right: O'Bannion, in a picture taken before Prohibition made him a success, and he started dressing like a dude.

The Montmartre Club was one of Capone's many joints. This picture was taken just after it had been raided by Federal Revenue agents.

Capone's last establishment, his emperor-sized masoleum in Chicago. Capone died of a diseased brain in 1947.

A typical Prohibition era speakeasy, which, from the inside looked like any bar, but which from the outside might resemble a laundry or a shoe shine shop. The police were seldom fooled, but, in most cases, they turned a blind eye.

Revenue Agents Izzy Einstein and Moe Smith have just raided an illegal distillery on Washington Street, in New York. This particular distillery even printed its own fake labels of well-known "imported" brands.

CHAPTER ONE
The Crime Network Today

The American public hardly needs films like *The Godfather* to give it a glimpse of organized crime. Almost daily somewhere in the United States a gang leader is shot through the head or a minor hoodlum is rubbed out. If you'd been eating in a restaurant in New York's Little Italy one April night in 1972 you'd have had to duck the bullets as the Colombo gang finally caught up with Joey Gallo, the Brooklyn mobster. At this writing at least 21 men have been killed in New York's latest gang war.

In Chicago's most recent crime feud, 46 hoodlums wiped each other out over a two-year period. They bomb each other in Detroit, blast away in Cleveland, and sling lead all over New Orleans. At the 1972 funeral of slain New York gang leader Tommy Eboli, one of the mourners, a blonde woman in a polka-dot dress said, "And now somebody will take his place, until he's wiped out. That's the kind of life they seem to want."

It may not be what gang leaders want, but that's the way it seems to work out. An organization, even a criminal one, must have a leader. And when utterly ruthless men struggle for power, people get killed.

Not all of gangland's killings are over the leadership of a mob or control of a city's crime, of course. Some are merely considered enforcement exercises, or as example-setting that should be helpful in maintaining discipline in the future. Nor is power the only prize; the struggle is also over money—an incredible amount of money.

Organized crime is the biggest and most successful business on earth. It is estimated that every year it grosses more than the entire automobile industry, and certainly its profits are higher. Crime is today are considered standard operating procedure by gangs in cities across the nation. By taking over one union, Lepke practically ran the garment business in New York, and New York at the time produced 60 percent of the clothing made in the United States. Lepke's "take" added about $1,000,000 per year to the price people paid for clothes that eventually reached the shops. By controlling drivers' unions, Lepke added to the price of bread. He took money from the businessmen who hired workers and from the wages of the workers they hired. During his trial, it was estimated that $10,000,000 per year from a variety of sources went into Lepke's pockets. We all paid it to Lepke, yet he earned it for no other reason than because he had guns.

Today, most of the manipulating, enforcing, collecting, and smuggling in organized crime is handled by a "staff" of approximately 100,000 crooks, big-time and petty. These troops are in organized crime, but they do not run it. The high command consists of about 5,000 Sicilians and/or Italians, who belong to 24 "families" spread from coast to coast. (There are a few non-Sicilian/Italians, such as Meyer Lansky, in the high command, but they are the exception.) Each "family" has a "don," whose word is law.

To settle disputes and arrange cooperative ventures, the 24 families have a commission, which consists of nine elected members. Until recently, when New York's Don Carlo Gambino started rubbing out rival New York gang leaders, five of the nine men on the National Commission were from the New York area.

Nobody is surprised any more when a politician is exposed as having Mafia connections. Fortunately, when this fact becomes too well known, he usually loses the next election. But not always.

In Donald R. Cressey's book, *Theft of the Nation*, he quotes a retiring police official as saying, "organized crime will put a man in the White House some day, and he won't know it until they hand him the bill." Cressey adds, "*We* won't know it until they hand *us* the bill."

The nationwide take from organized crime runs into the billions. The profits from illegal off-track betting alone are estimated to be about *$20 billion annually*. In one year New York State lost $50 million in revenue from the sale of untaxed, smuggled cigarettes. The income from heroin, prostitution, gambling houses, extortion, insurance swindles, labor racketeering and a host of other enter-the only big business that daily touches the lives of most of us —whether we realize it or not.

The bookie down on the corner is part of organized crime; so is the elevator boy who takes numbers bets. The neighborhood beauty parlor, the laundry, the liquor store and thousands of other legitimate businesses, may be owned by criminals. Buying an honest business is the approved way for the modern mobster to put his illegal profits to work. It "washes" his money, and it helps him to explain his high standard of living to the tax man.

In the 1,622,600 feet of tapes made by a secret bug in the headquarters of a New York gang, there is evidence that organized crime owns and operates at least 200 otherwise legitimate businesses in the New York area. Brooklyn District Attorney Eugene Gold, whose plainclothesmen planted the listening device in the now-famous Mafia headquarters in a Brooklyn junk yard, said that New York's mobs own almost every kind of firm. Florist shops, garages, funeral parlors—you name it.

Elsewhere in the United States, according to the report of the President's Commission on Law Enforcement, the mobs own jukebox companies, cigarette vending machines, restaurants, hotels, bars, nightclubs, factories, garbage collection services, linen supply houses, laundries, trucking companies, in fact, just about every sort of business you can think of.

The Brooklyn tapes revealed that among organized crime's illegitimate interests, these were the most popular: prostitution, smuggling, bookmaking, hijacking, extortion, counterfeiting, labor racketeering, insurance frauds and the selling of hard drugs.

Perhaps the most insidious thing about organized crime is not the blatantly illegal acts or the legitimate businesses that are criminal-owned, but the fact that many seemingly honest, upright citizens are really in the employ of the mobs. The Brooklyn tapes contain the names of at least 20 New York politicians and judges who frequented the gang's headquarters. Another 100 or so regular visitors were policemen.

Every time you pay a nickel on a number, place a bet, or do any of the score of things that are organized crime's chief support, you are helping it to grow.

Until he was finally electrocuted in 1944, Louis (Lepke) Buchalter, one of the founders of organized crime, was the biggest union racketeer of them all. He invented various labor shakedowns that prises cannot even be estimated, but it runs into even more billions of dollars.

We know all these things, yet some people, many of them in high places and presumably informed, still refuse to admit that crime is so totally organized. Nor do they see it as one of the most pressing problems facing the United States today.

Nevertheless, through the years we repeatedly have had ample evidence that there *is* a national crime cartel. Unfortunately, on every occasion that this proof has surfaced, there has been a brief flare of publicity, lots of ''outraged'' political speeches, and perhaps a television ''circus'' hearing or two, and then society has mentally swept it all under the carpet until the next time.

Look at the record:

As early as 1928, Cleveland police stumbled onto a hotel room meeting of 23 Sicilian gang leaders from cities all over the United States. This was during the height of Prohibition, and newspapers speculated as to whether bootleggers and racketeers were organizing on a national level.

In 1929 police and the press were made aware of a second national organizational meeting, in Atlantic City, New Jersey. This one featured not only Sicilians, but leaders of other gangs. Thirty of the biggest crooks of their day, from twelve different cities, attended the three-day convention.

In 1934 there were two separate meetings. The one for the East Coast mobsters was held in New York. The second, for the Midwest bunch, was held in Kansas City. Both meetings were chaired by Johnny Torrio.

In 1940 Abe (Kid Twist) Reles, thanks to brilliant handling by Brooklyn prosecutor Burton B. Turkus, turned state's evidence and shocked the nation with his blood curdling revelations about organized crime. Reles admitted that Murder, Inc. was the nationwide enforcement arm of the syndicate, and that at least 1,000 murders committed during the 1930s were ''contract'' jobs! Reles told who ran what, and how, and his testimony helped put seven organized crime figures into the chair. Other syndicate hoodlums squealed as well, and if there was anyone who still doubted that there was a national crime conspiracy, his doubts should have been quelled.

In 1950-51, the Kefauver hearings once again established the existence of an underworld government. While not nearly so revealing as the Reles testimony, they confirmed many of the things that Reles had said and for the first time, thanks to television, the public got an intimate look at the unsavory characters involved.

In the middle fifties, the McClellan Committee, with its ace counsel, Robert F. Kennedy, explored organized crime's intrusion into labor unions. Once again the Reles testimony and testimony developed during the prosecution of Lepke were borne out.

In 1957, following the killing of Albert Anastasia, 63 mob leaders from all over the country were found together in the small town of Apalachin, New York, at the home of one of their friends.

In 1963 a Cosa Nostra "soldier," Joe Valachi, told everything to investigators and a Senate committee. He too confirmed most of what had been learned before, and he added to it, revealing even more facts about the national crime syndicate.

You might think that in the face of this mountain of documentation regarding the existence of a nationwide crime network that society might at last be aroused and determine to break mobdom's tightening grip on the economy and politics of the country.

Well, not exactly. On May 25, 1973, there was this unsurprising item in *Newsweek* magazine:

La Cosa What? The Mafia seems to be last year's issue as far as Congress is concerned. The committees have put the topic on the back burner—despite widespread belief that organized crime has stepped up its efforts to penetrate legitimate business. "We have enough to investigate for four years," one disgruntled Senate staffer says, "but senators are backing off." The reason: lack of interest, lack of leadership and possible pressure.

CHAPTER TWO
1880-1900

Poverty in southern Italy and in Sicily, plus America's growing reputation as the land of opportunity, brought about a mass migration to United States shores. Most of the new immigrants settled in the poorest sections of New York and Chicago, and then tried to find work. Not all of them found it, and not all of them were actually looking for legitimate jobs. Some Sicilians brought with them a centuries-old tradition of robbing the rich, not necessarily to give to the poor. It was not so much a method of sticking a gun to someone's head and demanding his money, as it was a simple shakedown—send us some money or we will blow your house up with one of our homemade bombs. Crude, but effective.

Then just as now, the people who suffered the most from ghetto-based criminals were ghetto dwellers themselves. The Black Handers, which is what the original Mafia types in America were called, practiced their trade among their fellow Sicilians and Italians, in other words, people who knew all about the Mafia, and who feared it as much in America as they had in the old country.

The term "racket," as applied to crime, supposedly comes from old-time New York political fund-raising parties. They were called "rackets" because of the noise they made. Later, hoodlums gave their own "rackets," for which merchants were made to buy tickets.

Sicily is where the Mafia was born. In Arabic the word means "place of refuge," and the Mafia organization has given its friends a place of refuge for centuries. For a long time Sicily was, of course, a colony of Rome, and the Sicilians were used as slaves on great farms to grow corn for Rome and its empire. When Rome fell, the

Church took over Sicily and it too used the big farms, with the Sicilians continuing as slaves. Next came the Arabs, who allowed the Sicilians to own small farms themselves, and to be in business.

Unfortunately, in the eleventh century the Normans conquered Sicily and practically made the Sicilians slaves again, taking away their property and forcing them to work on the reassembled huge farms. It was somewhere along in here that the Sicilians, seemingly always ruled by a far-off, disinterested government, began to develop "our thing," Cosa Nostra, as the Mafiosi put it even today.

Certain Mafia traditions were begun in the eleventh century. The code of silence, *omerta*; the vendetta; the kiss of death; the respect for the senior Mafia leader; the togetherness—"us" against "them,"—"them" being any government, including an Italian or even a Sicilian one.

All of these things developed in a land that, one way or another, was ruled by outsiders for two thousand years, and was conquered or reconquered 16 times. The natives learned how to stick together, and to ignore or even subvert whatever government was in power. In many places in the Sicilian hills the Mafia was the only government; sometimes it actually enforced law and order, mainly because the only crimes the Mafia has ever approved are its own.

The Germans and the French came and left. Then, with the arrival of the Spanish, Sicily suffered from the Inquisition for almost three hundred years, or until 1787.

Mafiosi are bound by primeval laws which go even deeper than blood ties. Many Mafia rituals are curiously akin to those practiced by some African tribes in the Republic of Mali, whose members are governed by laws that go back to prehistoric days.

In one district of Sicily two clans became involved in a vendetta between the years 1872-78 which practically depopulated the whole area. The clans involved were the Fratuzzi and the Stoppaglieri. In 1872 a Fratuzzi denounced a Stoppaglieri to the police. By Mafia law, this misdemeanor called for the execution of the informer by his own family. When the Fratuzzis failed to kill him, the feud was on. Very soon all near male relatives of both clans had been killed, and the area's population was in terror as the remaining members of the clans searched wider and wider for remote relatives.

The ritual requires that the continuation of the vendetta be entrusted to the senior female member of the household, and by 1878, the Fratuzzi-Stoppaglieri feud had so decimated the two families that a man in the area might be approached by a black-shrouded old woman whom he'd never seen before, and told that he was now the surviving head of one of the families. She would tell him he must consider himself responsible for killing some complete stranger.

Reconciliation of the two families and an end to the feud was finally brought about by a member of the Fratuzzi. He went to the police and told them all he knew about the Stoppaglieri. He was aware that this was tantamount to suicide, but his entire family had already been wiped out in the feud and he felt that the sacrifice must be made. This time the Fratuzzi family did the right thing and killed the informer, making sure his body was properly displayed.

Many of the southern European families who emigrated to America in the 1880s came from the same sections of Sicily and Italy, and when they settled in the United States, they usually picked the same neighborhoods. Brooklyn had a very large contingent from a place called Castellammare del Golfo, located on the northwest coast of Sicily, some 40 miles west of Palermo. Names that were important there and were later transferred to America included Bonanno, Magaddino, Maranzano.

From Naples, Italy came the Lucianos, the Capones, the Torrios; they went to the Lower East Side of New York.

At the turn of the century in New York, the large gangs were Irish; at least they controlled gambling, elections, prostitution and the protection rackets. They also handled the large robberies. Working with them were some Germans and a few Poles and Jews. It was at this time that Arnold Rothstein got his start. Rothstein thought of himself as a gambler, which he was, running several large books in New York, but even more than that, he was practically the inventor of the loan-shark racket. Whenever Rothstein lent money, he liked to get what he called "juice," or "vigorish"—interest of anything from 25 to 100 percent. Rothstein also ran some of the largest crap games in town.

On the Lower East Side, there was the Five Points gang, composed mostly of southern Italians, of which Johnny Torrio was a prominent member. The Five Pointers made their money from robberies, some of the smaller protection schemes, and by doing odd jobs for the bigger gangs uptown; they also found employment on election days, coercing voters, shooting at opposition candidates, and bombing polling places.

Across the river in Brooklyn, Frank Uale, known as Frank Yale, a Sicilian, was running a few gambling houses and a small extortion racket. He occasionally hired other Sicilians to work for him.

In Chicago, the other main breeding ground of the national crime syndicate, the Germans, the Poles, the Irish and the Jews were in charge. There the Sicilian crooks' main activity was the Black Hand extortion racket, just as it was in New York.

The Illinois Crime Commission has a whole collection of the Black Hand's threatening letters of this period. Here are two samples:

Most Gentle Mr. Silvani:

Hoping that the present will not impress you very much, you will be so good as to send me $2,000 if your life is dear to you. So I beg you warmly to put them on your door within four days. But if not, I swear this week's time not even the dust of your family will exist. With regards, believe me to be your friends.

The English wasn't very good, but the meaning was clear. One of the characteristics of the Black Hand's notes was the excessive politeness, a sort of Old World courtliness.

We took your boy from your house this morning at ten o'clock, and he is in good care with us now. All we want is five thousand dollars and the boy will be sent back. If you value your boy's life, don't miss this. Give your money to some friends who will pass the house. Don't forget. . . . La Mano Nera.

That letter was sent to a Mr. Anthony Marino of Chicago, shortly after his six-year-old son was kidnaped.

Violence, however, was nothing new to Chicago. In 1860 the *Chicago Journal* was saying, "We are beset on every side by villains." In the early part of this century, long before Capone and the real mobsters moved into Chicago, there was a murder every day, a burglary every three hours, and a stickup every six hours. The arrival of the Black Hand on the scene merely made life in Chicago more exciting.

New York, too, had problems with the Black Hand. Jack Petrosino, a New York cop, was born in Italy and had emigrated to the United States when he was 13. When he joined the police he became a member of the Italian Squad, a department which was formed to combat the growing menace of Mafia-run rackets.

In 1909 Petrosino persuaded his superiors that the best way to learn about the workings of the Mafia would be for him to go to Sicily. His companions for the trip were two ex-Black Handers from the States. There is little doubt that they informed their compatriots of his plans.

On the evening of the day Petrosino arrived in Palermo, he left his hotel for a secret rendezvous. As he walked across the plaza, the street lights of the town went out. When they were turned on again, Petrosino was found dead, shot in the head.

One of the acknowledged heads of the Mafia in Sicily for many years, Don Vito Cascio Ferro, was said to have admitted taking only one life (although he had been accused of over sixty murders). The acknowledged victim was Jack Petrosino. Don Vito claimed, "My action was a disinterested one, in response to a challenge I could not afford to ignore."

Chicago had the biggest whorehouses and gambling joints in America, along with off-track betting shops, many of them owned by a man named Monte Tennes. The same Tennes later furnished a wire service of racing information to other bookie joints all over the Midwest.

Prostitution in Chicago was not just prostitution, but white slavery as well, with girls being kidnaped from places like Kansas City and St. Louis, and then forced into prostitution in Chicago's red-light district. Others were tricked into going there to work as domestics, only to be told the real nature of the job when they turned up for work, usually lacking bus fare home.

Another entrepreneur of the time was Mossy Enright, a labor racketeer. Usually, he worked for the unions, helping them to organize certain reluctant industries. Bombs and guns were employed frequently. Enright was a pioneer in the field of labor negotiations, being able to call off a threatened strike if his palm were greased. Most members of Enright unions paid their dues and did what Enright or his puppet union presidents said.

Legitimate unions often got involved with Enright when they tried to organize a new factory and found that the management had hired goon squads to break the strike. For a fee, Enright could provide much tougher goons than management could.

He also provided small packages that went boom!

CHAPTER THREE
1900-1910

Big Jim Colosimo, who emigrated in the 1800s from Italy, got his first job in America as a water boy for a railroad construction gang. His next job was that of a janitor in Chicago's First Ward, where he met two almost legendary figures: Michael (Hinky Dink) Kenna, and John (The Bathhouse) Coughlin. Both were city aldermen and apparently scoundrels at heart.

Hinky Dink and The Bathhouse were the fix-it men at City Hall for the gambling houses and red-light establishments in their ward. Hinky Dink himself ran the Working Man's Exchange, which was more or less a beer parlor. His friend, The Bathhouse, would sit there night after night, drinking beer and writing poetry.

The aldermen promoted Colosimo in ward politics and even occasionally gave him money. In exchange, he helped to deliver the votes on election day and he did odd jobs. In 1902, Colosimo married the owner of a popular Chicago whorehouse. From there, by easy stages, he rose to the top of Chicago's gambling-drinking-whoring café society.

By 1908 he owned the "swellest joint in town," Colosimo's Café, at 2128 Wabash Avenue. Here he blossomed into a fat, jolly figure, wearing expensive suits, with diamonds in his tie and on his fingers. In addition to his main saloon, he owned a whole chain of brothels in Chicago's Tenderloin. Every night in Colosimo's he would hold court at the bar, passing out favors as a precinct captain, handing out bribes and telling jokes to the hangers-on.

This wealthy citizen in their midst did not escape the attention of the Black Hand, then run by Sunny Jim Cosmano. The Black Hand was not impressed with Colosimo's importance. Sunny Jim decided it was time that Big Jim made a donation.

First Cosmano sent Colosimo a friendly but threatening letter. Big Jim refused to believe that he was really being shaken down. Cosmano became more insistent, and finally Colosimo, in order to avoid a lot of trouble, coughed up $5,000. He could stand it; he was making $500,000 a year from prostitution, booze and gambling —and that was just about tax free in 1910!

The Black Hand, keeping its eyes on Big Jim's growing operations, decided that it was time for a little more share-the-wealth, and this time demanded $25,000 from Colosimo. Big Jim left almost immediately for New York, where, during a brief vacation, he looked up his nephew, Johnny Torrio.

The latter was running his own splinter group of the Five Points gang called the James Street gang. Torrio was 29, and felt that he wasn't getting anywhere; all the "good" rackets in New York were dominated by others, and the Italians and Sicilians got only what was left.

Colosimo mentioned his little problem with the Black Hand in Chicago, and offered Torrio a job, second in command, if he could get the Black Hand off Big Jim's back. Within a week Torrio left for Chicago and his new career.

One afternoon in 1919, shortly after Torrio arrived in Chicago to help out his uncle, three Black Handers, sent by Sunny Jim Cosmano, walked into the Café and told Big Jim that if he didn't deliver the $25,000 by the next day he would be filled with 1,000 bullets. Big Jim called Torrio, his new "manager," over to the table and the two men agreed to deliver the money the next day.

Torrio and his men kept the appointment, but instead of money all they delivered to the Black Hand was death. All three of Cosmano's henchmen were blown apart by sawed-off shotguns, wielded by four Torrio soldiers.

This was Torrio's debut into Chicago's gangland and things were never to be quite the same again. Cosmano, the Black Hand leader, was visibly shaken. The Black Hand's victims were not supposed to shoot back.

In New York authorities had got so alarmed at the amount of shooting in the streets that the Sullivan Law was passed in 1909. This made the carrying of concealed weapons without a license illegal. Some hoods managed to pull strings and get gun permits; others simply broke the law.

As one gangster put it, "I'd rather explain it to twelve than be carried by six," meaning that he'd rather face a jury than be dead.

Much pressure was put onto the New York gangs in the early 1900s by vigilante committees such as Dr. Parkhurst's "Society for the Suppression of Crime." This sort of public outcry resulted in a state investigation that netted a number of grafters and big-time Irish crooks. Much of this inadvertently helped to clear the way for the far rougher crowd which was to follow.

One of those who escaped attention at this time because he was just getting started was gambler and loan shark Arnold Rothstein. In his heyday Rothstein was to be a prince of Broadway society, a darling of the press and a leader of Manhattan's underworld.

Rothstein was born in 1883 and raised on East 47th Street. Although his father was a wealthy dry-goods merchant, young Arnold had little taste for proper schooling, and spent much of his time in pool halls and penny-ante gambling dens. By the time Rothstein was 16 in 1899, he had his own horse parlor and loan shark business, and he was employing one Monk Eastman as his "heavy" for the collection of usurious loans.

By 1902 Rothstein had come to the attention of Big Tim Sullivan, the Tammany boss, who decided that the young gambler was a man who could prove useful. By 1903 the Rothstein bankroll of "walking-around money" was $5,000. By 1906, when he was only 26, Rothstein was known never to have less than $12,000 in his pockets.

In 1909 Rothstein married a 19-year-old actress, Carolyn Greene. Their wedding present from boss Sullivan was his protection for Arnold's latest venture, a swank gambling house co-owned with former ward leader Willie Shea. Shortly thereafter, Rothstein hit the gossip columns for the first time: he won $10,000 in a 34-hour poker game.

One night, after a particularly long game, Rothstein discovered that his partner had made off with the house winnings, claiming it was his compensation for certain of the house's funds that Rothstein had used for other ventures. In any case, the partnership was dissolved and Rothstein continued to run the casino alone.

CHAPTER FOUR
1910-1920

In Chicago Big Jim Colosimo soon recognized his nephew Johnny Torrio's potential, and together they began to establish themselves in Chicago's already existing protection rackets. Federal investigators tried to curtail this growing endeavor, and in the process found a former Chicago whore willing to testify against Colosimo and Torrio. She was stashed away in Bridgeport, Connecticut, but before her evidence could be heard she was found dead, her throat slashed. Torrio's old New York gang was suspected of her murder, but nothing was ever proved, though the link between New York and Chicago hoodlums was clearly evident.

Alderman Robert Merriam is reported to have said, "Chicago is unique. It is the only completely corrupt city in America." And certainly in the early years of this century almost every activity of the city's life was under the "protection" of organized crime, although corruption was nothing new in the history of the Windy City.

From the middle of the nineteenth century, when Chicago was the "Mudhole of the Prairies," and a busy Indian trading post, it tolerated all sorts of villains. Even in the early days it was not always easy to distinguish the good guys from the bad guys. In 1876 a whorehouse owned by a superintendent of police was described in *The New York Times* as "an epitome of hell." An English journalist, W.T. Stead, wrote a book in 1893 in which he told of many highly respected citizens whose apparently blameless lives were supported by the proceeds from brothels and gaming houses. In 1906 the *Chicago Tribune* claimed, "A reign of terror is on the city." Indeed, Chicago was worse than some of our big cities are even today.

Of course, attempts were made to curb vice. In 1911 Mayor Harrison, a Democrat, ordered the closing of several brothels. The state's attorney, John Wayman, then began grand jury investigations, and followed with a decree abolishing the whole red-light area. The madams thereupon sent all their ladies into the streets, some wearing bizarre and exotic costumes, to knock on every door in the district and ask for lodgings. Needless to say, they were refused at every house, which presented the ward with the insoluble problem of hordes of homeless women. This led to the inevitable reopening of most of the brothels.

Law-abiding sections of the Italian and Sicilian communities in Chicago also took steps to offset the results of the Black Hand's trafficking. In 1907 a society called the White Hand was founded, dedicated to good deeds and to helping victims of the Black Hand.

During the early years of the century many gangsters, whose names later became notorious, started operations in Chicago: Monte Tennes, bookie and racetrack racketeer; Joey D'Andrea, who as head of the Sewer Diggers and Tunnel Miners' Union, was a leading labor racketeer; Izzy (The Rat) Buchalsky, another labor racketeer; Sunny Jim Cosmano, who ran the Black Hand protection rackets; and Dion O'Bannion, who led one of Chicago's strongest gangs, and whose murder in 1924 triggered off the beer wars.

Some of the gangs in Chicago were led by Irish gangsters: O'Bannion was an Irishman; there were two O'Donnell gangs—the South Side O'Donnells and the West Side O'Donnells. Each was led by a group of brothers, but the two O'Donnell gangs had no relationship to each other, and they gave each other no quarter in gang feuds. Terry Druggan and Frankie Lake were two Irishmen who ran a gang started in the 1890s. Frank and Mike Ragen founded Ragen's Athletic & Benevolent Association in 1902, mainly for the Irish, and although its aims were allegedly philanthropic, the club was little more than another gang. A Pole, Joe Saltis, and a homicidal maniac, Frank McErlane, ran the Saltis-McErlane gang, and on the West Side Mike (The Pike) Heitler built up his organization.

These gangsters exploited every human weakness including prostitution, gambling and drugs, and made such huge profits that they were able to exploit yet another human weakness and bribe police and city officials to ignore much of Chicago's vice. Any resistance was dealt with by violence. Soon a pattern emerged: different types of operations in various areas were carved up between the gangs, and in each area the gang boss saw to it that sufficient funds were extorted from "his" brothels, gaming-house, and racetracks for funds to be available to pay the right bribes in the right places. In Chicago the law was for sale.

Cooperation at higher levels was assured by the gang boss's control of votes at election time. One example was Alderman Hinky Dink Kenna, of the First Ward Democratic machine, who floated into office again and again on Big Jim Colosimo's bloc votes. Colosimo operated numerous "businesses", in all of which his candidate would be heavily endorsed. Once Big Jim himself briefly took refuge from the law among the city's street sweepers, whom he promptly organized into a union. Their bloc vote was also at his disposal.

On another occasion a policeman was found carrying a list in his jacket of all the vice establishments in his precinct, each carefully graded—"not to be raided"—"only raid infrequently"—together with the exact amount of extortion money to be expected from each, and the number of ways it would be cut, up to and including the officers in charge of the precinct.

With the law and its officers so closely linked with organized crime, the gangsters and hoodlums were able to attend to their business unhindered. Very few of the leading crime bosses were ever charged, even with the crimes they were known to have committed. If a zealous officer got his man as far as the courts there were so many loopholes known to corrupt attorneys and judges that convictions were rare. Sentences when passed were usually only partially served before the offender was released on one pretext or another.

Even the White Hand organization found the odds too great, and in 1913 it was disbanded. Dr. Joseph Damiani, White Hand president, said that his members would not advance any more money to help combat the Black Hand; they were too discouraged by the lax administration of justice. According to a statement published by the White Hand Society in 1911, there were also other factors which made arrests difficult. Many Sicilian and Italian families were still governed by an alien psychology which they brought with them from their own countries. In one murder hunt in Chicago the identity of the murderer was known to the police: he and his victim were both Italian. An intensive search for the criminal went on for several weeks, until one day he was spotted coming out of the house of the murdered man's brother. On being questioned, the brother said that his home had been the man's refuge since the killing. He had been wounded, and the victim's family wished to nurse him back to life, so that they might themselves avenge the brother's death by killing the murderer as soon as his health was restored!

Between 1910 and 1914 the Chicago Vice Commission uncovered 77 cases of white slavery, and estimated that 5,000 prostitutes were employed in Chicago's 1,020 brothels. A wave of reform spread through the city in 1912, and Chicago's red-light district was closed. Big Jim Colosimo and Torrio moved out to Cicero, a Chicago suburb, and opened the first brothel there. They needn't have bothered; of the more than 1,000 brothels closed, 712 reopened within two months.

Many gang bosses "looked after" the families living in the neighborhood of their brothels and gaming houses. This meant that they were often surrounded by compliant neighbors only too willing to keep indoors and see nothing and know nothing in the event of trouble. Johnny Torrio would send his flunkies to all the houses in his districts, and it was up to them to find out all they could about the family problems and hardships. One man in financial trouble would find his mortgage payments brought up to date and being paid regularly. Another in trouble with the police would have the charges against him suddenly dropped. No wonder that the local boss was held in high esteem, and often appealed to for help. If it suited the gang's purpose, help would be forthcoming.

And at the same time, opposition was ruthlessly eliminated. In 1910 the Black Hand alone killed 25 people in Chicago; in 1912 the total was 31.

In 1914, the police in Chicago's red-light district started demanding even larger payoffs, accompanied by threats of arrests and closures. Torrio responded with threats of violence and sent for Roxie Vanilli, a New York hoodlum, and Chicago triggerman Mac Fitzpatrick. In the gun battle which ensued with the police, one policeman was killed and three were wounded. Vanilli himself was also wounded. Colosimo and some of his men were arrested, but all charges were soon dropped for lack of evidence. One of Colosimo's henchmen, Duffy the Goat, killed a police informer, Isaac Hengow. Duffy was actually brought to trial and convicted of murder. Several eyewitnesses testified that Hengow had been walking along the sidewalk and had not seen Duffy approach. He hadn't even had time to raise a hand as Duffy gunned him down in cold blood, the witnesses testified. However, Duffy the Goat managed to secure a retrial, and the second time he was acquitted on the grounds of self-defense.

It was in 1914 that Anthony D'Andrea first ran for election as Cook County commissioner. He and his brother Joey, a forger and president of the Sewer Diggers' and Tunnel Miners' Union, were Italians who had emigrated to Chicago. Tony was a lawyer, and president of the Chicago branch of the Unione Siciliano, an organization set up by immigrant Sicilians and Italians for charitable work. Its membership included many eminent men, judges and politicians, and it was established in major cities throughout the nation. It was also claimed that the Unione existed to control gang rivalries and to allocate fair distribution of areas for extortion and other rackets.

Tony D'Andrea fought the election with gunmen and rigged votes, but he was exposed as a defrocked priest, a convicted bank robber, and a counterfeiter—and he was not elected. His brother Joey was later killed in a labor dispute.

Tony D'Andrea's defeat at the polls did not discourage him. In 1916, he ran for the Democratic nomination for alderman, and again he lost. This was a violent election, and one of D'Andrea's opponent's aides was shot dead while voting. In 1921 D'Andrea tried again. This time John Powers was his opponent and Powers won, but the polling was bloodier than ever. Two houses were bombed and 30 people killed. In this election an old Sicilian custom was observed, and the names of the intended victims were posted in advance on Dead Man's Tree, a poplar growing in Chicago's Little Italy.

In New York in 1912, the "Crime of the Year" was the slaughter of gambler Herman Rosenthal, a competitor of Arnold Rothstein's. Rosenthal was killed by two hoodlums known as Gyp the Blood and Lefty Louie, who took care of Rosenthal for New York detective Charles Becker. It seems that Rosenthal was about to expose Becker for being on the take from various Manhattan gambling houses.

Strict new United States immigration laws, which many called unfair, were instituted in 1914, and this slowed to a trickle the immigration of Italians, Sicilians and other people from southern Mediterranean countries. From then on, many imported Mafia types had to enter the country illegally. Many years later this was to prove useful to federal authorities desperately looking for some means of deporting hoods on whom they could get nothing else.

One of the leading members of New York's Five Points gang after the departure of Johnny Torrio was a Sicilian named Salvatore

"Lucky" Luciano, who by 1915 was already pimping for a string of prostitutes. The Five Points gang itself was run by Paolo Antonini Vaccarelli, otherwise known as Paul Kelly, and his associate, James (Biff) Ellison. The major Brooklyn rackets in 1918 were handled by Ciro Terranova, known as the Artichoke King because of his legitimate business of wholesaling artichokes, of which he had a monopoly. Terranova was related to Ignazio Saietta, known as John Lupo, "the Wolf." Lupo the Wolf and Frank Yale, president of the national Unione Siciliano, were able, between them, to pack the Unione with hoods to their liking.

Yale himself in addition to being a gun for hire, ran a string of sleazy nightclubs-cum-gambling joints in Brooklyn. In 1919, one of his bartender-bouncers was Alphonse Capone, a cousin of Johnny Torrio's. Within a year, young Capone, who was only 20 at the time and known for his vile temper and brutality, had been arrested once for disorderly conduct and was suspected of having committed two murders.

Just as things were getting a bit too hot for Capone in New York, he was invited to Chicago by his cousin Torrio, who said he needed a trusted man to help him run Big Jim Colosimo's empire. Capone left for Chicago on the next train.

Prohibition became law in 1920, and soon bootlegging, the biggest racket of its time, was launched. It was destined to bring untold wealth to a few and unbridled violence and death to many.

CHAPTER FIVE
1920

There was always plenty of crime in the United States—everything from armed holdups and burglary to extortion, graft and fraud, but it was the advent of Prohibition that gave criminals the impetus and the vast sums necessary to make their first tentative steps toward organization.

Exploitation of the nation's drinking habits was complicated and something that simply couldn't be handled by one desperado, or even one large gang. Booze had to be made, transported and sold. This called for businesslike methods, accountants, drivers, loaders—not to mention armed guards, armed "salesmen" and police payoff agents.

The hoodlums of New York, Chicago and other big cities were not slow to realize the potential of Prohibition any more than they were slow in later years to take advantage of the nation's narcotics laws. However, in the beginning there were certain growing pains, as in any new industry. The difference here was that in legitimate business, the losers either merge or go bankrupt; in crime, they either quit or get killed.

In New York in the year before the Volstead Act, there were 15,000 legal bars. One year later the bars were all closed and there were 23,000 speakeasies. Chicago didn't even put a good face on it, as New York dld, and close all its bars. Many Chicago joints simply stayed open and competed with the thousands of new ones.

It is safe to say that people who'd never had a drink before in their lives started drinking during Prohibition, simply because it was chic and somehow glamorous. Within a few months of the beginning of Prohibition, magazines and newspapers were running feature articles on how to make your own hooch. There were specialist shops selling—against the law—all the equipment necessary for making rotgut in your kitchen or bathtub.

Legitimate breweries forced out of business by the Volstead Act were bought at knockdown prices by hoodlums or people with hoodlum connections. Some breweries, such as the five taken over by Johnny Torrio in Chicago, converted to making legal near-beer, and the real stuff on the side. Bathtub gin, made in hidden stills in New York and Chicago tenements, was sold as either bourbon or gin, depending on how much coloring was added. Some real booze came across the Great Lakes from Canada to Chicago, Cleveland, Detroit and Buffalo. Frank Costello, the first of the Italian-American crooks to hit the big time, ran a fleet of fast launches that took booze from freighters anchored far at sea.

Arnold Rothstein's gambling house in New York became a speakeasy overnight. At this time Rothstein was already a famous figure due to his huge bets and the fact that he was the man credited with having "fixed" the World Series of 1919, in the notorious Black Sox scandal. (The Chicago White Sox were alleged to have taken a dive against the Cincinnati Reds.)

Another New York figure of the period was Nicky Arnstein, a gambler. Both he and Rothstein were suspected of engineering a Liberty Bond racket in 1920, in which $5,000,000 in bonds were "borrowed" from legitimate brokers and sold again. Arnstein, accused of being the "master mind" of the bond racket, was charged and released on $100,000 bail, put up by Rothstein. At his first trial, which was nonconclusive, Arnstein was defended by William Fallon, the "Great Mouthpiece." Fallon was busy elsewhere when Arnstein was tried again in Washington, and Arnstein was convicted and sentenced to a stretch in Leavenworth.

These adventures, however, were mere sidelights to the main events; the real villains were not quite onstage. Lucky Luciano was still a mere lieutenant in New York's Five Points gang; Frank Yale owned only a few cheap speakeasies in Brooklyn; Dutch Schultz was operating a lottery and extortion racket; Legs Diamond was winning a dance contest in Chicago; Al Capone was Johnny Torrio's henchman in Chicago, but as yet completely unknown to the press.

In New York Sicilians and Italians such as Joseph Profaci, Joseph Magliocco, Stefano Magaddino, Frank Labruzzo, Frank Garofalo, Salvatore Maranzano, Joe Masseria, Peter Morello and

Vito Genovese were known as "Mustache Petes" by the Irish-Jewish-Polish gangs which dominated the city's gambling, extortion and prostitution rackets. The established hoods thought the relatively new immigrants were too wild and excitable to last long.

The Chicago scene was much the same in 1920. While the Colosimo-Torrio and Genna gangs were chiefly comprised of Sicilians and Italians, the other major gangs in the city were not, and no one gang had dominance over the entire city.

Johnny Torrio and Al Capone would change all that.

When it had become apparent that the Volstead Act would become law, Torrio immediately began making plans for the Colosimo mob to cash in on it. Unfortunately, Colosimo wasn't interested; he was happy with his brothel and casino empire as it was. He had just married a much younger woman after having discarded his first wife, who'd set him up in business, and he was content to flash his diamonds and show off at his own bar, entertaining his friends. Torrio found this lack of ambition annoying.

In May 1920 Colosimo was waiting in his restaurant for a consignment of bootleg whiskey arranged for him by his trusted lieutenant and nephew, Torrio. But what Uncle did not know was that Torrio had also sent Frank Yale, New York's gun-for-hire, to the casino along with the whiskey, and in the confusion of unloading, Colosimo was shot through the head. No charges were ever made, but the police questioned Yale at the Chicago train station the next day, just as he was leaving town.

After Colosimo's elimination, Torrio was finally his own boss. He quickly made the youthful Capone his No. 1 henchman and gave him 25 percent of Colosimo's existing Chicago brothel and gambling business (which netted $100,000 per year) and 50 percent of the expected bootleg profits. Capone sent to New York for his brother Ralph, and his cousins Rocco, Joseph and Charles Fischetti, all of whom joined him in the mob. At this time Torrio was 39 and Capone only 23.

Torrio also recruited the Druggan-Lake gang and had them run his five Chicago breweries. These breweries supposedly were producing legal near-beer with an alcohol content of only one-half percent. Torrio sold real beer produced in the near-beer plants to other Chicago gangs at $50 a barrel. His profit was $35 per barrel.

The six Genna brothers, Angelo, Michael, Tony (The Gentleman), Sam, Peter and Jim, a family of Sicilians known as "The Terrible Gennas", ran a $5,000,000 business in moonshine liquor. They employed hundreds of poor Sicilian families living in tenement buildings in one area of the city. In their kitchens the gang installed portable stills: the families had only to stoke the stills and strain off the raw alcohol, which was collected by the bosses, for which the man of the house was paid the princely wage of $15 a day. For such a wage in those days, families were coming over from Sicily to go into the Chicago alky business. The Gennas then bottled the raw alcohol, nicely colored and flavored, and sold it labelled whiskey or gin. Even after all expenses had been met, it is estimated that the monthly net profits were about $150,000.

The Gennas had arrived in the States when their parents emigrated in 1910. They were a wild, brutal lot, with all the stubborn pride of generations of Sicilian banditry. The only exception was one brother, Antonio, "The Gentleman." He lived a quiet, sober life, and was always immaculately dressed, hence his nickname. He was never known to be armed or to be implicated in any killing. He educated himself, and became an architect; he was a great reader and operagoer, but was always present at family conferences and acted as counselor in Genna enterprises.

When the Gennas' affairs later came under government scrutiny some interesting statements were made by one of The Gentleman's office managers: he said that the warehouse was in operation 24 hours daily, in two shifts, quite openly. Heavy trucks used in the distribution of the liquor ran in and out unchecked. The warehouse was raided occasionally, but the police never failed to give the Gennas 24 hours' notice, which gave them plenty of time to get things cleaned up, and after the raid it was business as usual. The Genna manager's statement went on, "During all the period that I worked in the warehouse the entire Genna enterprise was done with the full knowledge, consent and approval of the police of Chicago. . . ."

It was also stated that by 1925 the amount paid to the police for their protection was about $6,500 a month, plus large amounts of cut-price alcohol. So that there could be no question of policemen from other precincts coming in to collect from the Gennas, police headquarters supplied the warehouse each month with a list of the badge numbers of the men assigned to their area; in this way each man could be checked when he called for "pay."

For a time where was trouble when the warehouse was sending large consignments of alcohol to areas some distance away—the Genna trucks were often intercepted by the police in those other areas. But this difficulty was soon overcome; when a truckload was due to leave the warehouse for some other district the local precinct would be informed and the home squad would provide a police convoy to see the truck safely through.

After Policeman Harold F. Olson had been murdered, and Scalise and Anselmi were on trial for killing him, Attorney Patrick H. O'Donnell produced some documents taken from the Gennas including a list of the names of police who had been in their pay. Nearly two hundred policemen were transferred, and many promises of full publication were made, but, in fact, the list vanished when the trial was over.

Sunny Jim Cosmano, the Black Hander, was still around, but after his bitter experience losing three men to Torrio's blazing guns, he was more or less leaving other hoods alone and picking on fellow Sicilians who didn't pack guns of their own. His outstanding feat in 1920 was the rub-out of Mossy Enright, the pioneer labor racketeer. Cosmano is said to have done this as a favor to Big Tim Murphy, another labor gangster, and an Enright rival.

One of the kingpins of the Cleveland bootlegging operations was Alfred (Big Al) Polizzi, another immigrant from Sicily, who ran his organization with help from his associates in Chicago and Detroit. He was very friendly with Pete Licavoli, a notorious gang leader in Detroit. Johnny Torrio and Al Capone had opened many more brothels and speakeasies in Cicero and other suburbs of Chicago and had virtually taken over that territory.

Mayor William Hale Thompson (Big Bill) was elected mayor of Chicago three times during the 1920s, and during his terms it was widely known that payoffs would be accepted at City Hall and that he was prepared to ignore any evidence of crime if approached in the proper manner. His official salary was never very high, but when he died of natural causes in 1944 at the age of 75, Treasury officials searched his home, and boxes of tightly wedged banknotes were found amounting to about $1,750,000. He had, it seems, launched many fund-raising drives "for charity" during his lifetime, although the small amounts collected had often occasioned surprise and disappointment in many quarters.

One of Big Bill Thompson's pawns was Len Small, who was first elected governor of Illinois in 1921. On taking office he granted pardons to about 1,000 known killers and other hoods.

There were a few ripples to disturb this tranquil scene, among them the hostility between the Irishman, Dion O'Bannion, and the other gang leaders. O'Bannion had been allowed by Torrio to cut in on some of his Cicero operations, but O'Bannion was not an easy man to get along with. His parents were poor Irish immigrants, and he had been brought up in tough slum surroundings. Born of a Catholic family, he sang in the choir at the Holy Name Cathedral, and served as an altar boy. Unfortunately influences outside the church were stronger, and in his teens O'Bannion had already joined one of the vicious street gangs of his area. He had by this time a pronounced limp, as one leg was several inches shorter than the other due to a street accident when he was ten.

Later, O'Bannion worked as a singing waiter at a notoriously seedy dive where the waiters sang as they systematically robbed the tipsy customers. At 17 he was convicted on a burglary charge and served a short sentence, but he quickly learned how to avoid such pitfalls. O'Bannion took lessons from a convicted murderer and practiced gunslinging until he was a crack shot with both hands. He always carried three guns, and was ready at any time to fire them at anyone who bothered him.

At the same time he had amassed a fat fortune and learned how to bribe effectively. He was so active in politics that in 1921, when he was actually caught in the act of robbing a safe at the Postal Telegraph Building by tough Detective Sergeant John J. Ryan, the O'Bannion influence—and $30,000 in bribes—was enough to get the charges dropped for "insufficient evidence."

One of O'Bannion's lieutenants was Earl "Hymie" Weiss, a Pole, who as early as 1909 had coined the phrase, "take 'em for a ride."

O'Bannion also loved flowers, and was a skillful florist. He owned a florist's shop, which served as an admirable front for his illegal activities. The shop was well patronized by the general public, to be sure, but the big spenders were the hoods who ordered flowers for their rivals' funerals—sometimes in advance.

O'Bannion charged into the bootlegging business with his usual lack of subtlety, both guns firing, and was soon established as one of the richest and most powerful gang leaders and possibly one of the most hated; between him and the Genna brothers there was deep-rooted antagonism.

Johnny Torrio also hated O'Bannion, but he was a very different kind of enemy. He ruled ruthlessly, but never let it seem so. Torrio was a small man, always quietly and conservatively dressed. He lived a simple life in a small house on Michigan Avenue where he made a point of returning early each evening to sit in slippered ease listening to the radio, or playing opera records. According to Mrs. Torrio, life with Johnny was "one long unclouded honeymoon." Torrio didn't smoke or drink, spoke quietly, and never used bad language.

CHAPTER SIX
1921-1923

Big Jim Colosimo's swank den was located at 2128 South Wabash Avenue in Chicago. His offices, from which his nephew Johnny Torrio ran Jim's gambling and prostitution empire, were on the first floor of a place called the Four Deuces, only a block away at 2222 South Wabash. While the Colosimo place got the celebrities and "nice people" out for an evening of slumming, the Four Deuces got the dregs of Chicago society. It was just too rough for anything else—12 unsolved murders had been committed there by 1921.

The first floor of the Four Deuces contained a seedy bar-café, with Torrio's offices in the rear, the second and third floors had the gambling and the whorehouse was on the top floor. Among those who hung out at the Deuces were some of the roughest men Chicago and organized crime would ever know. There were the trigger-happy Genna brothers; John Scalise and Albert Anselmi, who were destined to become Capone's execution squad; Vincent (The Schemer) Drucci, who was to die while kicking an ambulance attendant in the face; Samuel J. (Nails) Morton, the gunman who loved horseback riding; Dion O'Bannion; Earl (Hymie) Weiss; Louis (Two-Gun) Alterie, a former cowboy who thought Chicago was Dodge City; Sam (Samoots) Amatuna, who put garlic on his bullets to insure infection if he only wounded; the West Side O'Donnells, whose nutty machine-gunner, James (Fur) Sammons, often sprayed slugs in the wrong direction.

Not a nice crowd in 1921, and they hadn't even achieved top form.

Torrio spent the first few months of Prohibition expanding into Chicago's suburbs, taking over such towns as Cicero, Steger, Chicago Heights, Stickney, Posen and Forest View.

Torrio's plan was double-barreled. First, he knew that at any time an election could go against him in Chicago itself, and a reform mayor might replace the "reasonable" Big Bill Thompson; he decided it would be better to control a few small towns as insurance. In addition, he wanted more outlets for the beer he planned to make in the breweries he was buying up. Each of the Torrio dives in Cicero, for instance, was a little empire in itself, containing a speakeasy, a gambling den and a whorehouse. That way, someone looking for sin needn't shop around; he could get all his vices attended to at once.

Another facet of Torrio's grand plan was to insure peace within the business. As he explained it patiently to the other gang leaders, there was going to be more than enough money in the bootlegging business for everyone; there was no point in killing each other. In fact, he said, there was more to be gained from cooperation. With this in mind, the hoods, many of whom were simply glorified burglars, holdup men and extortionists, agreed to divide Chicago between them and go into business in a big way.

Torrio took the Loop district and most of the "best" part of Chicago; on the fringe of this territory were the Saltis, the Ralph Sheldon and the Spike O'Donnell gangs. The Druggan-Lake gang, Torrio's partners in the brewery business, got the territory between Chicago and Cicero. The Gennas controlled a small area just off the Loop; the Klondike O'Donnells operated north of the Gennas. Torrio's partners, Guilfoyle and Maddox, were between the O'Donnells and the territory of Roger (The Terrible) Touhy, who ran his outfit from Des Plaines. Dion O'Bannion and Bugs Moran had the area north of the Loop, along the shore of Lake Michigan.

While all this organizing was going on, a secondhand furniture dealer was setting up next door to the Four Deuces. His card said:

Alphonse Capone
Secondhand Furniture Dealer
2220 South Wabash Avenue

His stock, which, oddly enough, never sold, consisted of bric-a-brac, leather novelties, an upright piano, three cheap oak tables, a rocking chair, an aquarium, some books, several rugs and a Bible.

All of the gangs smuggled in whatever real booze they could from Canada. Mostly though, their beer came from Torrio, who owned those five lovely breweries and who agreed to sell it to the other gangs in exchange for no trouble, i.e., infringing on his territory, and/or hijacking his beer trucks. The Gennas, with their incredible network of home distilleries all over Chicago, furnished moonshine to anyone who had the price. A few of the gangs had their own distilleries and breweries located out of town, and this was later to cause a lot of trouble.

For a few months the truce seemed to be working. The kindly Big Bill Thompson was elected to a second term as mayor in 1921, and his stooge, Len Small, was elected governor of Illinois. Crime not simply overlooked by Thompson was pardoned by Small.

The same election that installed Thompson and Small saw the remarkable ''Alderman's War'' in Chicago. Here the public was treated to an almost unbelievable spectacle as hoodlum Tony D'Andrea ran for alderman against a man named John Powers. Both sides employed gunmen and bomb throwers, not to mention hired assassins brought in from New York and Buffalo. The Genna brothers, who were on D'Andrea's side, brought in a gunman all the way from Sicily. He was Antonio Spano, otherwise known as The Cavalier, who already had had a bloody career as a Mafia executioner in his homeland.

After the Genna crowd managed to kill two of Powers's campaign workers, 28 other people were killed on both sides, among them D'Andrea himself. As stated in a previous chapter, some of the names of intended murder victims in the ''election campaign'' were actually posted on a famous tree in Chicago's Little Italy. It was altogether one of the most bizarre episodes in American political history.

Along about this time Capone, of all people, was made a deputy sheriff of Cook County! This fact alone should give the reader some idea of the influence of the mobs on Chicago's officialdom.

Capone was Torrio's No. 1 business associate, but there were other well-known Torrio lieutenants. Among them were Frank (The·Enforcer) Nitti, who handled day-to-day operations; Mike (The Pike) Heitler, who did much of the strongarm stuff; and Jake (Greasy Thumb) Guzik, so called because he was the treasurer, accountant and payoff man.

By 1922, Capone had still not come to the attention of the press. However in August, driving while drunk, he smashed his car into a taxicab. He jumped from the car and threatened the cab driver and onlookers with a gun. Eventually the police rolled up and arrested him, charging him with assault with a car, driving while drunk and carrying a concealed weapon. The small item about it in the next day's paper even got his name wrong: "Alfred Caponi, 25 years old . . ."

All three of the charges against Capone were serious ones, which, if proved, could have gotten him years in jail. However, the case never even came up and Capone never appeared in court. The whole thing was just squashed.

It was not until 1923 that Al Capone, finally nicknamed Scarface, really came to public attention. (Capone, who had been in the army during World War I, sometimes told admirers that he was wounded on the front. Actually, his long facial scar came from a bottle fight with a customer in Frank Yale's Brooklyn bar, where Capone had been a bouncer.)

Not all of Chicago's hoodlums were in one mob or another. Some were still trying to be independent. One of these was a man named Joe Howard, a gun-toting safecracker. A loud-talking, bragging type, Howard claimed to have three notches on his gun. Considering the men he was about to pit himself against, Howard's three notches were not all that impressive.

Howard, blearily eyeing the profits of the booze business, decided to cut himself in on it. First he tried robbing a bonded distillery, only to be caught by the police. The case eventually was dropped, proving, if nothing else, that even a small-timer like Howard could put in the fix in Chicago. Next he hijacked two beer trucks, which was to prove his downfall. They belonged to Torrio.

The following evening Howard sat around in a place called Heinie's, not far from the Four Deuces. He'd been barred from the Four Deuces on the simple grounds that he was a slob. In tones easily overheard, Howard told his friends how easy it was to steal from the bootleggers. The next night Howard was again in Heinie's when two men entered.

"Hello, Al," Howard said, sticking out his hand to shake.

The man he spoke to shot him six times, smiled at everyone, and walked out.

One witness, a carpenter, said the killer positively was Al Capone. Within 30 minutes, police had an all-points lookout for him, and the next day the Chicago newspapers ran Capone's picture for the first time.

On May 8, the day after the shooting, there was an inquest at which all three of the witnesses suffered a sudden loss of memory.

Meanwhile Capone had dropped out of sight. He reappeared a month later by walking into a police precinct station and blandly asking, "I hear the police are looking for me. What for?"

Capone was questioned by Assistant District Attorney William H. McSwiggin, who said he planned to prosecute, but eventually gave up.

By 1923 the peace that had prevailed in Chicago's gangland was about to be broken. Spike O'Donnell, leader of the South Side O'Donnells, was in prison when Torrio and the others were cutting up the city. When he was released, O'Donnell decided that his gang hadn't gotten its fair share.

O'Donnell decided to improve on the arrangement and this seemed like a good time to press Torrio. Big Bill Thompson, the bootleggers' friend, had just been defeated by a reformer, William E. Dever, who'd vowed to clean up Chicago. With Torrio's connections with City Hall temporarily cut, Spike O'Donnell thought Torrio would not want to make waves.

The South Side mob's first move was to start making their own beer, and forcing it on saloonkeepers in the nearby territory of the Saltis-McErlane gang. In addition, O'Donnell brought in New York gunman Harry Hasmiller and hired paroled convicts to hijack Torrio beer wagons. At first Torrio behaved as expected, and refused to get into a shooting war. His only retaliation was to cut the price of his beer by $10 per barrel.

Unfortunately for the O'Donnells, they made the same mistake that Joe Howard made: they went too far. Not content with muscling in on Saltis-McErlane joints and hijacking Torrio beer trucks, they started trying to get even Torrio speakeasies to take their beer. An affront like that could hardly be ignored if Torrio were to remain in power.

On the night of September 7, 1923, Steve, Walter and Tommy O'Donnell, along with Jerry O'Connor, George (Spot) Bucher and George Meeghan beat the living daylights out of Jacob Geis, a Torrio beer user, and his bartender. Then, feeling their oats, the O'Donnells smashed up five other Torrio spots. Finally, somewhat exhausted by their strenuous "selling" efforts, they repaired to one of their own places on South Lincoln Street.

They had been there about an hour or so, drinking beer and munching sandwiches, when the door flew open and in walked Deputy Sheriff Daniel McFall and four other men.

"Stick 'em up, or I'll blow you to hell," McFall yelled, and he sent a shot over Spike O'Donnell's head. The O'Donnells began diving out of doors and windows just as another man carrying a shotgun appeared. McFall and the shotgun wielder chased the O'Donnells outside, where there was a great deal of shooting for several minutes. When the smoke cleared, the O'Donnells' man, O'Connor, lay dead. The police claimed that the man with the shotgun was McErlane.

Only ten days later, the O'Donnells' other henchmen, Meeghan and Bucher, were ambushed in their car as they waited for a traffic light. They were killed by machine-gun fire from a car that moved slowly past; McErlane was beginning to favor the tommygun over the shotgun.

Reform mayor Dever was shocked at this outburst of gang violence and ordered a police crackdown on all known speakeasies. This had little or no effect, as even the police cheerfully ignored him. During his three years in office, Dever was to see 135 men slaughtered in gang wars in the streets of Chicago.

Al Capone was questioned about the Meeghan-Bucher murders, but he said he was only a secondhand furniture dealer who needed his license to carry a gun because of all the crime in Cicero. Businessmen have to protect themselves, he said. Torrio went away for a short vacation, leaving his lawyer to present his alibi. It seems that Torrio was at a wake at the time of the killings. So-called Deputy Sheriff McFall was indicted for the death of O'Connor, but was quickly acquitted, because of a mix-up over the bullets found in the body.

At this point, the frustrated O'Donnell complained to the police, who were questioning him at the time, "I can whip this bird Capone with bare fists any time he wants to step out into the open and fight like a man."

Spike O'Donnell finally realized that the odds were against him when his prize gunman, Hasmiller, and his brother Walter O'Donnell were shot to death in a roadhouse. Spike decided to retire, at least until he regrouped his forces.

CHAPTER SEVEN
1924

By the fall of 1923 when Mayor Dever was trying to cut down on gang violence, Johnny Torrio and Al Capone had a small army of some 700 men. On election day in Cicero in April 1924, the Torrio battalions were victorious.

During the elections the Torrio syndicate had had to fight not only law and order, such as it was, but other gangs who were trying to put their own puppets into office. In one of the shootouts, Frank Capone, Al's brother, was killed. So were some 12 other men.

With the installation of Torrio's slate, Cicero became the most wide-open town in all of Prohibition America. The commuter trains ran back and forth between there and downtown Chicago. Greeting the trains and the tourists were barkers who yelled, "Step right in, folks, and wet your whistles." "Hey, mister, would you like a girl?"

At one of the casinos, Lauterback's, there was as much as $100,000 on the dice table at one time. In this one small suburban community there were 161 speakeasies and gambling dens. Capone—handling affairs while Torrio was touring Europe with his family—and depositing a cool million in banks overseas—gave the Cicero slot-machine concession to Eddie Vogel. Dion O'Bannion got the beer rights in exchange for his help with men, arms and ammunition during the blazing "election campaign." The West Side O'Donnells got a large share of the gambling clubs and speakeasies.

In nearby Stickney, Illinois there were dozens of brothels, with as many as 60 girls in each. Capone and Torrio owned virtually all of these, and got their cut of much of what happened in Cicero and other nearby towns as well. According to federal investigations, Capone and Torrio took profits of $100,000 per week each just from their suburban operations.

Now and then there was trouble. Take the case of Eddie Tancl, a fearless ex-prizefighter who ran the Hawthorne Inn in Cicero. He had his own source of beer and hard liquor and he refused to buy at inflated prices from the mobs. In answer to being told to go along or get out of town, Tancl growled, "Try and put me out. I was in Chicago long before you guys came!"

When Tancl did leave Cicero, shortly afterwards, it was in a long, narrow pine box.

Tancl was in his saloon talking to one of his waiters, Leo Kilmas, when Miles O'Donnell of the West Side gang and gunman James J. Doherty picked a fight with him over the quality of the food. When the guns came out, Tancl fired back. Finally, mortally wounded, Tancl flung his empty gun into O'Donnell's face and yelled, "Kill the rat! He got me!" Kilmas jumped onto O'Donnell's back, but was dispatched with a shot from Doherty.

Both killers were brought to trial, but were acquitted. The district attorney who failed to prove his case was the same man who had failed to get Al Capone into jail on the Howard murder: William H. McSwiggen.

The Hawthorne Inn, Tancl's place, then fell to Al Capone, who expanded it and made it his Cicero headquarters. It became so well known that the bus drivers referred to it—to the gawking tourists —as Capone Castle.

Shortly after the April election, the Chicago Crime Commission published a list of public enemies. Al Capone was in the No. 1 position. Others on the list were: Tony (Mops) Volpe, Ralph Capone, Frank Rio (alias Frank Kline, alias Frank Gline), Jack "Machine Gun" McGurn, James Belcastro, Rocco Fanelli, Lawrence (Dago Lawrence) Mangano, Jack Zuta, Jake Guzik, Frank Diamond, George (Bugs) Moran, Joe Aiella, Edward (Spike) O'Donnell, Joe (Polack Joe) Saltis, Frank McErlane, Vincent McErlane, William Niemoth, Danny Stanton, Miles O'Donnell, Frank Lake, Terry Druggan, William (Klondike) O'Donnell, George (Red) Baker, William (Three-Fingered Jack) White, Joseph (Peppy) Genero, Leo Mongoven, and James (Fur) Sammons.

Along about the middle of 1924, the *real* beer war began. The truce between the gangs that Johnny Torrio had arranged was only a working arrangement. Between the Sicilian-Italian hoodlums and the non-Mediterranean crooks, particularly the Irish, there was deep-seated antagonism, much of it for ethnic reasons. In addition, men like Dion O'Bannion resented Capone and Torrio, thinking that, despite their success, they were newcomers to Chicago. It was also a question of envy and greed.

O'Bannion, Capone and Torrio were known as the Big Three of Chicago crime, but O'Bannion was always of the opinion that it should have been the Big One—himself. As the general grumbling grew, the Irish, Poles, Germans and Jews more or less rallied around O'Bannion. Capone and Torrio could only be reasonably certain of the Gennas, and they didn't trust them very far.

Things started to go wrong between Torrio and O'Bannion when the former realized that he'd made a big mistake giving O'Bannion the entire beer concession for Cicero. At the time, Torrio and Capone had thought it would be worth about $20,000 per month. Instead, thanks to the boom in Cicero, O'Bannion was taking profits of $100,000 per month.

Another thing that bothered the Sicilians was the fact that O'Bannion had a big mouth. Once, when his beer trucks were stopped by two policemen who demanded a $300 bribe to let them pass, O'Bannion exclaimed, "What! I can have them bumped off for less than that!"

This telephone conversation was actually overheard in the early days of wire taps by the Chicago police. O'Bannion's next call was from Torrio's office. The caller said: "Johnny says give 'em the money. He don't want no trouble." At this point, the police, afraid that O'Bannion would simply send a squad of men to kill the policemen, sent a posse to rescue and arrest them.

On another occasion, when told that the Gennas were upset about his operating in their territory, O'Bannion was quoted as saying, "To hell with them Sicilians." This one remark, as much as anything else, is probably what hastened Dion's demise.

But O'Bannion was a man who lived dangerously, and if he had any sense of public relations he kept it well hidden. Once O'Bannion's lieutenant, Yankee Schwartz, complained that Davy Miller, a gambler-gangster and former Torrio-O'Bannion bootlegging partner, had refused to speak to him. At this time, Miller was a prizefight referee.

One night O'Bannion waited for Miller outside a music hall in Chicago's Loop, and in front of at least 1,000 sidewalk witnesses O'Bannion opened fire. Miller's life was saved by his belt buckle, the bullet spending most of its strength against it. Nevertheless he was severly wounded. O'Bannion was never even charged.

Things came to a head when Torrio, realizing how much money O'Bannion was making out of Cicero's beer concession, asked him for 25 percent of it in exchange for a piece of Torrio's brothel business in Stickney. O'Bannion's reply: "Johnny, go peddle your papers."

At this juncture O'Bannion tried an extreme ploy to rid himself of Torrio for a few years, at least. O'Bannion, Torrio and Capone owned the Sieben Brewery, one of the biggest in Chicago. It was one of those supposedly making near-beer. The police in their kindly way had allowed it to operate with their protection for three years, but then Special Agent Eliot Ness and the federal authorities insisted that it be raided. The bust was scheduled for May 19, 1924. The cops warned O'Bannion, but he failed to tell his partners about it.

Instead, O'Bannion saw the raid as a heaven-sent opportunity for him to get Torrio. The Irishman went to Capone and Torrio and said that the animosity of the Gennas was making him nervous. In fact, he said, he wanted to retire from the rackets and go live on a ranch in Colorado with his pal, Two-Gun Louis Alterie. All he wanted was $500,000 for his interest in the brewery. Capone and Torrio were surprised and happy to get rid of O'Bannion so easily, and agreed on the price immediately. O'Bannion said they would work out the details while overseeing a shipment from the plant on the night of May 19.

To allay suspicion, O'Bannion planned to allow himself to get caught in the raid, too. He craftily thought that as a first-time offender he would get only a fine, but that Torrio, who'd been caught once before, would draw a stiff prison sentence. At the same time, the Torrio-Capone outfit could hardly suspect him, since he was caught in the same net.

It was a neat plan, but Torrio smelled a rat the moment the police cars appeared. However, the legal aspect worked out almost exactly as O'Bannion planned. As it was, he never lived to see Torrio pull his nine-month prison sentence.

The climax approached when, in retaliation for O'Bannion intrusions into their territory, the half-mad Genna brothers began selling their homemade gin in O'Bannion country. O'Bannion repeatedly complained about this to Capone, but Capone failed to give him any satisfaction. Some reporters of the day decided that Capone and Torrio wanted the Gennas and O'Bannion to fight it out between themselves.

O'Bannion finally decided that "them Sicilians," meaning the Gennas and Capone-Torrio (who were actually Italians) were out to make a sucker of him. He thereupon told his men to hijack *any* booze trucks they felt like, regardless of whose they were. As it turned out, many of them belonged to the Gennas.

The Irishman was reaching the pinnacle of his success in other ways as well. He was deeply involved in politics, and in the local and state elections in November 1924 he did everything he could to ensure that his friends got in. At this point there occurred a social event that left reform Mayor Dever almost speechless.

At a dinner at the Webster Hotel where political boss Dion O'Bannion was the toast of the evening, several of the city's leading politicians sat down to eat and drink with some of the best known gangsters and murderers of the day. One of those who joined the head table was no less than Colonel Albert A. Sprague, the Democratic nominee for the United States Senate. Another was County Clerk Robert M. Sweitzer, a former unsuccessful candidate for mayor, and two police officials.

The funny thing about the dinner was that O'Bannion and his henchmen were actually against the election of Sprague. They had attended the dinner merely to keep an eye on him and make sure he didn't get too many votes in their precinct, which he didn't.

After the election, in which O'Bannion's people outpolled the others, the Irishman was jubilant. During the daylight hours in his florist shop, he kept bragging to friends how he had "pulled it off." O'Bannion wanted to be known as a man with election power.

Just as this was going on, Mike Merlo, president of Chicago's Unione Siciliano, died a natural death, and for several days mourners—mostly gangsters—dropped by O'Bannion's shop to order flowers for the funeral. On November 10, Carmen Vacco, a city official, and James Genna, one of the six brothers, came in and ordered flowers for Merlo. The two men told O'Bannion to stick around because some more friends would be in for flowers. Then they left.

A few minutes later, over the phone, O'Bannion was told that these other customers were on their way. He was alone in his shop, with only a black porter, William Crutchfield, in the back sweeping up. About ten minutes passed and then a large sedan containing four men pulled up outside. One of them remained at the wheel.

According to what Crutchfield told police later, when the three men walked in O'Bannion seemed to recognize them, and said

87

"Hello, boys, you from Mike Merlo's?" He had his flower shears in his left hand, and he extended his right to shake hands. One of the men took the hand, held it tightly, and the other two pumped six shots into O'Bannion's head and body. He died instantly.

Witnesses gave descriptions, and Torrio, Capone and the Gennas were all pulled in for questioning. Naturally the gang leaders had alibis. The coroner's report said only this:

"Slayers not apprehended. John Scalise, Albert Anselmi and Frank Yale of New York suspected, but never brought to trial."

From those names, one might gather that it was a Torrio-Capone job, rather than a Genna one. Perhaps it was a joint venture. In any case, this was the second time that Frank Yale was coincidentally on the scene when a really big job needed doing. The first occasion had been the murder of Big Jim Colosimo.

It's possible that the coroner was wrong in his conclusion about Yale. As best as can be determined, Frank Yale just happened to be in town that day, possibly on Unione Siciliano business due to the death of Mike Merlo. Yale was the national president of the Unione. Or he may have been the man at the wheel of the car.

O'Bannion's crowd learned however that Anselmi and Scalise, Torrio-Capone men, were paid $10,000 each for the deed. They also each got a $3,000 diamond ring, which they flashed every-where. The third man—the one who grasped O'Bannion's hand —was none other than Mike Genna. One theory has it that Capone and Torrio knew about the execution, but had nothing to do with it. Anselmi and Scalise would kill for anyone, even the Gennas, if the price was right.

O'Bannion was planted in a $10,000 coffin, with $50,000 in flowers, including a basket of roses bearing a card, "From Al." There, across the open grave, Torrio, Capone, the Gennas, Hymie Weiss (O'Bannion's bosom sidekick), Vincent (The Schemer) Drucci, Louis (Two-Gun) Alterie, and many others stared at one another, each with his own thoughts.

Torrio's first thought was to get out of town fast before Hymie Weiss fulfilled his vow to get O'Bannion's enemies, or Two-Gun Alterie made good his challenge to shoot it out with O'Bannion's killer on the corner of State and Madison streets. Immediately after the funeral Torrio departed on a trip to Hot Springs, Arkansas, New Orleans, the Bahamas and Cuba. He managed to stay one jump ahead of Weiss & Co. until he reached his own front door in Chicago. There they caught up with him.

Al Capone, Chicago's most powerful ganglord, is shown in this police "mug shot" taken just after he'd been arrested in Philadelphia for carrying a gun. Note how the police allowed him to keep his hat on; Capone was very vain about his receding hairline. It was theorized that Capone had himself incarcerated in order to avoid enemies who were gunning for him in Chicago.

Mayor William E. Dever, who tried in vain to clean up Chicago.

The old Seiben Brewery in Chicago was supposed to make "near beer," but, under Torrio and O'Bannion, it made stuff far stronger than that. Torrio himself was caught there in a Federal raid allegedly set up by O'Bannion, who wanted his "partner" out of the way, in jail. O'Bannion was blasted into eternity shortly after that, but whether it was Torrio's men or the Genna gang who got him has never been clear.

Revenue agents Moe Smith, Izzy Einstein and Jack Gosnell at the scene of a still that's been raided in New York.

Dion O'Bannion's flower shop, where he was shot in 1924 by several men who came in pretending to want flowers.

His body being carried away.

Yet another speakeasy being raided, this one in Detroit.

Frank Uale, otherwise known as Frank Yale, a New York killer and speakeasy operator who occasionally worked as a gun for hire. Police found him at the railroad station, leaving Chicago, on the day after O'Bannion's killing. He was questioned, but released.

A bootlegger attempts to jettison his illegal load as a police launch closes in.

James Genna.

Sam Genna, along with James, managed to go into hiding and avoid being slaughtered in the Chicago wars.

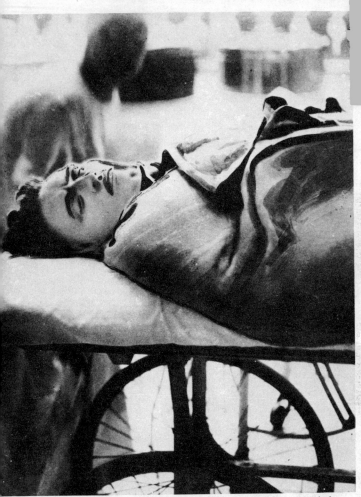

Tony Genna lies on a stretcher after being mortally wounded by gunmen waiting in ambush.

Important on the New York rackets scene during Prohibition was the boyish-looking Dutch Schultz, who distributed the worst beer in New York and who would kill a man if he didn't like his looks.

Waxey Gordon, a cometing ganglord who lived to tell the tale.

An up-and-coming Lucky Luciano, whose main business in the early 1920's was running a chain of New York brothels. Here, he's at the races.

Another still being raided, this time in 1926.

Legs Diamond, a New York gangster, was essentially just a holdup man and "protection racket" salesman. Here, he's seen in one of his many courtroom appearances.

Diamond was never really part of organized crime and, eventually, when he stepped on the wrong people's toes, he was eliminated. But only after many attempts.

When Legs Diamond wasn't shooting at people or "protecting" them, he was in court or recovering from wounds. Here he is seen in court. . . .

In the hands of police . . .

leaving a hospital . . .

and leaving a courthouse. By accident or design, he kept himself
in the news.

Legs Diamond making one of his final appearances in court, this time on a holdup charge.

The Aratoga restaurant in New York's Catskills, the scene
of one of many attempts on Diamond's life. He received chest
wounds when men armed with shotguns blasted away at him
as he left the roadhouse.

The funeral of Legs Diamond, in 1934.

Al Capone smiles confidently on his way to the Atlanta Federal pen following his 1931 conviction for tax evasion. He thought they wouldn't keep him inside for long, despite his 11-year sentence, but he did eight years in Atlanta and Alcatraz.

Vincent "The Schemer" Drucci, a member of the Bugs Moran gang who was suspected of rubbing out Angelo Genna. Drucci himself was killed in a shootout with police during the Chicago elections of 1927.

George "Bugs" Moran, the gangleader that the Capone mob was after at the St. Valentine's Day Massacre, but missed. Although Moran lost the war for Chicago's crime supremacy to Capone, he was one of the few rivals of Capone to live. In the St. Valentine's Day Massacre of 1929, seven Moran gang members were mowed down by machineguns in a Chicago garage. Moran, luckily for him, was late in arriving. Capone himself was in Miami. The crime has never been solved.

This speakeasy was found in an abandoned church.

Louis "Two Gun" Alterie, one-time O'Bannion bodyguard, was standing under the canopy of the building at right when a machinegun opened up on him from a window in the building opposite. He was killed instantly. The year was 1935.

Bugs Moran, seen here in court, when questioned by the police about the St. Valentine's Day Massacre in which seven of his cronies died, forgot the underworld code of silence in his rage and exclaimed, "Only Capone kills like that!"

The legendary Arnold Rothstein, gambler, loan shark and backer of shady enterprises, reputedly was the man who fixed the World Series. He should have stuck to crooked gambling; when he tried to move into other rackets, such as narcotics, he was hit.

His accused killer, one "Titanic" Thompson, is at right. New York police always thought that Dutch Schultz had something to do with Rothstein's sudden death.

Dutch Schultz was probably the best-known and certainly the most ruthless gang leader of York's Prohibition years. Schultz, who tried to have Special Prosecutor Thomas E. Dewey killed, once complained about the way the press put his name in headlines. "If I'd stuck to my real name," he said, "Arthur Flegenheimer, nobody woulda ever heard of me!" In this photograph, Schultz, on the right, is talking to his lawyer, James L. Noonan.

CHAPTER EIGHT

1925—Chicago

This was the year that was to see the beginning of two simultaneous gang wars in Chicago. One was the battle for supremacy between the Irish-Jewish mobs, formerly closely associated with O'Bannion, and the Italian-Sicilian element, the generals of which were Torrio, Capone and the Gennas.

The second war was over the control of Chicago's Unione Siciliano. Here Torrio and Capone were pitted against the Gennas. The presidency of the Unione was not just a matter of prestige; most of the 15,000 home brewers on the Gennas' payroll—their alky cooking empire—were members of, or believed in, the Unione. It was their "thing." Whoever had the presidency of the club could do business with them. Torrio and Capone had long coveted the Gennas' bathtub gin monopoly, but they knew that the only way to get through to the "distillers" was through the Unione. Aware that Mike Merlo, the Gennas' friend, was ill and not destined to remain long as the Unione's president, Torrio managed to make a deal with his old associate, Frank Yale. Yale was the founder and national president of the Unione. He gave Torrio the right to appoint the next Chicago Unione president.

Since neither Torrio nor Capone were Sicilians, and therefore not eligible for Unione presidency themselves, they decided to appoint someone cooperative with them and not too displeasing to the Gennas. On Merlo's death, Torrio appointed Antonio Lombardo. This did not go down at all well with the Gennas. While Lonbardo was a partner of Joseph Aiello, one of their associates, they knew that Lombardo himself was much closer to Torrio. They could see that Torrio was trying to ease into their alky business.

Even before Lombardo could take office under Torrio's sponsorship the Gennas quietly talked to the entire Unione membership and got them to endorse their man, young Angelo Genna. He was installed in the Unione office with an armed bodyguard to see that he wasn't ousted. Capone and Torrio did nothing about it at the time, because they had their hands full with O'Bannion.

Once O'Bannion was dead, the war with the Gennas over the Unione and with the late O'Bannion's allies and avengers got under way.

Hymie Weiss, a small, shrewd man with a pugnacious disposition, struck first. On January 12, 1925, Weiss, Schemer Drucci and Bugs Moran tried to get Capone. Al, who was running things for Torrio while the latter was on vacation and buying a home in Italy, had just alighted from his car in front of a restaurant and gone inside. At that moment, a large touring car with curtained windows drove past and poured machine-gun fire into Capone's vehicle. His chauffeur was wounded, but Al was safe inside the building.

It was this incident that caused Capone to order the first of his famous bulletproof cars, with armor-plated bodies and windows three inches thick. The first one cost him $24,000 and when photographers took pictures of it, he pleaded with them not to show the license plate, since this would make the number known and he'd be a marked man. (As if the huge, tanklike vehicle weren't distinctive enough!) When a newspaper finally did run a photo of the car showing the license plate, Capone immediately ordered another and gave the first one to a friend.

The next Weiss foray against Capone-Torrio came only 12 days after the attack on Capone's car. The day following Torrio's return to Chicago, the gang leader went shopping with his wife. As the Torrios got out of their car and approached their house another car rolled to a stop and two gunmen, one with a pistol and one with a shotgun, rushed toward them. One of the gunmen was Bugs Moran. Torrio ran for his front door, but was cut down by several blasts. The man with the automatic ran over to give him the coup de grace when the escape car's horn sounded. The man with the pistol tried to get off one more shot at Torrio, but he was out of bullets. He ran for his car and the murder team roared off.

Torrio made a swift recovery from his wounds, but even before he went inside to serve his nine-month sentence for bootlegging, he announced that he was giving up Chicago and moving with his whole family to Italy. It is alleged that Capone, in addition to giving Torrio a vast sum of money, agreed to send him occasional "royalties" once he was out of jail and settled overseas.

122

Capone was now sole boss of the firmly established Torrio-Capone domain. His only problems were Hymie Weiss, and that worthy's associate, Bugs Moran, and the Genna brothers, with whom he was battling for control of the Chicago branch of the Unione. But for a while, Capone needed time to reorganize. Besides Weiss and Moran were having their own argument with the Gennas, whom they blamed for their pal O'Bannion's death, and there was always the chance that they'd kill each other off.

The first favor the Moran-Weiss crowd did for Capone was wiping out Angelo Genna, the president of Chicago's Unione Siciliano. Moran, Weiss and Drucci practically blew young Genna apart as they pulled up beside his open roadster one morning. They used three shotguns. Angelo was buried in a coffin costing $12,500, and the funeral was attended not only by gangsters, but by much of official Chicago as well. There were 300 cars in the procession and the flowers alone were estimated to cost $40,000.

Before Capone had a chance to maneuver his own man into the suddenly vacated Unione presidency, the Gennas once again outsmarted him, and installed one of their own: Sam (Samoots) Amatuna, the hoodlum owner of a popular restaurant. He only lasted four months. In November Drucci and Jim Doherty, whom Weiss had borrowed from the West Side O'Donnells, killed Samoots while he was seated in a barber's chair. Weiss, it is theorized, continued to think that he was reducing the number of Sicilians against him, but what he was really doing was helping Al Capone.

Weiss's next two victims were two associates of Amatuna, Eddie Zion and Bunny Goldstein. They were dead within two weeks, probably because Weiss had heard that they were out to get him for the Amatuna job.

Finally Capone was able to get his own man, Lombardo, in as president of the Unione. At the time, the Gennas were too busy coping with Weiss. (Lombardo was to live longer as president of Chicago's Unione than most—almost two years.)

The Gennas counterattacked. Drucci and Moran were ambushed in their car by Mike Genna, Anselmi and Scalise, but escaped with flesh wounds. While fleeing the job, the Genna car attracted the attention of the police, who gave chase. When the Gennas wrecked their car, two policemen were killed, and one was wounded in the gun battle that followed. Since it was broad daylight, there were hundreds of eyewitnesses to the Genna gang's cutting down the cops.

One policeman who was not wounded gave chase to Mike Genna—Anselmi and Scalise having escaped—and cornered him in a basement. Assisted by two off-duty cops, patrolman William Sweeney wounded and disarmed Genna. As he was being carried out to an ambulance, Mike Genna kicked the attendant in the face, said, "Take that, you son of a bitch," and promptly died.

The police at this point were enraged at the whole gangster element in Chicago. Five policemen had been killed in the single month of June 1925. Things were so bad in Chicago that Vice President Dawes read a petition from leading Chicago citizens to the United States Senate, asking for federal help.

Anselmi and Scalise, who were caught a mile or so from the shooting scene, were charged with cop killing. The Gennas set about raising funds for their defense and managed to get about $100,000, mainly with threats of violence and death. Anyone who objected to the Anselmi-Scalise shakedown was killed. This happened to Henry Springola, a Genna brother-in-law, who gave $10,000, but refused to give more. The next to die were Augustino and Antonio Moreci, who objected to the killing of their friend Springola. The Gennas also killed Vito Bascone, a wine merchant, who refused to make a third payment of $2,000 to the defense fund.

In some cases, friends of the victims struck back. Four "defense fund" collectors for the Gennas were shot dead: Orassio (The Scourge) Tropea, Little Joe Calabriese, Eddie (The Eagle) Baldelli and Tony Finalli.

All of this killing simply to raise money to defend two known murderers!

But while all this was going on, Capone had begun his own offensive. Sensing that the Gennas were weakening, with two of the six brothers already dead and their two best gunmen, Anselmi and Scalise, in jail, Capone engaged Antonio Spano, known as The Cavalier. Spano had been brought from Sicily originally by the Gennas, but in both his native land and in Chicago he was simply a hired gun, available to the highest bidder. When Spano telephoned Tony the Gentleman Genna, saying he had something important to tell him, the dapper Genna went to meet him right away. As they shook hands on a street corner two gunmen came out of the shadows and filled Genna's back with lead.

He lived long enough to tell his wife in the hospital that his killer was The Cavalier. Police, who were listening, said he named a man called Cavallero. At least this was their excuse for making no arrests; they couldn't find a hood named Cavallero.

The death of Tony took the starch out of the Genna family. Two of the brothers, Sam and Pete, disappeared to a hideout in downstate Illinois, and Jim went back to Sicily where he was arrested on an old charge and incarcerated for five years.

Other gangs were doing their own sorting out. Including the Genna-Weiss war, and the Capone-Genna war, there were 76 gang killings in Chicago between the summer of 1925 and the summer of 1926.

It was in 1925 that Al Capone complained to a reporter friend that he couldn't get his life insured. He said he's applied to several legitimate companies and offered to pay any premium they asked, but was refused every time. He apparently couldn't understand why they thought a policy on his life would be a bad risk. Had a company charged a high enough premium, it probably could have made money on Al Capone—he was to live another 22 years!

As the year 1925 drew to a close, there had been a subtle change in the balance of power in Chicago. While the Italians and Sicilians were not in complete control, they were at least as powerful as the Irish-Jewish element and definitely a force to be reckoned with. No longer were they laughed at as being "Mustache Petes," Black Handers, or "gun-crazy kids."

Some of the Irish-Jewish gangs were linked in a subordinate role to the Capone gang. The remaining O'Bannion loyalists were embattled and running scared. While Bugs Moran and Weiss had been successful in reducing the Gennas' power, the Gennas were replaced by the Aiellos and Capone, who through Lombardo had seized the Chicago Unione Siciliano.

And whether Weiss and Moran realized it or not, the organization of Chicago had begun.

CHAPTER NINE
1925—New York

The situation in New York was much the same as that in Chicago despite the fact that much of the city's real talent had been exported to the Windy City. Al Capone and Johnny Torrio were both New York boys who went to Chicago and made good.

As in Chicago, the big gangs that got immediately into bootlegging stemmed from gangs that had been formed during the labor wars of 1900-1919. Usually it was the employers who hired the gangs to break strikes by threatening or committing violence on union leaders. Two early enlistees in pre-World War I gangs were Louis Buchalter, affectionately called "Lepke" by his family, and his apelike associate, Jake Shapiro, who started out in crime as a sneak thief. Lepke, who was born in 1897, had honest parents who worked desperately hard to educate their children. One son became a rabbi, one a pharmacist and one a dentist. Lepke's sister became a teacher.

Lepke himself became an unsuccessful burglar. He had been arrested twice by the time he was 18, and when he was 20 he was sentenced to a year in Sing Sing for yet another failed burglary. No matter; he eventually managed to control a gang that was responsible for the deaths of 70 people, and by 1939, Lepke was named by J. Edgar Hoover as the "most dangerous criminal in America." Thomas E. Dewey's accolade was that Lepke was "the worst industrial racketeer in the United States."

By 1922 Lepke, released from prison, was with the labor enforcement gang of Li'l Augie Orgen. Jake Shapiro, known as "Gurrah" for his colorful way of saying, "Gur outa here!" was in the mob with him, along with another character soon to achieve fame, Waxy Gordon.

It wasn't long before the unions realized that they needed to hire some muscle of their own, and by 1922 both sides had gunmen in their ranks. Some gangs hired out to both sides in the same dispute.

Eventually there was competition among the gangs for business. The mob of one Kid Dropper, from Manhattan, tried to take over some of Orgen's jobs, but Curly Holtz, an Orgen lieutenant, got his man Lou Cohen to shoot Dropper in the head—right in front of the courthouse while the hoodlum was seated in a cab talking to a police captain! Cohen got a prison term, but not the chair. (Eventually released from jail, Cohen was killed by one of Lepke's men in 1939.)

The waterfront labor rackets were controlled by the notorious Paolo Vaccarelli, otherwise known as Paul Kelly. Before Prohibition, as mentioned in a previous chapter, he'd had Johnny Torrio in his band. Kelly himself was president of the International Longshoremens' Association. Albert Anastasia, who was also to work for Kelly, arrived in the United States in 1920, by jumping ship in New York. It didn't take long for young Anastasia to begin working his way up on the waterfront. Along with his associate, Jimmy Florio, Anastasia killed longshoreman Joe Turino. They were both convicted and sentenced to die in the electric chair, but 18 months later a new trial was granted. By this time four of the state's witnesses had been murdered, and Albert became a free man again. Only four months later Anastasia was arrested again for murder; this case was dropped. A year later he was arrested for shooting a man dead; this case was dropped. In 1928 he was charged with killing a man with an icepick. He beat this rap too. Anastasia was to go on to become the Lord High Executioner of Murder, Inc.

While clubbing his way to the top of the labor rackets, Anastasia made friends with some tough kids who hung out in Brownsville, a section of Brooklyn that's been the breeding ground of some of the nation's most wanted men. One of the favorite gathering spots was a coffee shop and bakery run by Louis Capone (no relation to Al). It was here that Capone, destined to become a killer himself, and Anastasia met and impressed younger punks like Abe (Kid Twist) Reles, Happy Maione, Pittsburgh Phil and The Dasher. In those early days they were simply petty thieves and errand boys for the mobs, but Albert could see that they were capable of handling bigger things, such as Brooklyn enforcement problems.

The head of the Black Hand in New York in the pre-Prohibition days was the well-known Lupo the Wolf, real name Ignazio Saietta. As previously stated, his pal was Ciro (the Artichoke King) Terranova, who made a habit of buying all the artichokes in New York. Then, as Joe Valachi put it years later, "Since Italians have got to have artichokes to live, he simply charged whatever he liked." Lupo the Wolf had come to the United States after being accused of a murder in Italy. In the early twenties his gang controlled the Italian numbers racket, narcotics in the Italian community and the Black Hand shakedowns of immigrants. Unfortunately for Lupo, he decided that he could print his own money faster than he could steal it, and soon Lupo was pulling 30 years on a counterfeiting rap. He was to be set free a few years later by none other than President Harding. However, Lupo continued to be careless, and shortly was back inside, serving his full sentence.

With Lupo the Wolf out of circulation for the duration of Prohibition, a number of other Italian-Sicilians stepped up to claim leadership of the Italian rackets. One of these was Giuseppe Masseria, whose criminal record stretched back to 1907.

Masseria, a small, rather inconspicuous-looking man, simply announced that he was the boss of Italian rackets, and that was that, so far as he was concerned. At first other racketeers jokingly referred to him as "Joe the Boss." They stopped joking when it turned out that he had the guns to back up his claim. Joe the Boss was the last of New York's "Mustache Petes," but he was to survive for some nine years as one of the city's most powerful crime overlords.

Prohibition provided the opening for immigrant Sicilians and Italians to break into the really big money of United States crime. Heretofore, in New York as in Chicago, the labor rackets, gambling and prostitution were dominated by Irish, Jewish and Polish mobsters. Distilling whiskey and making beer, however, was a talent that the Sicilians in particular had in abundance. For centuries they had been brewing their own untaxed stuff in the hills of Sicily without the hindrance of government regulations. This is why, for instance, the Gennas in Chicago had had such a ready-made labor force available, a bathtub gin industry that was never improved on throughout Prohibition, and one which gave the Gennas a flying start in bootlegging. In New York it was much the same story, with Joe the Boss Masseria in charge.

However, he had lots of competition. Neapolitan Frank Costello and Big Bill Dwyer were smuggling the real stuff in from Canada and from boats at sea. Waxy Gordon and his mob, along with the Diamond brothers, were sticking up bonded government warehouses, where spirits were kept for medicinal purposes.

Throughout Prohibition you could still buy booze if your doctor prescribed it, but such permits weren't easy to come by, and doctors were closely watched. There was also a flourishing market in stolen and counterfeit whiskey permits, with which real hooch could be purchased.

Naturally all of this home-brewed, stolen, smuggled and fraudulently obtained liquor had to have a market, and an exchange market at that. If you were supplying "your" speakeasies, it was no good just having 600 cases of hot bourbon; you needed Scotch and gin as well. An unofficial, but very real, liquor exchange grew up. It was a "curb exchange" in the purest sense of the word, since all of the transactions took place in the street, on streets directly behind police headquarters in Lower Manhattan, as a matter of fact.

Shortly after Joe the Boss announced that he was the No. 1 hood for his people, in 1922, another bootlegger, Umberto Valenti, decided to debate the point. One fine, sunshiny day in August, two men took up a vigil in a restaurant facing Masseria's house on the Lower East Side. When Joe the Boss finally emerged, both gunmen dashed out, firing as they ran after him down the street. Masseria dodged into a nearby hat shop, cursing the fact that he was alone and unarmed. For what happened next, here is the account of the shopkeeper, Fritz Heiney:

The one with the gun comes right up to the other fellow. Just as he fires, the little fellow jumped to one side. The bullet went through the window of my store. The man fires again and the little man ducks his head forward. I don't know where that bullet went, except it didn't hit him. The man shoots again. The other man ducks again. This one made another hole in my window.

The gunman eventually fled in disgust with an empty gun. Masseria was shaken, but unharmed. After that, he was considered almost a legendary figure by his countrymen—the man who was faster than bullets.

The next move was Masseria's. He arranged a peace conference with Valenti. The two of them talked it over alone in an East Side spaghetti joint. After the conference they came out together, joking and laughing. They even shook hands and parted. A minute later, two of Joe the Boss's men pumped Valenti full of slugs as he opened the door to a cab. The Masseria crowd considered the peace conference a great success, and Joe the Boss went on to set up his operation.

His rackets in Brooklyn were run by Frank Yale, the national president of the Unione Siciliano. In the downtown area of Manhattan, Joe the Boss placed a young whoremonger who was beginning to show promise, Charles Luciano. One of Luciano's henchmen was Vito Genovese. Both men were destined to be No. 1 gang leaders in their day. Luciano, like Anastasia, had also arrived in the States illegally. One of his first jobs had been in a hat factory, but he quit it, he said, "Because I didn't want to wind up being just a crumb." For a short time he worked for the Diamond brothers, Eddie and Legs, rather simpleminded gunmen whose main forte was hijacking beer trucks, sticking up stores and shaking down small businessmen. The Diamonds were never really accepted into the underworld, being regarded as mere holdup men with no class.

Another early Luciano employer was George Uffner, who was deeply involved in a narcotics ring funded by gambler and loan shark Arnold Rothstein. Luciano gave all that up when he went with Masseria because he could see that Joe the Boss was a man of destiny. Luciano became known as "Lucky" after some rival hoods kidnaped and tortured him to learn the whereabouts of some dope he was handling. He wouldn't talk, and they left him badly cut and burned, but he surprised them and survived.

Joe the Boss knew, though, that there was a limit to his plans for expansion. Lepke, Costello, Dwyer and Gordon were too big, and had too many guns. Nor was he about to take the Harlem numbers rackets and the beer bootlegging business from Dutch Schultz. The latter was simply not a man to be fooled with. Throughout Prohibition Dutch Schultz made probably the worst beer of any in the country. At the same time, he had the biggest beer bootlegging operation in New York for the simple reason that anyone who tried to compete with him seriously wound up dead. The Dutchman would tolerate a certain amount of imported beer, and a few small beer breweries here and there, but nothing big.

Dutch Schultz's real name was Arthur Flegenheimer, but he was nicknamed by his Bronx teen-age buddies after one of their old-time heroes, a prizefighter of the early 1900s. By the time Arthur was 17, he'd done time for burglary. In the early twenties, Schultz started up in the numbers rackets in Harlem, taking as a sidekick a man named Joey Rao. The Schultz gang rapidly became known for its ruthless tactics. A man of fiery temper and sometimes uncontrollable rage, Schultz more than once was known to have blown a man's head off simply to win an argument. He also was fond of having an enemy maimed, rather than killed.

In addition to his beer monopoly, Schultz added plenty of water to the booze he bought from Costello and Dwyer, and then forced speakeasy operators to buy it. The slot machines in Harlem were also part of the Schultz empire in the twenties. As for the numbers business, Schultz even had a way of improving the odds for himself.

The numbers game works like this: players can pick any number from 000 to 999. That's 1,000 numbers, but the numbers operators only pay off at a rate of 600 to 1. An edge like that should be enough to satisfy anyone, and it was enough, and is today, to satisfy the rest of gangdom. But not Schultz. He managed to find a crooked mathematical genius who could "fix" the number day after day, making certain that numbers with a lot of money bet on them did not win.

The winning number was picked then, just as it is now, from the figures in the mutuel handle at whatever park the gangs agree on. Say the number is taken from the results of the first three races at Tropical Park. The winning horse might pay $22.40, $12.60 and $4.00. The second horse might pay $6.00 and $3.20. The show horse, $1.20. All of those figures would add up to a total handle for the first race of $49.40. The first number was always the first digit to the left of the decimal in the first race. In this case, the first number would be 9.

This was done for the next two races as well. At the end, the number might be 943. Since the race results and the mutuel handle are published in newspapers every day, anyone who knows the system and which track the number is taken from can tell the winning number.

Schultz's human computer, one Abbadabba Berman, would go out to the track and watch the amounts bet on the tote board. From this, at the last moment, he would be able to compute the price that would be paid on any horse that might win the race. He not only had to figure that out, but he had to figure out all the combinations of win, place and show that went to make up that single number. If it appeared that a heavily played number had a chance of coming up, he would place one bet that would change it, a truly prodigious feat of quick calculating, and one that enriched the Dutchman by millions.

Extortions, killings and all-around rough stuff for Dwyer, Costello, Lepke, Gurrah, and sometimes even for Schultz and Masseria, were handled by the firm of Bug and Meyer. The Bug and Meyer mob was named after its two founders, Meyer Lansky and Bugsy Siegel, two of the most ruthless hoods to come down the pike in years. (They didn't work for Waxy Gordon though; they were hired to shoot him.)

By 1925 crime in New York was not yet organized, but there was a certain amount of cooperation between the gangs. Just as in Chicago, however, there were periodic outbursts of rivalry during which hoods bumped each other off and left bodies in the streets, about 500 of them in New York between 1919 and 1925.

Not all gangland victims were killed, however. Dutch Schultz often merely maimed. One of his victims was left tied up with infected bandages over his taped-open eyes; he went blind within a few months.

CHAPTER TEN
1926

One of the 64 men to die by violence in the year of the Great Chicago Bloodbath was District Attorney William H. McSwiggen. On the night of April 27, 1926, while seated in a car at a roadhouse in Cicero, he was blasted into eternity by machine guns. Killed with him were the notorious Jim Doherty and Tom Duffy, both of the West Side O'Donnell gang. Two others in the car were Miles O'Donnell himself and former policeman Edward Hanley, Doherty's driver.

Two questions came immediately to the mind of the public and the press: who killed McSwiggen and what was he doing in that car? Chicago officialdom advanced the theory that McSwiggen was "trying to get information," which, on the face of it, does not seem likely. Very few people believed that a whole carload of gangsters would sit around in a car lot and confess to a lone prosecutor.

Others suspected Al Capone on the theory that he was not getting along too well with the O'Donnells, who'd been overstepping the territory granted them in the Torrio days. If Capone was just after the O'Donnells, then McSwiggen was killed accidentally. Another theory had it that Capone had been paying off McSwiggen for years, but that he discovered that McSwiggen was also getting paid off by the O'Donnells. Rather than lose his "fix," Capone decided to get them all at one of their meetings.

McSwiggen did have a good record for prosecuting hoodlums, although he never managed to get anything on Capone. Nobody knows whether he tried hard or not. Capone himself, questioned about McSwiggen's death, perhaps said more than he meant to. Certainly he revealed that he knew McSwiggen better than anyone had suspected.

"Of course I didn't kill him," said Capone. "Why should I? I liked the kid. Only the day before he got killed he was up to my place and when he went home I gave him a bottle of Scotch for his old man. I paid McSwiggen, and I paid him plenty, and I got what I was paying for."

The next bit of information came from the owner of the Pony Inn, in whose car lot McSwiggen and the hoodlums were killed. He said that when he'd wanted to start a saloon in Cicero, Al Capone had said he couldn't. Finally Capone said he could open, if he bought Capone beer. A few months before the McSwiggen killing, "Doherty and Miles O'Donnell came to me and said they could sell me beer better than Capone beer, which was then needled. They did, and it cost only $50 a barrel, where Capone charged me $60. I changed, and upon my recommendation, so did several other Cicero saloonkeepers."

That sounded like enough motive for a Capone killing. As for McSwiggen, if Capone was paying him, it was speculated that maybe McSwiggen wouldn't stay bought, and was switching to the O'Donnells. In the early days after Torrio left, many people doubted that Capone was strong enough to carry on alone.

And then there was the statement of A. V. Korecek, a hardware dealer, known to be the main supplier of machine guns to the gangs of Chicago. (He claimed that he was "forced" to buy the Thompson guns from a firm in Valparaiso, Chile, and consequently had to dispose of them any way he could.) He said he sold two such guns to men named John and Charlie, but he wouldn't identify them further. He would not say whether they were John Capone or Charles Fischetti, of the Capone gang. He said he feared for his life, and that probably was no exaggeration.

Mr. Korecek also said that he'd sold machine guns to Charlie Carr, manager of Capone's famous Four Deuces hangout on Wabash Avenue.

The next witness was a man who said that on the night of the killings he was in a Cicero restaurant and that he saw Al Capone, Ralph Capone and three other hoodlums in an animated conversation. Following the discussion, Al Capone went over to a cupboard, took out a machine gun and some revolvers and that the gang then went out, just about one hour before the shooting.

Capone disappeared for four months. When he returned and surrendered to the law, the charges against him were dismissed for insufficient evidence!

Meanwhile Capone increased his personal bodyguard to 18 men, many of them hired in New York. He then went gunning for Hymie Weiss, the O'Bannion avenger who'd vowed to wipe out all the Italian and Sicilian mobsters.

He had to wait until August 10 before his troops had a clear shot at him, though. Weiss and Schemer Drucci, carrying $13,000 for a "settlement" with the Chicago Sanitation Department, were about to enter the Standard Oil Building downtown, where the sanitation people had an office. The traditional touring car, carrying the traditionally armed men, raced toward them. As the gunmen inside fired, the noon-hour crowds ran in every direction. Weiss and Drucci took cover and returned the fire. The gun battle lasted for several minutes, but no gunman on either side had been hurt by the time police rolled up.

Drucci and Weiss, true to the gangsters' code, refused to identify a Capone gunman named Louis Barko, who'd failed to make the getaway car. They also refused to say it was a murder attempt. "They was after my roll," was Drucci's explanation.

A week later Capone's band tried again. This time one of his cars forced to the curb a car containing Drucci, Weiss and one of their lawyers. As it happened, this, too, took place in front of the Standard Oil Building. Once again, despite lots of shooting, no one was hurt.

Capone, on advice from the absent Torrio, tried to make peace. He and Weiss met at a "neutral" hotel, with an unnamed police official as referee. Unfortunately for the peace and quiet of Chicago, the two gang bosses failed to reach any sort of agreement.

It took only three weeks for Weiss to mount his next attack, and what it lacked in results it made up for in style. On September 20, Capone and his chief bodyguard, Slippery Frank Rio, were finishing lunch in Capone's Hawthorne Inn in Cicero. It was just before the first race at nearby Hawthorne Racetrack and the town was jammed with people.

Weiss and Co. rolled down the street toward the Inn in an 11-car procession. The first car went by and fired machine-gun blanks in front of the restaurant. When it had passed, Capone started to rise from the floor to run outside. Rio flung himself across Capone to keep him down and yelled, "No, boss, it's a trick! They want you outside!"

Rio couldn't have been more right. The remaining 10 cars in the Weiss cavalcade stopped, and from them machine-gun fire ripped into the restaurant. A man from the last car got out and sprayed machine-gun bullets all over the front of the building and directly into the door. Then Weiss's men drove quickly away. One Capone man and an innocent bystander were wounded.

The inn was practically blown apart. About 35 cars in the area had bullet holes. Yet Capone wasn't touched. Barko, the wounded man, failed to identify Weiss and Drucci, although police asked him to do so and knew he'd seen his attackers. (Since Weiss and Drucci had failed to identify Barko after his attack on them, it was only common criminal courtesy.)

The following month, on October 11, Capone finally won the war with Weiss. The way he went about it was at least a departure from the usual touring-car-with-guns-sticking-out technique. The day after the Weiss armada had invaded Cicero, one of Capone's men rented a room that overlooked O'Bannion's old flower shop, now taken over by O'Bannion's successor, Weiss. A mysterious woman rented another room that overlooked the street beside the flower shop. Both "tenants" disappeared, and soon three machine gunners took up stations at the windows and waited. For a week they watched Weiss and his men go in and out. Apparently they were waiting until the streets were clear of honest citizens. Capone had no desire to upset the whole community by blasting innocent folk.

Weiss was walking into the building with four companions when Capone's boys began blasting. Weiss fell dead, 12 bullets in his body, without ever knowing what hit him. So did his bodyguard. The other three men were seriously wounded, but eventually recovered.

"I'm sorry Weiss is dead," Capone told the police the next day when they called. "I knew I'd be blamed for it. But there's enough business here for all of us, without killing each other like animals." Police could hardly be blamed for yawning as they took his statement.

Some of the other hoods in town decided that it might be prudent to make peace with Capone. After all, with O'Bannion and Weiss both gone, the Gennas out of business and both McDonnell gangs badly shot up, there was a scarcity of people left who were big enough to stand against Capone. Only Bugs Moran still talked tough, but not many people were ready to follow him.

A document found on Weiss's body indicated that he had been in cahoots with the Saltis-McErlane gang to raid the Capone empire.

Since Saltis and McErlane were supposed to be Capone's allies, they were terrified as to what might happen when word of the document got out. They sent an emissary to Capone to see if he was serious about making peace and he said he was.

The peace pipe was passed at the Hotel Sherman in Chicago on October 20, 1926. In attendance were representatives of the following gangs: Capone and Jake Guzik, representing themselves, and Ralph Sheldon who ran an associated Capone gang; Schemer Drucci, who'd inherited the Weiss (formerly O'Bannion) mob, and their cohorts, Ed Vogel and Jack Zuta; Maxie Eisen, representing Saltis and McErlane, temporarily in jail on murder charges; Klondike and Miles O'Donnell, now desperate to make peace before Capone shot up their gang any more.

The spirit of the agreement hammered out was that Capone was to be the boss of Chicago. There were no objections—out loud, anyway. Any territory which had been stolen from Capone by O'Bannion, Weiss and Moran was to go back to Capone. Chicago was redivided, with Capone taking an even larger share than Torrio had the first time "peace" was declared. Furthermore, Capone ruled, there was to be no more shooting. Any disputes were to be brought to him for arbitration.

Amazingly enough, the truce held for 70 days. In a city that had seen 71 gangsters wiped out in a single year, and 300 killed since 1920, it was almost unbelievable.

Mayor Big Bill Thompson was running for office again, and with the armistice, Chicago's hoods could see nothing but salad days ahead.

The truce was broken on December 30 when Hilary Clements, a Sheldon truck driver, was killed on orders from Saltis. It seems that Shelton had overstepped his territory again. To show Saltis that he really meant business about no shooting, Capone had two Saltis men shot and killed.

Things were reasonably quiet again until April 4, 1927, when Big Bill Thompson was once again elected mayor of Chicago, defeating reform Mayor Dever.

Anselmi and Scalise, meanwhile, had been granted a new trial. At their first trial, they were found guilty of manslaughter only, despite the eyewitnesses who had seen them shoot two policemen dead. Their $100,000 worth of legal talent seemed to have paid off.

As the year 1927 began, faint clouds began to gather for hoods in Chicago and New York. The U.S. Supreme Court decided in the case of New York bootlegger Manley Sullivan, that taxes must be paid on all earnings, even if these earnings were illegal. Sullivan's lawyers had claimed that for him to declare his illegal earnings would be the same as testifying against himself, something which the Fifth Amendment of the Constitution says that a man need not do.

When the Supreme Court ruled otherwise, it opened the door to a counterattack against hoods by the federal government. At last there was a weapon that might be used against big bosses who couldn't be convicted any other way.

CHAPTER ELEVEN
1927

The cease-fire arranged by Capone at Chicago's Sherman Hotel on October 21, 1926, was violated three times—there were three deaths over Christmas. In January 1927 Bugs Moran, who was still smoldering over the deaths of his partners O'Bannion and Weiss, and who was annoyed at the size of the territory allotted him by Capone, reopened the war.

Unable to get at Capone through his massive bodyguard, Moran tried to attack him from another direction. One of Capone's favorite eating places was Tony Anton's, a gourmet establishment in Cicero. Capone was fond of sitting in Tony's private dining room in the back, having his steak and chatting with the owner about baseball. One night as they were thus engaged, the doorbell rang. "Late customers," Tony said, "I'll get rid of 'em." He never came back.

His body was found on the outskirts of town. Why the gangsters didn't just go into the place and shoot Capone where he sat is somewhat of a mystery, but it was thought at the time that they probably believed he had several bodyguards with him.

At any rate, this was one of the few Chicago killings that really reached Capone. He is reported to have cried and vowed vengeance.

The next development was a potshot Vincent the Schemer Drucci took at Capone while Capone was vacationing and doing a little gambling in Hot Springs, Arkansas. The spa was a wide-open town and well known as a resort catering to hoods from all over. Drucci, who had been tailing Capone, got his chance but missed.

Capone was alone for once, and driving himself in a borrowed roadster. Drucci and pals pulled up beside him and began spraying Capone's car with lead. Capone was fat, but quick as a panther when necessary. No sooner had Drucci's car overtaken him than Al touched his brakes and tumbled out of the still-moving car on the far side. He was rolling into the ditch as his car hit a tree. Drucci's car sped on, the occupants jubilant in the thought that they had got him.

Retaliation was called for, but before Capone could arrange something unpleasant for Drucci, the cops did the job for him.

On April 3, the day before the Chicago elections, with the wet Big Bill Thompson once again pitted against the dry Mayor Dever, the gangs were out to ensure a Thompson victory, which, as it turned out, they did. Capone missed Thompson's being in office, and had showed his enthusiasm for Thompson's campaign by contributing $250,000.

Drucci and other members of the Moran gang were in the 42nd Ward of Chicago, making sure that everyone planned to vote for Thompson. One of their ideas was to wreck Dever's local campaign office. As it happened, the police heard of this scheme, and the order went out to pick up Drucci at once. He was arrested and relieved of his gun, by the police, who found him talking to a nightclub owner and another man. All three were taken to the station, but within half an hour Drucci's lawyer had got an order for his release.

Drucci was being taken to the Criminal Courts Building, where his lawyer was waiting for him, by Dan Healy, a policeman who had very little use for hoodlums. A fight broke out in the car. Drucci was handcuffed to Healy, another officer was beside Drucci, with a third policeman driving. Nevertheless Drucci, the officers said, tried to get the policeman's gun. All he got were the bullets—four of them in the stomach. Instead of going to the Criminal Courts Building, the car went to the morgue.

Drucci's lawyer demanded that policeman Healy be charged with murder. The police ignored this, saying they were thinking more in terms of giving Healy a medal.

Drucci's funeral was the typical gangland extravaganza. The mourners at the graveside included Drucci's friends, enemies and political connections. Bugs Moran, who must have been feeling rather lonesome, was there, along with a tearful Al Capone, whom Drucci had only recently tried to kill.

At this point Capone might have turned his full attention to Moran, except that he suddenly found himself with some determined new enemies, the Aiello family. They were much like the Genna family, and were, in fact, the inheritors of the Genna alky-cooking empire. They'd been minor partners of the Gennas until that group was decimated by gunfire and/or sent into hiding. The Aiellos' problem was that they were having trouble hanging onto the thousands of alky cookers who were members of the Unione Siciliano. Capone's man Lombardo was president of the Chicago Unione.

Until he was taken under Capone's wing, Lombardo had been an associate of the Aiellos. He drew away from them when Capone offered him the presidency. The Aiellos' first move was to send delegates to various cities, such as Cleveland, Milwaukee, St. Louis, New York, Pittsburgh and Detroit, to talk about setting up another Unione in Chicago, on the grounds that Capone, a non-Sicilian, had "corrupted" the original one.

Two Aiello men were on just such a mission in Springfield, Illinois, near St. Louis, when persons unknown shot them to death as they dined on spaghetti. The resulting retaliations caused 12 more deaths on both sides in St. Louis.

The Aiellos then formed a partnership with the desperate Bugs Moran, and a few other Capone-ophobes, and plotted to get Capone once and for all—before he got them. They decided to hire out-of-town killers. The fee was $1,000 traveling money and $50,000 cash to the one who actually got Capone.

The first citizen to take up the offer, Antonio Torchio, of New York, was reportedly a Luciano gunman. He was found machine-gunned to death the day after he got off the train in Chicago. The only clue was a nickel found clutched in his hand.

The next volunteers were the team of Anthony K. Russo and Vincent Spicuzza, both of St. Louis. They were found dead the day after they got off the train to Chicago. Machine-gunned to death. Each had a nickel clutched in his hand.

Next came Samuel Valente of Cleveland. Dead. Day after arrival. Machine-gunned. Nickel in the hand.

A monotonous story, to be sure, but Capone is said to have been amused by it.

The killer in all of these instances, it was later reported, was the aptly named Machine-gun Jack McGurn, whose real name, James de Mora, has almost been lost to history. He was Capone's chief assassin.

The Aiellos persisted. They tried to bribe the chef at Capone's usual restaurant, the Little Italy Café, to put prussic acid in Al's soup. Instead the chef told Capone.

Along about here, Capone stopped being "Mr. Nice Guy," and got serious about going after the Aiellos. Between June 1 and July 17, 1927, McGurn and friends killed six Aiello henchmen. This slaughter embarrassed even the Chicago police department, and the chief of detectives formed his own group of raiders, all of them former soldiers with World War I combat experience. He equipped them with machine guns and armored cars. And, ignoring little niceties such as due process of law, he ordered them to shoot first and shoot to kill, whenever they saw known hoodlums up to no good. Considering that there were 500 men in the chief's band, ranged against some 1,000 or so armed hoodlums, it was a good time for innocent bystanders to dig foxholes.

The chief's first engagement with the enemy came before the year was out, when his men killed a bodyguard of Joe Saltis. Police then arrested 45 gangsters and charged them with operating a protection racket against candy store owners, of all people. An anonymous tipster then told the police that they should look closely at a house opposite that of Capone's puppet Unione president, Lombardo. There the cops found an abandoned machine-gun nest. A hotel bill left there led them to a cache of bombs intended for Capone's house. A check on a house across the street from where Capone got his cigars every day revealed another abandoned machine-gun nest.

In the hotel raid where the cops found the bombs, they also found four gentlemen who strongly protested their innocence of any wrongdoing: Joseph Aiello, himself, and three of his coworkers. While Aiello and his band were being questioned, the police noticed a taxicab army assembling around the station house. The cabs were filled with armed Capone men. More police were called for, and eventually, after lots of fighting, three Capone men—New Yorkers borrowed for the war from Luciano—and the Aiellos were in jail, in adjoining cells. Outside in the dark, the Capone mobsters continued to lurk, but the Aiellos got a police escort home.

Just the same, the night of terror at the police station had had quite an effect on Joseph Aiello, the would-be Unione president. He fled to New Jersey, without even stopping to pack his bags. Just in time, too, because his brother Dominick, who stayed to sell some of their properties, was rubbed out.

From New Jersey Joseph Aiello continued to offer $50,000 to anyone who would get Capone, but there was an understandable shortage of takers.

In the meantime, Capone, for all his good relations in New York, was having a bit of trouble with his old pal, former employer and part-time assassin, Frank Yale. He was the Brooklyn manager of Masseria's mob and the conduit for real booze smuggled in from Canada, and shipped to Capone. After several of the loads were stolen between Brooklyn and Chicago, Capone began to think that Yale might be selling the stuff to him and then stealing it back.

Capone sent his gunman, James De Amato, to New York as an investigator. He was killed there before he had learned much about Yale. However De Amato's death in itself had told Capone what he wanted to know.

On the New York scene there also was a bit of a labor dispute. One of Lepke's underlings, Li'l Augie Orgen, had broken away from the main mob to get into narcotics on his own. However he was tempted back into the labor extortion racket when the painters' association offered him $50,000 cash to keep the painters' union from going on strike for more money. Orgen accepted the money without clearing the operation with Lepke, and when it turned out that Lepke wanted to keep out of the affair, for reasons of his own, Li'l Augie refused to give the money back.

In fact, he ordered the painters not to strike, and to enforce his edict, Orgen hired Legs Diamond to intimidate the painters and to protect him from Lepke. This infuriated Lepke and his gorilla, Jake (Gurrah) Shapiro. Not only was it insubordination, but they didn't like Legs Diamond anyway. They considered him merely a holdup man, who had no business in the rackets with them.

On the night of October 15, 1927, Diamond and Orgen were walking along in Manhattan when Lepke and Jake overtook them in a car. Lepke's instruction to Jake was "Only Augie." He saw no real reason to kill Diamond, unless the latter got in the way. Leaping from the car, ready to fire, Shapiro growled, "Move over, Diamond!" Legs, who had survived a number of assassination attempts, instinctively reached for his gun. That got him a bullet in the shoulder. Orgen got one through the head.

Lepke and Gurrah were questioned by the cops, but none of the witnesses could remember exactly what had happened, or what the killers looked like. The Lepke-Shapiro mob grew rapidly in 1927, eventually numbering about 250 men who worked in the labor field alone.

That November there was a famous Chicago episode: a well-known singer, Joe E. Lewis, refused to work in a club jointly owned by Capone and Machine-gun Jack McGurn. He even ignored threats. One night McGurn and henchmen walked into Lewis's dressing room in the rival club and slashed his throat from ear to ear, ruining his vocal chords. Lewis eventually recovered, but never regained his singing voice. Despite that, he went on to a brilliant career as a comedian, knocking out jokes in a harsh, gravelly voice.

In December Capone left for Florida and announced that he might even retire there soon. He was not warmly received by the Miami police, but, by pulling strings, he was eventually allowed to buy a huge house and take up residence, after promising not to cause any trouble. During this time Capone foolishly answered a lot of questions for a Florida district attorney about the source and amount of his income. Capone had not taken much notice of the new ruling by the Supreme Court regarding the necessary declaration of all income, illegal or not.

With Capone in Miami, business in Chicago carried on. He'd left some good men in charge: Frank (The Enforcer) Nitti, Jake (Greasy Thumb) Guzik, Tony Accardo, Felice De Lucia (otherwise known as Paul the Waiter Ricca), Sam (Mooney) Giancana and Machine-gun Jack McGurn. Through them, he ran crime in Chicago, with only a minor objection now and then from Bugs Moran.

The year ended on a humorous note. Mayor Big Bill Thompson, the bootleggers' hero, announced that he planned to run for President, on the America First ticket. He made speeches all over the country, pledging to "punch King George in the snoot." Not many people could see what he was talking about, and there was no noticeable clamor for his nomination.

CHAPTER TWELVE
1928-1929

Newly inaugurated President Herbert Hoover began the year by instructing Treasury Secretary Andrew Mellon to find some way to get Al Capone into jail. Hoover said he didn't care how it was done, just so long as Capone was behind bars. Shortly thereafter the Internal Revenue Service discovered, much to its delight, that Al Capone had never filed a single tax return in his entire life, despite the fact that he was obviously spending millions.

As the IRS began its investigation, Capone, seemingly unbothered, continued to expand. He moved his general offices from the Metropole Hotel in Chicago to the Lexington, where he took the entire fourth floor, part of the third floor and various other rooms around the hotel. Years later it was discovered that he'd also had built a secret escape hatch from his office. It led from his fourth floor headquarters to the fourth floor of an office building next door, where he could be reasonably sure of exiting through a doorway not covered by enemy machine-gun fire.

But Al Capone, for all his cleverness, slipped up on some rather important things. First, he laughed off the IRS until it was too late. And he ignored his doctor's advice when he was told that his mistress had been found to have syphilis. Capone insisted on treatment for the girl, but refused any for himself, saying that there were no signs of it. Besides, the great Al Capone was afraid of hypodermic needles!

Throughout 1928 Capone was living high. He was gambling as much as $100,000 on an afternoon at the track, and once, or so it was reported, he actually got a racetrack to lend him $500,000 one afternoon when he was on a losing streak and had run out of money to bet. He had the cash sent round the next day. The IRS suspected that at this point, Capone was worth about $20 million, including real estate, breweries, securities and stock. But very little of it, on the advice of his lawyers, was in Capone's name. However, while he covered up his assets, he didn't cover up his spending, and that's what got him in the end. One quick result of the tax investigation of Al Capone was the uncovering of $100,000 cash in his brother Ralph's safe deposit box. This left Ralph with some explaining to do. The feds also suspected that Capone owned or controlled several banks through which he moved his funds.

Some of Capone's allies followed his lead and bought winter homes in Miami. Among them were Terry Druggan and Frankie Lake, who ran Capone's breweries. Hughey (Stubby) McGovern, a small-time gang leader, moved in, and lots of other smaller Chicago hoodlums decided that Miami was the "in" place to be in the winter. The Miami police's headache was the Chicago police's relief.

In Florida Capone was a minor celebrity, even more toasted than he was at home, and he was frequently photographed at the track, or chatting with important, honest people.

On July 1, Frank Yale, who had developed the bad habit of hijacking Capone liquor trucks on their New York-Chicago route, was driving along in Brooklyn, going about his business. Suddenly another car, bearing Illinois license plates, pulled alongside Yale's new Lincoln and machine-gun fire spurted from it.

This was the first time that the machine gun had been used in New York, although it had been the standard gangland weapon in Chicago for several years. Yale, with 100 bullets in his body and dead at the wheel, crashed in his car across the sidewalk and into a nearby house. His killers were never found.

Johnny Torrio, who just happened to be in New York at the time, became the new national president of the Unione Siciliano, despite the fact that he was Italian. The link between New York and Chicago was now complete, and for the first time, Torrio, the original "Mr. Organization" of Chicago, suggested that there be a national bootlegging and rackets conspiracy. The Sicilian-Italian underworld of most of the big cities in the Midwest and in the East began thinking about the idea.

In August the diehard Aiello brothers returned to Chicago from their New Jersey hideout in despair and desperation. They realized that with Torrio at the head of the national Unione, and Capone's man Lombardo presiding over Chicago's, the Aiellos' chances of regaining their lost alky fiefdom were diminishing fast.

On September 8, Aiello gunmen put several dumdum bullets behind Lombardo's ear as he walked in broad daylight past State and Madison avenues, Chicago's busiest corner. One of his bodyguards, Joseph Ferraro, got a dumdum in his spine and died two days later, refusing to say who had got him. The other bodyguard, Tony Lolordo, was unscathed, and he chased down the sidewalk after the two gunmen, who were escaping through the noontime crowds. Police stopped and disarmed him and the killers got away.

Lombardo was followed into office by Pasqualino Lolordo, the elder brother of Lombardo's bodyguard. He was also a Capone man. He was to last four months, then he, too, was exterminated. The killers were three men who called by his home for a drink, had the drink and then shot him.

In New York, Arnold Rothstein had made the fatal mistake of crossing Dutch Schultz. The gambler and drug financier had finally got in over his head and ordered more drugs than he could pay for. He borrowed heavily from the Dutchman, but then the drug deal collapsed and Rothstein was left holding the bag. On the night of November 4, while he was in Lindy's, his usual late-night haunt, he was called to the phone and told that a business deal awaited him at the Park Central Hotel. When Rothstein got to the room, he was shot by one George McManus, who escaped in a car driven by "Bo" Weinberg, one of Schultz's lieutenants. Rothstein died two days later at the age of 46. (The average age of hoodlums killed in the gang wars of the twenties was only 28, therefore Rothstein was once said to have a charmed life.) Police were unable to hang a charge that would stand up in court on Rothstein's killers, and the matter was dropped.

On December 1, the Illinois District Attorney's office, under pressure from outraged civic groups, church leaders and the press, issued a report. It said that 91 of Chicago's unions were mob-controlled, and it estimated Al Capone's annual take from that and other crime as $105 million a year.

Capone paid little attention to such reports and public outrage. He just continued, calmly expanding his interests and cementing his relations with the Purple Gang of Detroit. The Purple Gang was tied in with Lepke in New York in the loan-shark racket, and with Capone in Chicago in bootlegging. The Detroit crowd smuggled in Canadian booze and then shipped it to Capone via the Great Lakes.

Moran and the Aiellos managed to hijack several of these boats in the fall of 1928.

This was ignored for a while by Capone, as he was busy expanding his business interests. He grabbed a chain of dry-cleaning shops by threatening the owner with death, and he opened several dog tracks that were illegal, but not really frowned on in Illinois.

On December 5, the first serious attempt to organize crime on a national level was held by Sicilian mobsters at the Statler Hotel in Cleveland. The idea was suggested by Johnny Torrio, but as an Italian, he was barred, as was Al Capone. The instigator of the meeting was Lucky Luciano, who had convinced his boss, Masseria, that it would be a good thing. Masseria and Luciano did not attend, but they sent their representatives.

There were 23 Sicilians in all from Chicago, New York, Detroit, Buffalo, St. Louis, Newark, Gary, Kansas City and Tampa. The largest delegation came from Chicago, with Capone being represented by his Unione president, Pasquale Lolordo (who was so soon to die), and Joe Giunta. The group from New York included Joe Magliocco, Joseph Profaci and Vincent Mangano, all theoretically Masseria men. Of the New York group named here, all of them later became territorial gang bosses, and two of them lived to attend the 1957 conclave at Apalachin, New York.

The main points discussed were cooperation in the shipping of bootleg booze here and there, similar cooperation on narcotics, although several gang leaders were against traffic in drugs, cooperation in rackets to exploit the union movement and the passing of racing information. Many new ideas were also exchanged during the two-day convention.

The press and public might never have known about the Cleveland powwow except for an informer, thought to be a rival non-Sicilian gangster, who told police that some gangsters were getting together in a certain hotel room. The cops raided it and pulled in all 23 of the Sicilians "on suspicion" and for questioning. They were freed quickly, but not before the press got wind of it, and the public had a chance to ponder on the significance of this meeting of leading hoods from cities all over America.

Shortly before Christmas, Capone went off to Florida. While he was gone, he continued to get reports of how Bugs Moran and the Aiellos were hijacking his booze trucks and his shipments from the Purple Gang in Detroit. He was less than pleased.

Moran's gang consisted of the tattered survivors of the old

O'Bannion and Weiss mob. He did have the alliance of the Aiellos, but the three remaining brothers had lost much of their following. Moran's chief assistants were Frank and Pete Gusenberg, gunmen and holdup artists; John May, a professional safecracker; James (Car) Clark, Moran's brother-in-law and chief bodyguard; Ted Newberry, the chief bootleg salesman; Albert R. Weinshank, who ran Moran's biggest speakeasy; Adam Heyer, who managed the Moran garage where the hooch was loaded and unloaded; Dr. Reinhardt H. Schwimmer, an optometrist, whose connection with Moran has never been clear; and Willie Marks, Moran's lieutenant.

As part of the Capone plot to get Moran, a member of Detroit's Purple Gang, unknown to Moran, made himself known to the gangster as a tipster for hijacked goods. On three separate occasions he managed to deliver to Moran dozens of cases of Capone's special whiskey, Old Log Cabin, which was then supplied only by Detroit's Purple Gang. Moran was delighted. He was getting Capone's prime stuff, and not having to do the hijacking himself. True, it cost more that way, but the risk was less.

On the night of February 13, 1929, the Purple Gang's planted man tipped Moran that he could deliver a truckload of Capone booze the following day at $57 a case. Since this was $3 less than the going rate, Moran jumped at it. They arranged that it be delivered to Moran's garage the next day.

That was St. Valentine's Day, and just about every crime buff knows what happened next. The Moran gang was waiting in the garage for the delivery and for Moran himself, who, luckily for him, was a bit late. A black Packard with a police bell on it rolled up to the garage, and five men got out. Two of them wore police uniforms and three of them wore long overcoats.

Just as the men were entering the garage, Moran, Marks and Newberry rounded the corner and saw the uniforms. Thinking it was a raid, they hurried away.

Inside the garage there was a terrible, deadly chattering as machine guns played back and forth behind the seven men who had been lined up against the wall. The fire was so concentrated that heads and limbs were practically severed from bodies. To make the job complete, shotguns were also employed.

Then, according to neighbors, the five men walked out of the garage, the three in civilian dress holding their hands over their heads as if under arrest, and the "policemen" carrying the machine guns. They got into their car and roared off. The whole thing had taken about five minutes.

When the police arrived, they found one Moran man miraculously still alive. He was Frank Gusenberg, who died some 30 minutes later without revealing the names of the men who shot him, although he talked to police until the end.

The other dead men were Gusenberg's brother, Pete, John May, Al Weinshank, James Clark, Adam Heyer and the mysterious eye doctor, Reinhardt H. Schwimmer.

Moran, so shaken that for once he forgot the gangland code and actually said who he thought attacked him, exclaimed to the press, "Only Capone kills like that!"

Capone, though, had an airtight alibi. He was in Florida and at the very moment of the execution was chatting in the office of the Miami district attorney.

For a brief time some people in Chicago actually thought that perhaps the police had done it in retaliation for numerous cop killings over the years. But this idea was soon rejected, especially when the police began developing clues in other directions.

It was discovered that up until three days before the massacre, Jake Guzik had been calling his boss in Florida daily from Chicago. Then the calls suddenly stopped. Another caller to Capone in Florida was Machine-gun Jack McGurn. Police also claimed that some of the machine gun bullets found in the body of Frank Yale, in New York, matched some used in the St. Valentine's Day job. That gun, according to police, was eventually traced to Fred Burke, a member of the Egan's Rats gang in St. Louis.

After about a month, the police said that the perpetrators of the St. Valentine's Day massacre were Burke, and his St. Louis sidekick, Earl Ray, Joseph Lolordo, and the famed murder team of Anselmi and Scalise. Police said that Burke and Ray played the parts of the policemen, because they were unknown to Moran. Lolordo was there to avenge the death of his brother, for which he blamed Moran and the Aiellos. Anselmi and Scalise were just doing their thing, killing for pay.

Lolordo immediately disappeared. Anselmi and Scalise, having been identified by witnesses, were indicted and then released on bail. Machine-gun Jack McGurn was arrested but released on bond. The case against him was dropped when the state failed to get enough evidence to take to court. Ray and Burke simply vanished.

As for Anselmi and Scalise, they eventually paid for their sins, but it was gangland that inflicted the penalty, and not the law. Joseph Giunta, a highly placed Capone man, became the new head of the Unione Siciliano in Chicago. He named Scalise as his assistant. And this seems to have gone to Scalise's head. With Capone in Florida, and beginning to have trouble with the tax men, Scalise made the suicidal announcement that he was the most powerful man in Chicago. Capone got word of that, and also of the fact that Giunta, Scalise and Anselmi were plotting to take over the alky cooking business and other Capone interests.

On May 7, the three conspirators were honored by the Sicilian community at a stag party just across the Illinois border in Indiana. As they leaned back with their cigars and brandy, they were hit from behind with baseball bats. Then they were shot. That was the end of their brief insurrection, and it was the end of police efforts to indict anyone else for the seven deaths in Moran's garage. The slayings of Scalise, Anselmi and Giunta were to remain unsolved, too.

CHAPTER THIRTEEN
1929-1931

From May 13 to 16, 1929, five months after the first national organizational meeting in Cleveland, there was a similar gathering in Atlantic City, New Jersey. The first meeting had been broken up by the police, but the next one, with Lucky Luciano and Longy Zwillman handling arrangements, had no interruptions.

Another difference at the second meeting was that the invitation list was not restricted to Sicilians. For one thing, Luciano wasn't a Sicilian himself, although he got along with them. For another, he had long been of the opinion that there was no sense being bigoted if there was enough money around to be made by all. Lucky's boss, Masseria, didn't totally agree with his protégé on this score, but he agreed to wait and see.

About 30 gang leaders from principal cities attended. A peek at the guest list would have revealed the following names: Max Hoff, Sam Lazar and Charles Schwartz, all from Philadelphia; Frank Costello, Luciano and Dutch Schultz from New York and Al Capone from Chicago.

At this meeting, just as Capone had sliced up Chicago and doled out territories to the various mobs, the national ganglords sliced up the country. They also decided which gangs would be "in" and which would be "out." Noticeably absent from this conclave were Bugs Moran and the Aiellos. Some cities, such as New York, were declared too big for any one gang to control, and they were divided between several gangs. An exception was made of Chicago, where one-man rule seemed to be a fait accompli. It was decided that while the Capone gang was in charge, no other gang would be recognized in Chicago. However, gangs from other cities could work with

Capone, or do something in Chicago, if the Capone outfit didn't mind or was willing to take a piece of the action.

Miami was declared an open city, with New York, Philadelphia and Chicago sharing in what happened there. Should other gangs want to try something in Miami, it was to be negotiated. At the Atlantic City meeting, Costello and Luciano outlined their plan for a nine-member national commission, which would rule on territorial disputes and other arguments between gangs.

On the way home from Atlantic City, Al Capone stopped in at a Philadelphia police station and turned himself in for carrying a gun. His reasoning was that with Bugs Moran still fuming about the St. Valentine's Day Massacre, which had all but wiped out Moran's army, the safest place for Capone might be in jail, until somebody did something about Moran. Then too, there were the Aiello brothers, who continued to offer $50,000 to any Capone assassin.

At the station house, Capone forced his bodyguard, Frank Rio, to turn himself in too for carrying a gun. Capone said he wanted company in jail, and besides, he said, they would get only 90 days. The judge surprised Capone, and gave him a year. Apparently Capone didn't have the pull in Philadelphia that he had in Chicago.

At first the press was stunned at the sudden and unexpected incarceration of Public Enemy No. 1. It soon became apparent, however, that during his absence Capone's gang would not be without leadership. In the first place, he'd left good men in charge, Fischetti, Nitti, Guzik, and brother Ralph. And then there was the fact that Capone would really never be out of touch with his mob; he would not only have his own private cell, and all the visiting privileges he liked, he would have his own phone to the outside world.

There was one man who did take advantage of Capone being away: United States Agent Eliot Ness. Along with his band of federal raiders, he hit 19 Capone distilleries and six breweries. In the process he destroyed about $1,000,000 worth of equipment, trucks and booze. Capone was furious and screamed down the telephone for somebody to do something about Ness, but nobody did.

Another thing that happened while Al was up the river: his treasurer, Frank (the Enforcer) Nitti, drew a sentence of 18 months for tax evasion. Jake Guzik was also being investigated and looked to be in serious trouble. Both men, it was said, had had opportunities to settle with the government out of court, but had been either too stingy or too stupid to do it.

In October 1929, with Capone still in jail, the stock market took its first shattering plunge. Capone laughed at that. The man who had sometimes dropped $100,000 at the racetrack had no money in stocks, because he'd always said the market was a "suckers' game."

The crash still cost Capone and his contemporaries a fortune; when people went broke they stopped having the money to buy booze. The gambling, hooch and whoring business across the nation was reported to be off by as much as 50 percent. That meant that Capone made only $50 million a year!

Jake Guzik was sentenced to five years for tax fraud in November 1929. (And here Bugs Moran fades from our story. Virtually put out of business by Capone, Moran began taking more chances in his quest for a buck. Several long jail sentences were to follow, and when he died of lung cancer, almost 30 years later in 1957, he was rotting in a federal penitentiary, all but forgotten.)

Al Capone, too, was almost at the end of the road, but he didn't know it. Nevertheless, from 1929 until today, the Capone gang and the organization he built up has controlled major crime in the Chicago area. No other gang has ever had a chance of operating there unless the action was approved by the main mob. The killing in Chicago has never stopped. Every now and then some new bunch, either local or from out of town, has tried its luck there and over the years, this has caused a lot of bodies to be left around.

In New York, meanwhile, there was still plenty of sorting out to do, just as there was in numerous other big cities. Crime had not been completely organized on a nationwide basis just yet. Nor had the Sicilians and Italians gained the ascendency everywhere.

In February 1930 Joe the Boss Masseria, began his expansion plan. His first move was to dub Peter Morello as the boss of bosses of all New York. Morello was an elderly Mafioso figure, who had much "respect" among his countrymen. And he was a leading Black Hander. Masseria controlled Morello and when he named him as the boss of all New York, he virtually set the old man up as a target.

The Masseria announcement was in direct conflict with the five-leader system for New York that Lucky Luciano and Frank Costello had worked out at Atlantic City. It was also in conflict with the plans of such noted Jewish gangsters as Bugsy Siegel, Meyer Lansky, Lepke Buchalter and Jake Shapiro. However Costello and Luciano, who were tied in with Masseria, bided their time and pretended to go along with it.

One of the first gang leaders to object seriously to Masseria's plans was a fellow countryman, Salvatore Maranzano, who led a gang composed chiefly of men with connections in an area of Sicily called Castellammare del Golfo. Masseria was not surprised when Maranzano and pals ignored his edict. He had long thought that the Castellammarese faction in Brooklyn was getting too big for its britches, and he viewed with suspicion the fact that new immigrants from Castellammare seemed to be arriving daily and swelling Maranzano's ranks. One of these "new" men was Joseph Bonnano, who had arrived in America by jumping ship in 1924. Another was Peter Magaddino. Both men had become Maranzano lieutenants by 1930, and had begun setting up subsidiary organizations in Brooklyn without even bothering to check with Masseria.

To bring the Castellammarese back into line, Masseria decided to show his authority by increasing the "take" he got from Brooklyn. When Maranzano paid no attention, Masseria had one Maranzano man killed and another kidnaped. The latter was ransomed for $10,000.

Still Maranzano refused to pay more tribute to Masseria. The older man's reply was to shoot up Maranzano beer trucks and Maranzano men. The first to go was Tom Reina, Maranzano's No. 1 lackey. He was shot to death by parties unknown on February 6, 1930. Then, to add insult to injury, Masseria sent his own replacement for Reina, a hoodlum called Joseph Pinzola. His job was to take Reina's place in the Maranzano mob and to see to it that the Maranzano forces paid tribute to Joe the Boss.

What has since become famous as the Castellammarese War was then on. In the next year or so, 60 men were to be killed as a result. The peaceful arbitration clause of the Atlantic City pact was temporarily shelved.

In contrast to Masseria, who, as stated, was an Old World-type "Mustache Pete," Maranzano was a reasonably cultured, elegant figure who loved opera and was a great student of history. In the beginning, the Masseria forces looked to be the certain winners, with more men, more money and bigger gang bosses on their side. There were Lucky Luciano, Vito Genovese, Joe Adonis, Carlo Gambino, Ciro Terranova, Albert Anastasia and Frank Costello, each with his own followers. In addition, Masseria was getting contributions of guns, money, cars and men from gangs in other cities. Al Capone sent him $5,000 per week.

Maranzano had a few allies himself. In addition to his local troops, Joseph Profaci, Joseph Bonanno, Joseph Magliocco, Gaetano Gagliano and Tommy (Three-Finger Brown) Lucchese, he had Stefano Magaddino, the Mafia boss in Buffalo, New York. Magaddino was the uncle of one of Maranzano's men, Peter Magaddino, and both Magaddinos were from Castellammare del Golfo.

The Buffalo Magaddino sent Maranzano about $6,000 per week. Another contributor to the Maranzano war chest was Joseph Aiello, who was hiding out from Capone. His thought was that since Capone was allied with Masseria, if Maranzano won he might help Aiello take on Capone in Chicago. Aiello sent Maranzano $5,000 per week.

Masseria's total army, including borrowed troops, and those of his allies, numbered about 600. Maranzano had only about 350 men, but what his side lacked in numbers it made up for in ferocity.

A good friend of the late Reina was Gagliano, a small mob leader. Without discussing it with Maranzano, he decided to wipe out Pinzola, Reina's replacement in the Maranzano outfit. To this end, he hired some new gunmen, such as Joe Valachi (known then as Joe Cago). He wanted troops that were strangers to Masseria so that the killings wouldn't necessarily be traced back to Maranzano or himself. Gagliano rather naively hoped that somebody else would be blamed for the job.

At the same time Maranzano decided to rub out Peter Morello, Masseria's so-called boss of bosses. The theory is that perhaps both Maranzano and Galiano thought that the Jewish gangsters would be blamed for both jobs.

Maranzano struck first, on August 15. One of his new gunmen was a citizen known only as "Buster from Chicago." To this day the police have never learned who he was. Joe Valachi has since been quoted as saying how Pete (The Clutching Hand) Morello got it. "Buster from Chicago looked like a college boy and carried his machine gun in a violin case. He said he got Morello in his office. He ran all over the office and Buster had to shoot him a lot before he went down. Some other guy was in the office, so Buster took him too."

The other guy was Giuseppe Pariano, a bodyguard.

A month later, Gagliano's men got Pinzolo. In this, Valachi had advance word. Joe Valachi had been recruited for the Gagliano mob by virtue of needing a job. In the early twenties, he had operated with a small gang called The Minute Men, because of the speed of their getaways. Some of them weren't quite so fast, however, and Valachi pulled a prison sentence. One of the men he'd met inside who had impressed him a great deal was Alessandro Vollero, an old hoodlum who had been serving life for murder since 1919. He gave Valachi the first tip that there was such a thing as a secret society behind some of the big mobs. Another thug who confirmed this for Valachi was his robbery partner, Dominick (The Gap) Petrilli. The latter convinced Valachi that when they got out of the pen, the best thing they could do to get ahead was to get "mobbed up."

It was Petrilli who eventually took Valachi to meet Bobby Doyle, whose real name was Girolamo Santucci. At the beginning of the Castellammarese War, Doyle had asked Valachi if he could find a few good shots in a hurry, and Valachi has said he could. Next, Doyle introduced him to Gagliano and Lucchese. Valachi was then told to rent a certain apartment and to keep himself available. Just before Pinzolo was knocked off, Petrilli had taken Valachi to meet him. Valachi later said he told Petrilli that he didn't care much for Reina's replacement, and that Petrilli had said that it didn't matter, because Pinzolo was going to die, and so were a few others.

On September 9, 1930, Pinzolo was killed by Bobby Doyle in an office rented by Lucchese, a fact which temporarily embarrassed Lucchese with the police. However, in the end, charges were dropped. At this point the small Gagliano mob and the larger Maranzano gang joined forces to protect themselves from Masseria, who had suddenly lost two of his best men.

Valachi was staked out in a flat opposite that of one Steven Ferrigno, a Masseria lieutenant. The idea was to hit Ferrigno one day as he walked out. Staked out with Valachi from time to time was Joseph Profaci, who later was to become one of the biggest gang leaders in New York. Some 30 years later, Valachi recalled Profaci walking into the ambush flat one day and saying, "We've lost the money from Chicago. Capone just got Aiello."

Aiello had been killed as he left his hideout on October 23, 1930. A machine gun opened up on him as he left his front door, but the gunner missed and Aiello ran back inside and out the rear. Another machine gunner cut him in half. At the time this was considered a big blow to the Maranzano forces, since they needed about $20,000 per week to pay gunmen, to buy guns and to rent hideouts.

On November 4, Valachi was entering the ambush nest again when he happened to get into an elevator with none other than Masseria himself. Valachi managed to get off the elevator without giving himself away, and quickly relayed the news. Within an hour Buster from Chicago, Bobby Doyle and Nick (the Thief) Capuzzi were all hovering around the window with shotguns, hoping to get Joe the Boss himself. They hadn't expected a break like that, at least not that soon in the war, and there was a lot of excitement.

Masseria's luck still held, however, because he spent the night in Ferrigno's flat. The next day, about 30 of his men arrived for a meeting. The assassins waited. When the meeting broke up, they still sat there, letting most of them go by, hoping to get Masseria. Finally, deciding that they must have missed seeing him leave, they cut loose on two of his lieutenants, Ferrigno and Alfred Mineo, as they walked past Valachi's pad. Both men were killed.

Soon afterwards Valachi was sworn into the brotherhood, Maranzano himself presiding. From Valachi's description of it in Peter Maas's book, *The Valachi Papers*, the affair sounds like a combination of a secret fraternal rite and some sort of Indian ceremony. There were oaths, and speeches, and blood-mingling routines. It might sound very silly to sophisticated people, but the evening was serious stuff to the men involved and made quite an impression on Valachi. His sponsor into the Cosa Nostra was Joseph Bonanno.

Following this, Valachi failed in one assassination effort, but was the driver for Buster from Chicago when Buster killed Joseph (Joe The Baker) Catania, another Masseria aide, on February 3, 1931. In order to do this, the Maranzano men had to hold three house painters at bay in an apartment and drill Baker from the window just after he kissed his wife good-bye outside. Not a bullet touched Mrs. Catania, apparently.

Valachi later quoted Buster as saying, "He kissed her in front of the office and I was afraid I wouldn't get a shot. But he turned and went for the corner. She was just standing there watching when I got him. I don't think I missed once. You could see dust coming off his coat when the bullets hit."

On another occasion, Valachi was driving when Steve Runnelli wounded Paul Gambino, brother of Masseria ally Carlo Gambino.

This seemed to convince Carlo that Maranzano had the best guns, and he immediately switched sides.

He wasn't the only one. As more and more Masseria men were dropped in the streets, Masseria's hold on the survivors weakened. Lucky Luciano and Frank Costello, still loyal, tried to talk Masseria into hiring some better killers, namely the Bug-Meyer mob; or Lepke. Unfortunately for Masseria, he would have none of it.

This decision was to cost him his two closest associates, Luciano and Costello. It also cost him the war and his life.

CHAPTER FOURTEEN
1931-1932

While the Castellammarese War raged in New York, things had not been going at all well for Capone in Chicago. He was up to his ears in tax problems with the government. The boss of Chicago had been released from jail in Philadelphia on May 16, 1930, where he had served ten months on the gun-carrying charge, and now it appeared that he was to go back inside again on a tax rap. For a while, Capone had seemed confident that he'd get only two years. Then his brother, Ralph, drew three years on a tax conviction, and some of Al's confidence seemed to leave him.

The big sensation of 1930 in Chicago had been the extermination of newspaper reporter Jake Lingle, who'd been known for his inside stories on the bootleggers, and for his contacts with the big men of crime. Few people seemed to have noticed that Lingle lived far above his means as a relatively poorly paid newsman, or that he played the horses with a reckless abandon. On the few occasions that anyone had expressed curiosity about his affluence Lingle had said either that he'd had a terrific run of luck at the track, or that an aunt had died and left him a packet.

At noon on June 9, 1930, Lingle had been shot and killed in a pedestrian underpass by a gunman dressed as a priest. Lingle had worked for the *Chicago Tribune,* and that august journal immediately offered a $25,000 reward for the capture of his killer, or killers. The rival *Chicago Evening Post* offered $5,000 and the *Herald Examiner* offered another $25,000.

All those papers were to be embarrassed when it developed that Lingle, on a salary of $65 per week, had managed to have a chauffeured Lincoln, a huge summer home, and a suite of rooms in a downtown hotel. He was 38 years old.

During the summer of 1930 it slowly developed that Lingle had been the payoff man between the Capone mob and City Hall. Not the only payoff man, to be sure, but an important one. No one ever found out who killed Jake Lingle, or exactly why, but theories abounded. Some people said he'd kept some payoff money for himself, or that he'd arranged a fix that fell through, and that the fixers thought he'd double-crossed them. That same summer it came to light, following Lingle's death, that several other Chicago newspapermen had apparently been in the employ of mobs.

And the killing in Chicago had continued unabated as Capone tightened his grip on the city's crime. During one period in 1930, there had been ten gang killings in as many days. (The total of all mob rub-outs in Chicago in the ten-year period between 1920 and 1930 was about 500.)

Another footnote to the year 1930 was the disappearance in New York of Judge Joseph F. Crater. While in Chicago they had been asking "Who killed Jake Lingle?" the papers in New York had been asking "Where is Judge Crater?" To this day, there has never been an answer to either question. Nobody even knows why Crater disappeared. He might have had something on one of the gangs of New York, Dutch Schultz's for instance, or he might have been in with them and been done away with because he knew too much. He might have been taken, or he might have disappeared on his own. All that is known about Judge Crater's disappearance is that he left his home on evening, and has never been seen since.

By April 1931 it had become obvious that Joe Masseria was losing his war with Maranzano. When he refused to call in outside help, as had been suggested to him by Luciano and Costello, these two switched sides. Genovese, Luciano's lieutenant, Ciro Terranova, Frank Livorsi and Joseph Straci (known as Joe Stretch) had also come over to the Maranzanos with all their men and had made a secret pact for peace. They agreed to take care of Masseria if Maranzano would then call off the war.

The end came for Masseria on the afternoon of April 20, 1931, at Scarpato's Restaurant on Coney Island. The man who had been faster than bullets fired from one gun was not fast enough to elude bullets fired from four guns simultaneously.

It was Masseria's old pal, Lucky Luciano, who set him up. Luciano invited Masseria to a private lunch so that they could "talk things over." At the end of a long and leisurely meal, they played cards for almost an hour, and then Luciano excused himself to go to the toilet. While Luciano was thus engaged, as he told police later, Masseria was killed.

Thirty years later Joe Valachi was to shed more light on the subject. Valachi told Peter Maas that four gunmen walked into Scarpato's that day and blasted Masseria before the old man could even get up from the table. Valachi said the gunmen included Vito Genovese, Frank Livorsi and Joe Stretch. The New York police had another version, at the time. Their case file No. 133-31 indicates that the main suspects in the Masseria murder were Albert Anastasia, Joey Adonis and Bugsy Siegel. Nobody was ever convicted of the job though, and today it seems reasonable to assume that we may never know exactly who, besides Charlie Lucky, got Masseria.

Five days after the Masseria slaying, according to Valachi, there was a big meeting in the Bronx. There were about 500 men in the room, virtually all of the top men and their close supporters in the Italian-Sicilian underworld. Valachi said that Maranzano spoke in Italian and laid it on the line about how things would be. He said he would be the boss of bosses and under him there would be five bosses with their own gangs. Those named were Lucky Luciano, Tom Gagliano, Joseph Profaci, Joseph Bonanno and Vincent Mangano. The five-gang rule over crime in New York has existed to this day, although death in one form or another has caused occasional changes in the leadership of the individual "families."

Underbosses that Valachi could recall being named that day included Vito Genovese, under Luciano; Thomas Lucchese, under Gagliano; and Albert Anastasia, under Mangano.

Missing from the meeting were obvious objectors to Maranzano's being the boss of bosses of all New York: Lepke, Shapiro, Schultz, Lansky and Siegel. They were Jewish, and according to Maranzano they would have to go. In 1960 Valachi related that Maranzano was also thinking about getting rid of Luciano, Genovese and Costello. He thought they were taking too much power into their own hands, and besides he didn't trust them because they were so friendly with the Jewish hoods.

For Maranzano to think out loud about getting rid of such cold-blooded, efficient killers as Lepke and Siegel was enough to give even Costello and Luciano white hair. They knew if talk like that got back to the Jews there would be a war that would make the Castellammarese War look like *Rebecca of Sunnybrook Farm*.

During the summer of 1931 there was a dispute within the

clothing unions. Lepke and his mob were hired to "represent" one faction, and the other side asked Luciano to give a hand. But Luciano refused, saying that Lepke was a friend of his. Maranzano, however, took the job. There were several killings before a truce was called, and Lepke was reported as being displeased. In a private meeting with Luciano, Lepke said that something was going to have to be done about Maranzano.

Luciano probably couldn't have agreed more. Maranzano's boss of bosses claim messed up everything Luciano and Costello had been trying to vis-á-vis New York and national crime. They were in favor of a five-man board to run New York and a nine-man national commission to rule on intercity disputes.

In addition, many of the Italian-Sicilian gang leaders were annoyed at the slice Maranzano was taking from the pie. Shortly after assuming control, Maranzano had held a huge banquet for himself in Brooklyn. Italian and Sicilian mobsters in New York and elsewhere in the country were "asked" to buy tickets and most of them had done so. Al Capone, according to Valachi, sent $6,000. It was guessed that Maranzano had collected more than $100,000 at the banquet, and that he had kept it all himself.

By September 1931 it became known in Maranzano's gang that in addition to killing Lepke, Shapiro, Schultz, Siegel, Costello, Luciano and Genovese, the boss of bosses wanted to be rid of Willie Moretti, a New Jersey boss, Al Capone in Chicago, and Joe Adonis, in Brooklyn. (Waxy Gordon probably would have been named, too, but he was in jail on a tax rap. Gordon, in fact, was never a power after that. In 1951 he was charged with being a common dope pusher, and put away by the government for a long, long time.)

When Maranzano started talking about hiring Vincent "Mad Dog" Coll to kill all his enemies, it became obvious, even to Maranzano's personal bodyguards, of whom Valachi was one, that the boss had flipped. The mobs didn't understand desperadoes like Coll, John Dillinger and Bonnie and Clyde. They put them down as stupid holdup artists who drew too much heat.

On September 11, 1931, while Maranzano and twelve of his men were in his downtown office, five strangers walked in and flashed police badges. They lined up the Maranzano thugs against the wall and relieved the gun-carrying ones of their weapons.

Maranzano himself then stuck his head out of his inner office and asked what was going on. Two of the five "detectives" pushed him back into his office, shot him several times, and cut his throat. In *Murder, Inc.*, a book written by Brooklyn prosecutor Burton B. Turkus and Sid Feder, the five assassins are named as Bo Weinberg, of the Dutch Schultz mob, two men named "Murphy," Allie, who worked for Longy Zwillman in New Jersey, and a man from the firm of Lansky and Siegel.

During that same 24 hours, other Maranzano allies and objectors to the National Commission scheme were eradicated all over the country. There were 40 deaths in all, during what later became known in crime folklore as the Night of the Sicilian Vespers. That was the last of the Mustache Petes.

Luciano then moved to cement relations between the gangs of New York and the gangs of other cities. His efforts were to lead to the two meetings of 1934 and the formation of the Cosa Nostra as it remains to this day.

On October 24, 1931, Al Capone stood up in federal court and received his sentence on tax charges—11 years. Nobody was more surprised than Capone, who ironically was at the height of his power, having at last squashed all objectors to his being the crime overlord of Chicago.

For a while it was theorized that he would still be able to run his mob from the pen, much as he had when he was in jail in Philadelphia, but this was not to be so. The government went out of its way to see to it that Capone had no special privileges in the pen, and as the years dragged on, Capone gradually lost control of the system he'd forged. At one point, he was even beaten up by fellow convicts. Late in his term the syphilis which he'd ignored too long affected his brain, and by the time he was eventually released from prison, in 1939, he was a broken, confused man. He was to die in 1947, at the age of 52.

In November 1931 Luciano and Dutch Schultz visited Al Capone in jail, where he was awaiting his appeal on the tax sentence. It seems that the New Yorkers were arguing over the territory given to Schultz and, in desperation, hoping to avoid another bloody gang war, Luciano hoped that Capone could get Schultz to be reasonable, and not claim all of Manhattan for himself.

As it turned out, Schultz refused to be reasonable, and Charlie Lucky made plans to exclude Schultz from the New York cartel. But for a while, Luciano knew they'd all have to put up with the Dutchman.

By 1932 there was a far bigger problem: Prohibition was ending, and all the lovely bootlegging money that went with it. The gangs knew that they could never compete with the legitimate breweries once they got back in business, and it was time to develop new sources of income.

Several young lads in the Brownsville of Brooklyn had already come up with one answer: they would kill people for money. Their names were Abe (Kid Twist) Reles, Buggsy Goldstein, Frank (Dasher) Abbandando and Happy Maione.

During Prohibition the three Shapiro brothers, Meyer, Irving and Willie (not related to Jake Gurrah Shapiro), had made a small fortune in bootlegging in Brownsville, with permission of the major Brooklyn mobs, of course. But by 1930 youngsters such as Reles, who was then 20, had decided that they were through being mere errand boys and that they wanted to move into the main arena.

At the time of this decision, Reles and Maione had been leaders of rival, punk gangs. They'd merged their outfits in 1930 in order to go after the Shapiros, whom they'd first approached for a cut, only to get turned down.

The first operation of the Reles-Maione combination was a disaster. While vandalizing the Shapiros' cars, they'd run into an ambush set up by one of their ''informants,'' Joey Silver. Reles and his pal Buggsy were both wounded, and George De Feo, Reles's chief gunman, was killed.

After that, Reles recruited Harry Strauss, also known as Big Harry, Pep, and more commonly, Pittsburgh Phil. Even for a notorious crime figure, Pittsburgh Phil was an extraordinary killer. Whereas a man like Machine Gun Jack McGurn simply blasted away and got the job done, or a man like Bug Workman went about his business nonchalantly, Pittsburgh Phil seemed to *love* to kill people.

Reles once said that when he'd landed Pittsburgh Phil, it had been like gaining a whole new mob.

From June 1930 until July 1931, the Reles combination tried 18 times to kill one or all of the Shapiros, and botched every attempt. It had not been an auspicious start for Murder, Inc.

Finally Reles and friends grabbed Meyer Shapiro in the street, and in December 1931, he was found dead. Next they killed Irv, and then Willie. Willie was found dead in a vacant lot, and police determined that he'd been buried alive.

By 1932 Albert Anastasia was taking a renewed interest in the young men he'd met in Louis Capone's pastry shop. Reles told prosecutor Turkus that he'd done his first job for Anastasia and Capone when he was only 18, in 1928.

Louis asks me to do this job for him. [Reles said] Happy and him drive me to one of them little streets near Pleasant Place, over in Ocean Hill. Louis points to the house and tells me what room the bum lives in. I go in and shoot the guy five times. One of the slugs goes in the back of his head and takes one of his eyes out. After that I do a lot of jobs for Louis when he tells me . . . Louis was always very nice to me.

Following the demise of the Shapiros, Reles, Buggsy and Pittsburgh Phil took Brownsville as their territory, and Happy, Dasher and Vito Gurino, known as "Socko," took Ocean Hill. However, to keep the two gangs from warring with each other over the rest of Brooklyn, Anastasia put Louis Capone on their "Boards of Directors" as a peacekeeper and liaison man with the main mobs.

By the time Prohibition was repealed, Reles and Maione were deeply involved in a loan-shark business that extended across New York State and into Pennsylvania. They also were getting more and more contract work from Anastasia. Pittsburgh Phil, in particular, relished it as a means of perfecting his skill.

"Like a ballplayer, that's me. I figure I get seasoning doing these jobs here. Somebody from one of the big mobs spots me. Then, up to the big leagues."

That was Pittsburgh Phil on the subject of killing people for a living. He was right about one thing; not only did he and Reles and the rest get spotted by Anastasia, the Brownsville bunch were to get most of the contract work for the entire syndicate for the next ten years. It is estimated that, between them, they were responsible for as many as 500 gangland killings in every state in the union. In most cases, they weren't paid by the job, they simply got a retainer to handle all the work for one mob. Reles disclosed in his testimony that Lepke sent him $12,000 per year, just to stand by and kill anybody Lepke wanted dead.

Frank Costello's solution to the loss of his bootlegging money was to move into legitimate gambling. Prior to 1939, when the parimutuel machines were installed at racetracks, anyone with a license could book bets at the track. Costello quickly bought a piece of several established, legal bookmaking operations and almost overnight he had a large, legal business. He also went into slot machines in a big way, installing them in the New York area and in Miami.

Lucky Luciano expanded his prostitution and narcotics operations, and got into the numbers game. (NOTE: In some places the numbers game is called the "policy" racket. This expression grew out of the fact that in the early twenties there were "penny" insurance policies. The machinery backing a numbers operation is sometimes called "The Wheel.")

Dutch Schultz expanded his Harlem numbers and slot-machine monopoly and also hit on a scheme to shake down restaurants. Large restaurants all over Manhattan and greater New York paid $2,000,000 a year for "protection." The Dutchman's men protected the restaurant owners from stink bombs going off at dinnertime, broken windows and mayhem upon the body of the restaurateur himself. Whenever a restaurant owner expressed doubts that such things could happen, the Schultz gang was quick to show him that they could.

Lepke used the strong-arm techniques that had been so successful in the clothing industry to penetrate the bakery, flour and trucking businesses, as well.

In Brooklyn the void left by the demise of Frank Yale was filled by Li'l Augie Pisano, whose real name was Anthony Carfano. Behind Carfano stood the shadowy figure of Joe Adonis, friend of Albert Anastasia, who in turn was a lieutenant in the Mangano gang.

The Brooklyn-Bronx crowd, Mangano, Bonanno, Profaci and Gagliano shared operations there—numbers, narcotics, slots, gambling—and a few ventures in Manhattan. Most of their efforts were coordinated by Lucky Luciano, who, though not a boss of bosses, was an arbitrator of disputes. At this time, the Sicilian-Italian element was lying low and looking with envy at the vast territories in New York controlled by Lepke, Shapiro and Dutch Schultz.

It was a good time for lying low, too, because in September 1932, Jimmy Walker, the tolerant, playboy mayor of New York in the twenties, was forced to resign after an investigation into government corruption led by Judge Samuel Seabury. Walker's replacement was Fiorello LaGuardia, who vowed to clean up New York, starting with slot machines. When a court surprised the Little Flower and ruled that slot machines were not illegal, the mayor sent cops around anyway to break them up with axes. New York's hoods were startled by this high-handed, illegal act. (By the middle thirties, this was enough to cause Frank Costello to move his entire operation to New Orleans, where Louisiana Governor Huey Long was more reasonable. Costello made a deal with Long that part of the take of the 5,000 slot machines would go to Long charities. The distribution of these funds was left to the governor. It has been reported that every year the poor and destitute of New Orleans benefited to the magnificent total of some $600—almost a penny per machine!)

Costello's manager in New Orleans was Dandy Phil Kastel. His manager in Miami was Frank Erickson.

The specialists, Meyer Lansky and Bugsy Siegel, remained available in Manhattan for enforcement assignments, and at the same time, expanded into Philadelphia, where they eventually established a brisk gambling, numbers and slot machine trade.

New Jersey was owned and operated by Longy Zwillman and his No. 1, Willie Moretti.

That was the lineup at the end of 1932, when the United States government suddenly got after Dutch Schultz about his tax returns, or lack of them. Schultz immediately disappeared, leaving Bo Weinberg in charge. He was to stay missing until late 1934, and when he returned, he found that Luciano and the other Italian-Sicilians had taken over most of his enterprises. This was to lead to a great deal of trouble.

In Chicago Al Capone was marched off to begin his 11-year sentence, and his two brewery partners Frankie Lake and Terry Druggan also drew sentences for tax evasion. The main men in Chicago, and the leaders of the Capone gang became Tony Accardo and Frank Fischetti.

In his heyday, Al Capone enjoyed the good life and his pose as a sportsman. Capone is at the Notre Dame-Northwestern football game in 1931 with former Chicago alderman Al Prignano.

Capone at a baseball game. This is one of the rare photographs taken from his left side, showing his severely scarred face.

Capone relaxes at his palatial estate in Miami.

Al Capone and his attorney, Michael Ahearn, shortly before Capone was surprised with a long prison sentence on tax charges in 1931. He was released in 1939 and went into retirement due to poor health.

The real Eliot Ness, a Special Prohibition Agent.

The real Frank Nitti, otherwise known as "The Enforcer."
It was Nitti, among others, who ran Capone's empire while
the latter was incarcerated. Nitti eventually went to jail himself on tax charges and, threatened with another prison sentence
in 1943, shot himself dead.

In the center of this group of men is a jaunty Johnny Torrio, who has just posted a record bond of $104,000 to be released from jail following the raid on his distillery.

The most sensational crime of 1931 was the slaughter of flamboyant newspaper reporter Jake Lingle, in a Chicago underpass. It was later learned that Lingle had some rather curious connections with mob figures and lived far above his means.

Leo Brothers, who was indicted for the murder of Lingle. Police suspected that Lingle had somehow double-crossed a leading mob boss.

Al Capone, who when questioned about Lingle's death, said, "I liked the guy!"

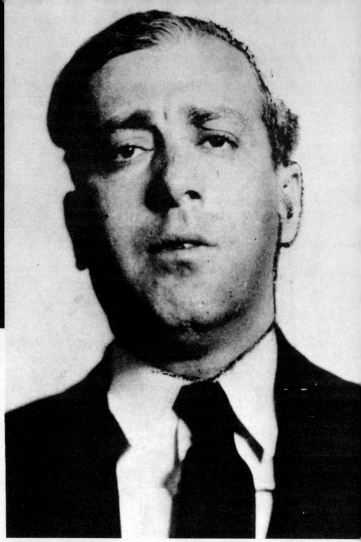

Among the inheritors of the Capone empire were the brothers Charles and Rocco Fischetti and Jake "Greasy Thumb" Guzik, so nicknamed because he was the mob's payoff man and was usually seen licking his thumb and counting out money.

Charles is shown above.

Rocco Fischetti.

Jake "Greasy Thumb" Guzik.

By the 1950s, three men were the presumed syndicate chieftains in Chicago: Sam "Mooney" Giancana . . . Murray "The Camel" Humphries . . . and Tony Accardo. All were graduates of the Capone finishing school.

Sam "Mooney" Giancana . . .

Murray "The Camel" Humphries . . .

Tony Accardo.

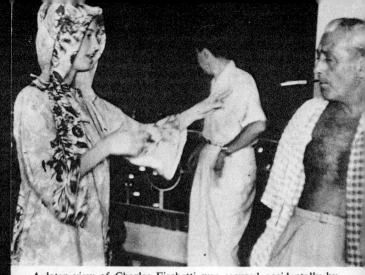

A later view of Charles Fischetti was secured accidentally by an alert fashion photographer who spotted him in Acapulco, Mexico, when, coincidentally, Fischetti was being sought by the Kefauver committee in Washington. The photographer has sent a model over to Fischetti to distract him while this photo is being taken.

The mobster, however, is having none of it and quickly walks away.

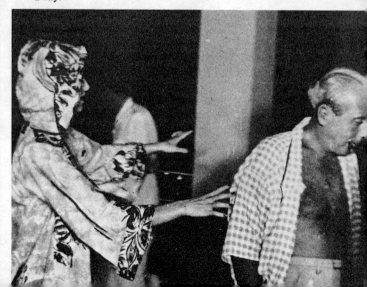

Special Prosecutor Thomas E. Dewey, who won a name for himself as the man who could put New York's leading hoods behind bars. His first big conviction was of the infamous Waxey Gordon.

Dewey's next targets were Dutch Schultz (above) and Lucky Luciano. It was during this period that the mobs gave serious consideration to having Dewey shot as he walked near his home.

Dewey, who eventually became Governor of New York and a Presidential candidate, is seen while campaigning in Manhattan.

Thomas E. Dewey's career was almost cut short by Dutch Schultz, who thought that the mobs' plan to kill the prosecutor was too good not to be used. Instead, the gangs decided that Schultz was a madman and had to go. Schultz confers with his attorney, J. Richard Davis, during the former's tax trial.

One of Schultz's henchmen, who was blasted into eternity with two others and Schultz himself in a New Jersey restaurant in 1935.

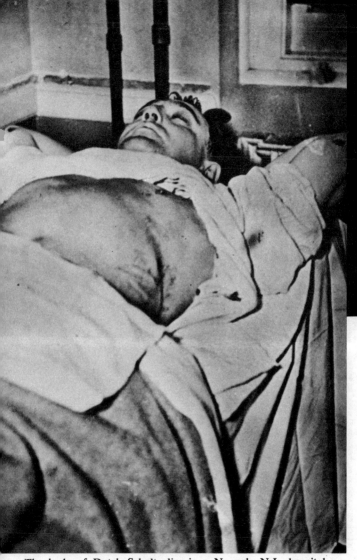

The body of Dutch Schultz lies in a Newark, N.J., hospital.

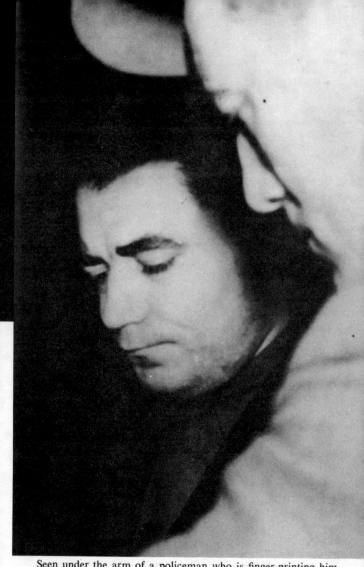

Seen under the arm of a policeman who is finger-printing him, is Schultz's killer, Bugs Workman, a syndicate triggerman. Workman wiped out the Schultz gang singlehanded.

Bugsy Siegel, a New York mobster and killer, who was sent to the West Coast and Las Vegas to supervise syndicate interests there. Here he is seen with his Hollywood lawyer, the famed Jerry Giesler.

Albert Anastasia, known as the Lord High Executioner of Murder, Inc.

Meyer Lansky, the supervisor of the syndicate's gambling interests in the Caribbean.

A profile and full frontal of the vicious Louis "Lepke" Buchalter, the man who, until he died in the electric chair in 1941, ran New York's union rackets with a firm hand and a gun. These are his FBI photographs.

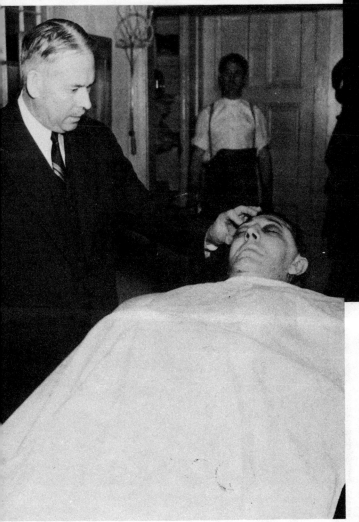

The body of George Weinberg, who once ran New York's numbers rackets. He may or may not have killed himself.

Thomas Lucchese, also known as "Three Finger Brown," was one of the five Mafia "dons" of New York when this picture was taken.

Abner "Longy" Zwillman, the reputed boss of New Jersey.
Here, he's testifying before the Senate Crime Committee in
1951.

It was at the California home of Virginia Hill that mobster Bugsy Seigel was wiped out in 1947. Someone blasted him through her picture window as he sat on the sofa. Here, in 1951, she's telling the Senate Crime Committee that most of her income in those days consisted of gifts from friends.

The Flamingo Hotel, in Las Vegas, which Seigel once had a hand in running.

Desert Inn, in Las Vegas, run by Wilbur Clark, alias Willie Bischoff.

Willie Bioff, a Hollywood union official, and one of the suspects in the famous shakedown of movie studios.

Although Dewey managed to get Lucky Luciano put into prison in 1936, the latter was released just after the war because of some mysterious "services" to the nation. It is thought that he might have helped to keep things peaceful and reasonably honest on the New York docks during World War II. Luciano here is being deported to his native Italy.

The Italian police have just declared Luciano "socially danger-ous" and have ordered him to remain indoors after dark.

In 1949, Luciano (top and bottom) is found at a house party in Naples.

Luciano attempts to avoid newsmen in a Naples street.

In this picture, two men are smiling, although it is hard to fathom why. Both are on their way to Sing Sing and the electric chair. From left to right, they are Louis Capone and Emanuel "Mendy" Weiss, two of the most prolific killers in the history of Brooklyn's organized crime. They died in 1941, the same year that Lepke himself got the chair.

Stefano Magaddino, the Mafia don of Buffalo. This portrait was taken while he was in police custody briefly in 1959.

Joseph Bonanno, a Mafia don of Brooklyn.

Frank Costello, who helped to run Lucky Luciano's mob when the latter was deported, shown here testifying before the Senate Crime Committee in 1951.

Mafia don, Joseph Profaci, who was questioned about the extermination of Albert Anastasia.

Joseph Barbara, at whose home in Appalachin, N.Y., police surprised a large group of syndicate bosses in 1957.

CHAPTER FIFTEEN
1933-1936

On February 15, 1933, the mayor of Chicago, Anton J. Cermak, was killed in Miami as he rode in a motorcade with the new President of the United States, Franklin D. Roosevelt. The killer, who was wounded and caught, was said to be an irrational anarchist, Giuseppe Zangara, who had in fact meant to kill FDR, instead of Cermak.

On his deathbed Zangara said that he'd killed Cermak on instructions from Al Capone. However, this eventually was discounted for several reasons. Zangara was a bit crazy, and Capone was in prison and had enough trouble without knocking off the mayor of Chicago. In addition, nobody could think of much reason for Capone to have done it, although there were rumors that Cermak was friendly to gangster competitors of Capone in Chicago.

The other major event in 1933 was the execution of John Bagdonowitz, a minor racketeer in New Jersey. One afternoon just after Repeal, he suddenly said he was giving it all up and going straight. The mob never did trust a man who wanted to go straight.

Bagdonowitz, of course, was aware of that, so he dropped out of sight. But it wasn't too long before he was spotted in a remote part of Long Island by Walter Sage, of Brooklyn's Reles-Maione mob. When this news reached New Jersey, the reply was as expected: put Bagdonowitz where he would be quiet—like underground.

Reles told the Brooklyn prosecutors years later that the assignment fell to Murder, Inc.'s Vito Gurino, Joe Marcaldo and Julie Catalino. Reles himself went along just to watch and enjoy. The quartet found Bagdonowitz at his mother's house in Long Island, just where Sage said he would be. When they rang the bell, the mother answered. They told her that they were detectives and that

215

they wanted to talk to her son. She fetched him, and when he came to the door, he met a firing squad.

For his good work, tipster Walter Sage was rewarded with a slot-machine concession for the Brooklyn mob. Unhappily for him, in 1939 they decided that he wasn't giving them a fair count on the receipts. One night his old pals Pittsburgh Phil, Gangy Cohen, Jack Drucker and Pretty Levine took him for a ride. Sometime during the conversation in the car they stuck an ice pick into Walter's chest 32 times. Then, as a symbolic touch, they tied his body to a slot machine and dropped it into a lake in the Catskills. Reles explained once that in order to keep bodies from floating to the top, an ice pick is very useful, because it lets the gases out as the body decomposes. In Sage's case, he floated to the surface in only ten days, slot machine and all. As the gang was baffled, and, always interested in perfecting technique, one hood asked a friendly doctor why. The answer was that ice pick wounds are fine for letting gasses out, but only if the holes are made after the victim is dead. Blood from a live victim, pumping through the holes, congeals and seals them. Pittsburgh Phil's comment: "Think of that. With this bum, you've got to be a doctor, or he floats!"

Johnny Torrio, having given up the rough stuff in Chicago, but also having tired of his sojourn in Italy, was back in New York and back in action. But no more guns and bombs for him. Instead he amused himself by being an elder statesman to the mobs, a top hoodlum with no gang and no territory. In other words, not someone they should worry about. Torrio advised Luciano and Costello on their plans for a national organization and kept himself available for assignments as a peacemaker between various rival mobs.

The millions that he took out of his Chicago operation were employed in a number of ways. He could always be counted on to back a loan-shark operation, or any number of other criminal activities that needed unofficial funding. And he dabbled in real estate, owning houses and vast tracts of land in Florida, New York and Maryland.

In 1934 police got wind of a big meeting in a swank New York hotel. Present were gang leaders from most of the big Eastern cities. The meeting was run by Torrio, with Luciano and Costello seated at either side. All the plans discussed at Atlantic City and Cleveland and briefly shelved during the Castellammarese War were brought out again, and this time the meeting endorsed a six-gang monopoly to run New York and New Jersey, with the Brooklyn boys as the official execution squad for jobs all over, and a nine-member National Commission to rule on disputes, to okay "hits" and generally to maintain order. There would be 24 gangs around the country, once certain other territories were opened up.

They also ruled that, for the time being, the membership would be closed, with no other mobsters being let in on the secret until their membership was approved by the National Commission. Outsiders could be employed, but they were not to be allowed in. Also, with few exceptions, the membership would be limited to Sicilians and Italians. The principal exceptions were Meyer Lansky, Bugsy Siegel, Lepke Buchalter and Longy Zwillman. Three of them had proved their loyalty and dedication. As for Lepke, well, he was there, and too powerful to be tangled with at the moment.

With the rise of Brooklyn's Murder, Inc., the mobs' old execution squad of Meyer and Siegel had a lot of spare time on their hands. However, there were plans for them, too. Meyer Lansky was to oversee gambling operations that were joint ventures of the mobs. Bugsy was to go west and open new territory. One man, one of the biggest up to that time, was left out of all plans: Dutch Schultz. The mobs were convinced that the Dutchman was going away for a long time on a tax rap, and they were already making plans to take over his empire.

Following the New York meeting, there was another meeting in Kansas City. The reports were that Johnny Torrio, Luciano and Costello were at that one too. This meeting included the Capone gang of Chicago, the Purple Gang of Detroit, the Mayfield gang of Cleveland and gangs from New Orleans, Kansas City, St. Louis and St. Paul.

When it was over, the national crime syndicate was formed.

In New York the mobs were busy dividing up Dutch Schultz's operations. He'd left Bo Weinberg in charge, but after a conversation with Lucky Luciano, Weinberg agreed that his chances of staying alive would be improved if he didn't cause any difficulties. Lepke took over Schultz's restaurant protection racket, which was worth a cool $2,000,000 annually, and Luciano took a large share of Schultz's Harlem numbers wheel. At this time Vito Genovese gave a small numbers operation there to Joe Valachi as a reward for services rendered.

Unexpectedly, in 1935 Dutch Schultz returned from his hideout, surrendered to the law and was out on bail. Still, the charges against him looked good and the odds were 10-1 against his beating the rap.

The Schultz lawyers persevered, though, and got the trial moved to Syracuse, New York, on the grounds that he was too well known and couldn't get a fair trial by jury in Manhattan.

In Syracuse, Schultz arrived early for the trial, took up residence, started throwing money around and donating to charity. Very soon the killer was a local celebrity and a lion of Syracuse society. His trial resulted in a hung jury. His second trial was moved to the tiny town of Malone, New York. Schultz went through the same routine, and this time he was found innocent! Judge Frederick Bryant was so annoyed that he remarked, "The verdict was dictated by other considerations than the evidence."

When Dutch returned to Manhattan, the gangs who'd helped themselves to his operations waited for the explosion. They didn't have long to wait. Schultz called in his manager, Bo Weinberg, and asked for an explanation. When, as it turned out, he wasn't satisfied with the answer, he stuck a pistol into Weinberg's mouth and pulled the trigger. At least that's what the cops think happened. They don't know for sure and the body of Weinberg has never been found.

As Schultz pondered his next move, he was suddenly given a new problem. A new district attorney, Thomas E. Dewey, was going after top criminals as though he meant it. Dewey had got the tax charge on Schultz in the first place and, when that had failed, he began looking at a numbers operation of Schultz's, one of the last ones that the Dutchman had left.

Schultz was beside himself with rage, feeling that he was being attacked and betrayed on all sides. Joe Valachi once related running into Schultz in a New York restaurant during this period as Schultz and Luciano were leaving together. Valachi quoted Luciano as saying, "All the Dutchman can talk about is Tom Dewey this and Tom Dewey that."

Schultz finally decided that Dewey had to be killed, and he asked the syndicate, of which he was not a member, to consider it. An exception was made and Schultz was allowed to attend the meeting. The syndicate couldn't make up its mind whether killing Dewey was the best move or not. Lepke and Luciano thought it might be better just to kill any witnesses that Dewey needed. Other mob leaders thought that killing Dewey might cause too great a stir, and bring even more heat. Finally, to be on the safe side, the meeting decided to have Albert Anastasia and his Murder, Inc. boys study Dewey's movements, in case the job had to be done in a hurry.

Two cars were stolen and hidden. One was to be the killers' escape car and the other was to be the "crash" car, for plowing into any pursuit. License plates were stolen. So were guns from a consignment of weapons bound overseas. A theft like that would remain undiscovered for a long time, if it ever was. Serial numbers were taken off the guns with acid. Filing numbers off, as the hoods had learned, left marks that could be read under certain lighting, and the guns were to be thrown away. Silencers were also made.

So far, all these preparations were standard, the things Murder, Inc. did for any really important rub-out.

Next came the casing of Dewey. He was followed from his home each morning and the gang learned that along with his bodyguard, he stopped off at a drugstore on the way to work. The gang planted a man and child in the drugstore as customers. The man learned that Dewey went into the drugstore to use the phone, to make his first check with his office each morning. (Dewey later explained that he got up early every morning and he didn't make the call from home, as it would wake up his wife.)

The plan was for the killers to be in the drugstore ahead of Dewey. When he went in, leaving his bodyguard outside, as usual, he would be killed in the phone booth. The druggist, a witness who might give the alrm, would also be shot. Because of the silencers, the bodyguard outside wouldn't even hear the shots and wouldn't realize anything was wrong until after the gang had had time to make a leisurely escape.

At the next syndicate meeting, the plan was gone over, but the assembled hoods, with the exception of Lepke's man, Gurrah Shapiro, decided to forget it, and just kill Dewey's witnesses. Schultz argued for using the plan, but the syndicate decision was final.

When Schultz got back to his New Jersey hideout, he was fuming. Finally he decided that the assassination plan was too good to waste, and he would have his own men use it. One of them leaked the news to the syndicate, and a hasty meeting was called. The Dutchman had to be stopped.

According to Kid Twist Reles, who gave all these facts to prosecutor Turkus, the death squad for Schultz consisted of three men: Charlie (The Bug) Workman and Mendy Weiss, both on Lepke's personal assassination staff. The driver was a hoodlum known only as Piggy.

As a killer, Workman was in a class by himself. He was an excellent shot and usually worked alone, apparently not needing any other guns to back up his own. When the car pulled up in front of Schultz's headquarters, which were in the back of the Palace Chophouse in Newark, New Jersey, Workman went in alone. Not many hoodlums would walk into the headquarters of Dutch Schultz alone, expect to kill him, and hope to walk out alive.

Workman, though, simply strolled through the restaurant and approached the office in the rear. At the office door, he noticed a men's room. Looking inside, he saw a man washing his hands. Thinking it was a bodyguard, he blasted the guy once, and then jumped through the other door and into the office. Three men were there, talking business. Workman shot and killed all three. One was Abbadabba Berman, the human computer. Annoyed that he hadn't seen Schultz, he went back to the men's room, and sure enough, it was the Dutchman himself on the floor. Workman went through Schultz's pockets for the stray thousand or two, and then calmly walked back outside, only to find the getaway car gone!

Apparently the whole slow-motion business had been too much for the other two hoods, and they'd panicked and fled, leaving Workman on his own in the middle of very hostile territory. But, by one means or another, Workman made it back to New York in one piece.

Dutch Schultz lived for almost 24 hours, with police stenographers by his side. This gave the syndicate some anxious moments, but, as it turned out, the Dutchman only raved about people stealing his rackets. His last coherent words were: "Mother is the best bet. And don't let Satan draw you too fast."

If Dewey was ever grateful to the syndicate for saving his life, he never showed it. With his prime target Dutch Schultz out of the way, Dewey was forced to turn his attention to Luciano.

The thing that finally got Luciano in trouble was compulsory prostitution, often called white slavery. The ironic aspect of it was, that of all the things of which Luciano was guilty, murder, extortion, gambling, narcotics peddling and bootlegging, prostitution was probably the thing he'd had the least to do with.

Luciano had got into the bordello business almost by accident. After Repeal, when the gangs were looking around for new business, it occurred to Luciano that the 500 individual brothels in New York were unorganized and in need of "management." Because

Lepke was grabbing the labor rackets and Schultz was grabbing the restaurant protection gimmick, Luciano had decided that he had to grab something. So he'd started "protecting" whorehouses. This led to ownership of whorehouses, and girls who worked for him —or else. That's where the compulsory angle came in.

The gangs didn't think Dewey could pin much on Luciano, so they were as surprised as the gang boss himself when Dewey had him arrested in Hot Springs, Arkansas. Dewey proved his case, and Luciano was sentenced to 30 to 50 years on July 17, 1936.

The mastermind of organized crime had been removed from the scene so suddenly, and with such seeming ease, that the entire underworld was shaken. It had only just got over the fact that Al Capone could be brought down, and Al, at that point, had been gone for four years.

Luciano was not destined to stay in jail for all that time, but nobody knew it then. The man who replaced him at the head of his gang was his old sidekick and lieutenant, Vito Genovese. The new "Big Six" in New York were: Genovese, Profaci, Bonanno, Lepke, Mangano and Zwillman.

Genovese was a man with almost as much guile as his former boss. He was born in Naples in 1897, and had come to the United States when he was 16. He then worked his way up in the rackets, sticking close to the rising star of Luciano all the way, and by 1930 he was a very rich man.

Genovese's first wife had died in 1929, but by 1932, he'd met another woman. The sad thing was that she was married. Then fate—or something—took a hand: her husband was strangled on a New York rooftop. According to informer Joe Valachi, the killers were Peter Mione and Michael Barrese, who were hired by Genovese. Valachi said, too, that when Barrese had started acting nervous about the whole thing, he disappeared. Forever.

One of Genovese's private, non-gang deals was with the famous "money machine." In this, Genovese and Mike Miranda, another Luciano man, swindled a businessman out of $160,000 with the old con trick about the machine that takes in paper and turns out money. Later the man who had steered the sucker to them demanded $35,000 as his share. His name was Ferdinand (The Shadow) Boccia.

Ferdinand should have kept his mouth shut, because he wound up dead—killed by Genovese-hired assassins. This assassination in

1934 was, years later, to cause Genovese a lot of inconvenience.

In Chicago Jake Guzik, released from Leavenworth on the tax rap, once again became co-director of the Capone mob, with Ralph (Bottles) Capone, also newly released from prison. Their assistants were Tony Accardo and Paul the Waiter Ricca.

In 1936 Machine Gun Jack McGurn finally got his, in a bowling alley in Chicago. His killers mowed him down with machine guns, fittingly enough. Police theorized that McGurn died at the hands of Moran gang survivors, who blamed him for taking part in the St. Valentine's Day massacre.

CHAPTER SIXTEEN
1937-1939

With Lepke on the lam from the feds, who wanted him on a narcotics charge, and from Dewey, who wanted him for murder, among other things, the administration of his rackets empire fell to Jake Gurrah Shapiro. The Luciano mob, meanwhile, was being administered by Frank Costello, since Luciano was in jail and Genovese in Italy. But Big Frank had so many interests, both legitimate and otherwise in New Orleans and Miami, that he hardly had the time or the inclination to worry about the day-to-day problems of mob control. Because of his legitimate speculations in oil and other businesses, particularly gambling, Costello was gradually growing away from the tough-guy stuff, and becoming the dapper Prime Minister of Crime, as the press called him.

As a consequence, the actual running of the Luciano operation fell to these hoods: Li'l Augie Pisano (whose real name was Anthony Carfano), Joe Adonis, Trigger Mike Coppola, Dominick (The Sailor) DeQuatro and Anthony (Tony Bender) Strollo. Each of them had their separate followers within the group. Costello was available to settle their disputes, and to relay orders from Luciano in prison.

Joe Valachi, at this time, was a soldier in the team run by Tony Bender, and not too happy about it. He'd never liked Bender, but had had no choice in the matter. Following the Castellammarese War, he'd been assigned to Bender, and that was that. Like many soldiers who were on call for assignments from time to time, Valachi was also given various concessions to help keep him alive between big jobs. He would be given a small numbers book, or a string of slots. Valachi also managed his own loan-shark business,

223

which eventually enabled him to take over half a large restaurant in return for a debt one of his creditors couldn't pay. He got a piece of a clothing firm in the same way.

At one point Bender had Valachi and two other men beat up a citizen with baseball bats in broad daylight on East 79th Street. The beating took place on the sidewalk. "If you want to know what the people in the streets were doing, they were just going on about their business as if nothing was happening," Valachi told author Peter Maas. Valachi was disturbed by this piece of work, however, because the man they'd beat up was a friend of Tommy Lucchese, also known as Three-Finger Brown, a boss in the Gagliano outfit. Valachi survived the complaint which followed, but this gave him even less reason to like Bender.

This was the state of things in New York when the syndicate decided to send Bugsy Siegel to California and virgin territory. It pained the mobs to realize that southern California, namely Los Angeles, was not organized at all. There was one good man out there, Jack Dragna, but he hadn't the capital or the experience to do much. Siegel arrived in Los Angeles in 1937, along with a friend, Mickey Cohen of Brooklyn. Dragna was signed on as the No. 3 man.

When Siegel looked over the situation, he quickly saw where other hoods had gone wrong. A shakedown of Hollywood and the movie industry was, of course, the obvious course. There was no huge aircraft and defense industry in California in those days. Previous efforts, however, had been aimed at threatening the movie studios. This hadn't worked very well because the movie moguls of the time were mostly tough businessmen from the garment and fur districts of New York. They'd either called the cops, or called "friends" back in New York.

Siegel decided, instead, to go after the movie stars themselves. The first thing he did was to take over the union of movie extras. Then he simply threatened name stars with an extra walkout in the middle of a big picture. A few thousand in Siegel's pocket would keep the extras in line. The odd thing is that instead of being generally loathed in the community, Siegel became a sought-after dinner guest, a so-called mystery man with exciting, sinister connections. Some of the female movie stars who fancied him in those days had no idea of how sinister Bugsy Siegel, boy killer, really was.

Shaking down the movie stars was only the beginning of the West Coast operation. The Mafia dons in New York, Chicago and Cleveland, delighted with his work so far, sent Siegel more trusted men to beef up his army. Siegel was engaged in "organizing," i.e., taking over California's bookmakers when he got his first murder contract from New York. It seems that Lepke, who was hiding out in Montreal, suddenly recalled the name of a man who might be able to give evidence against him: Harry (Big Greenie) Greenberg. Harry had helped Lepke with his industrial rackets, but lately had been running scared, all the way from New York to California.

The assignment was carried out by Bugsy himself and Allie Tannenbaum, Lepke's representative from New York. Two other men identified by witnesses were Champ Segal, a petty hood, and Frankie Carbo, the fight promoter. Carbo was later charged with shooting Greenberg, but got off with a hung jury. The case was eventually dropped, and Carbo went on to promote some of the most famous—and controversial—championship fights of the 1940s.

During 1939 Lepke, from his hideout, was ordering the deaths of witnesses left and right as Dewey's evidence against him mounted. The boys in Murder, Inc. carried out at least 12 contracts for him, adding to the 30 other men they'd killed for him in years past. These murders were all on top of the ones Lepke had his own men do, and ones that were done by friends, such as Bugsy Siegel.

As the deaths mounted, the manhunt for Lepke became the biggest in the history of the United States. During this time, the syndicate, of course, know exactly where Lepke was. There was even a large meeting with Lepke once, at the home of Tony Romero. Abe Reles, who drove Lepke there, recalled that others at the meeting were Longy Zwillman of New Jersey; Albert Anastasia, representing Vincent Mangano; Willie Moretti, with Zwillman; Jerry Rullo, also with Zwillman; and Three-Finger Brown Lucchese, representing Gagliano. The question before the house was whether Three-Finger Brown and the Gagliano outfit could dabble in one small area of the garment industry.

Lepke said no. Anastasia agreed that the garment business belonged to Lepke. The discussion was closed. Nobody wanted to annoy Lepke—not in the mood he was in at that time.

The price on Lepke's head eventually reached $50,000, and still nobody in the underworld would give him away. Finally J. Edgar

Hoover hit on the ploy that eventually produced Lepke. He told Frank Costello and Joe Adonis that unless Lepke was surrendered to the FBI posthaste, the FBI would pick up every Italian and Sicilian mobster in the country for questioning.

The syndicate decided that much as it loved Lepke, it couldn't afford an embarrassment like that. The syndicate informed Lepke that unless he turned himself in, he would be delivered to the FBI, one way or another. Lepke finally agreed to surrender, provided that the fix was in: he would take the federal rap on narcotics, if Dewey dropped his charges. Dewey at the time was saying that he had enough on Lepke to put him away for "500 years." The federal charge was worth only 10 to 12 years.

On being assured by his henchmen, Moey (Dimples) Wolinsky and Albert Anastasia, that Hoover had agreed to "protect" Lepke from Dewey (i.e., get Dewey to drop his charges in return for Lepke's surrender to the FBI), Lepke threw in the towel.

This, then, is how Lepke came to be captured by the late Broadway newspaper columnist, Walter Winchell. This author heard the story of the memorable night many times from Winchell, and it bears repeating:

On August 24, 1939, I parked my Cadillac in the warehouse district of the Lower East Side. My instructions were to sit there alone, until a car pulled up behind me. The second car was to be driven by Albert Anastasia. Lepke was to get out of Anastasia's car and get into mine. We were then to be joined by J. Edgar Hoover, who was waiting in another car nearby. Anastasia was to be allowed to drive away.

And that's exactly how it happened. One can only imagine the feelings of Winchell, regardless of how eager he was to score a scoop, as he sat there waiting for the most wanted man in America, on a dark night, with nothing but empty warehouses all around. Coming toward him in the shadows would be a man responsible for the deaths of at least 60 others, and he was being driven by an equally well-known killer. At any moment there might have been gunplay if Lepke had changed his mind, or if the syndicate had decided that it didn't want him in jail, where he might talk.

Once he was in FBI custody, Lepke learned that there was no fix. The FBI would prosecute him, and then he would be made available to Dewey. The syndicate had turned him around in order to save itself. (Moey Dimples, Lepke's trusted lieutenant, who'd lied to him, was blown to smithereens by a shotgun about three years later. When informed, Lepke, still in prison, smiled.)

Lepke drew 14 years on the federal narcotics charge, and then Dewey got him 30 years to life for his labor racketeering. That might have been the end of the Lepke story, except for a dramatic break in the fight against organized crime—the defection of Abe (Kid Twist) Reles, in 1940.

But that blow was yet to fall on the syndicate. In 1939 the main news, in addition to the arrest of Lepke, was the 30-month sentence given to Johnny Torrio for failing to pay the proper tax on his income.

And Al Capone finally got out of jail, after doing about two-thirds of his 11-year sentence. There was, of course, no question of his resuming control of his old mob. His mind was gone, due to syphilis. He was to spend the remaining eight years of his life sitting in the sun at his Miami home, often not even recognizing those around him.

Toward the end of 1939, M.L. (Moe) Annenberg, who for years had run the racing results wire service for bookies all over the country, retired. He was about to begin a sentence for tax fraud, and he just didn't want anything to do with the bookies' service any more.

Testimony developed by Senator Estes Kefauver's Senate Committee in 1950-51 revealed more of the story of Nationwide News Service, and its successor, Continental Press. Because offtrack betting was illegal, and because bookies need race results quickly in order to operate, there was a lucrative business opportunity for anyone who could get the results out of the racetracks around the country and into the horse parlors.

There are no telephone booths at racetracks, so various means had to be used to flash the results outside. One was for men to jot down the results and leave the track for the nearest phone after every race. But even this could be slow and called for lots of men working in relays.

Another method, at tracks with overlooking buildings, was to have a telephone man watching the tote board with high-powered glasses. Where this failed, sometimes a wigwag system could be used, from a man inside the track to a man outside.

When Nationwide folded, the manager, Tom Kelly, of Chicago, was unemployed. Happily for him, his|brother-in-law was Arthur B. (Mickey) McBride, a multimillionaire Cleveland property developer with numerous hoodlum friends. At the urging of Kelly, McBride started Continental Press, to take up where Nationwide left off. However, McBride made the operation slightly more legal. Instead of providing the information directly to the bookies, he sent it to 24 "distributors" around the country. They, supposedly, were in the business of printing racing papers and tip sheets. They called themselves "publishers." If they, in turn, sold the information to bookies, well, Continental Press couldn't help that, the Kefauver Committee was told. The information was sent to the publishers over regular telegraph and telephone lines.

McBride and Kelly were to make bundles of money out of this operation, until just after World War II, when the Capone mob and Bugsy Siegel decided to move in.

CHAPTER SEVENTEEN
1940-41

William O'Dwyer, later to become mayor of New York, was the new district attorney of Brooklyn in 1940. One of his first appointments was that of Burton B. Turkus, a young lawyer, to the post of assistant district attorney, in charge of homicide.

Turkus had barely settled into his job when a convicted thief, Harry Rudolph, then in jail, sent him a note. It said that he knew something about a murder. And indeed he did. The note from Rudolph set off a chain of events that eventually put seven men into the electric chair and got another one a sentence of 80 years. It also caused scores of deaths in the underworld as the mobs frantically killed potential witnesses and squealers.

Before Turkus was through, he'd discovered that 200 or so unsolved murders in Brooklyn were not only connected with the overall crime picture in New York, but part of a pattern of some 1,000 gangland killings spread from coast to coast. Turkus eventually confirmed the existence of the national crime cartel and he uncovered the previously unsuspected existence of Murder, Inc., the syndicate's firing squad. (The label Murder, Inc., now famous, was coined by the late Harry Feeney, the now defunct *New York World-Telegram*'s police reporter.)

Rudolph told the Brooklyn DA's office that Abe (Kid Twist) Reles, Buggsy Goldstein and Dukey Maffetore had killed his friend Alex (Red) Alpert. Alpert had been found shot dead six years before in a vacant lot. He was only 19.

When Reles and Goldstein heard that the DA was looking for them, they actually went into a police station and inquired why. Maffetore was arrested near his home. The three hoods were then placed in separate jails and each was told the other was talking. Eventually Dukey Maffetore cracked. He said he had had nothing to do with Alpert's murder, that the job had been done by Pittsburgh Phil, Frank Dasher Abbandando and Happy Maione. All Dukey did, he said, was steal the murder car, along with Pretty Levine, and deliver it to the killers.

The other thing he did, he said, was deliver some guy to Kid Twist's house. "They choked him there," Dukey said, "and then Buggsy sets fire to him on a lot."

Levine was picked up, and he talked in order to keep his young wife from being held in jail as a material witness.

As the story emerged from the testimony of Reles, Levine, and other witnesses, Red Alpert, a burglar, came to Pittsburgh Phil one day and tried to sell him $3,000 worth of hot jewelry. When Pittsburgh offered him only $700, Alpert refused—and for this he was killed.

At this point, much to everyone's surprise, Reles said he would tell all. To this day, nobody knows exactly what his motivation was, although there has never been any shortage of theories. Some think he merely wanted to escape the electric chair, and decided he would take his chances on staying alive as a "squealer" in prison. Others think that perhaps he simply wanted to be known as a big man. In any case, he was a godsend to the Brooklyn DA's office, and while nobody relished the idea of letting someone like Reles get away with murder, it came down to a question of priorities: Reles had what the DA desperately needed to convict others.

Reles himself, as described at the time, sounds almost evil-looking enough to scare his victims to death. He was a heavyset, squat man, with closely set eyes, thick lips, small ears, gorillalike arms and very large hands, with thick fingers.

When Reles began talking, the men in the DA's office could scarcly believe what they heard. He began by saying he knew the details of 50 separate murders, which he'd been in on, all over the country. At the end of 12 days, according to Assistant DA Turkus, Reles's revelations filled 25 shorthand notebooks.

At one point the amazed Turkus asked Reles if his conscience ever bothered him, or if he'd ever felt anything when he'd killed someone. Reles answered with questions of his own.

"How did you feel when you tried your first law case?"

Turkus admitted that he'd been nervous.

"And how about your second case?"

Turkus said he'd still been a bit nervous.

"And after that?" Reles asked.

Turkus said that eventually he got used to it.

"It's the same with murder," Reles said, "I got used to it."

Reles shed light on more things than murder. He gave the lowdown on organized crime across the United States: who did what, who controlled what, and who hired who to do what. He told about the "hideout network," and how it worked. Men on the lam from the law in their own cities could quickly get jobs—even new identification—through mobs in other cities. And if they really wanted to go underground, they'd get "respectable" jobs in legitimate businesses that were mob-owned.

When word of Reles's defection got out, the mob moved to kill anyone else whom it thought might possibly talk. Reles himself knew only too well the ganglords' efficiency in these matters: "Lep gave us eleven 'contracts' for witnesses when he was on the lam. We knocked off seven of them before Dewey put him on trial last year."

In many cases, the mob's exterminations actually drove ordinarily tight-lipped hoods to the DA's office, and the protection it offered. Many of them were afraid—because they knew too much—that the mob would have them killed just to be on the safe side. Many of the men who talked to Turkus at this time probably never would have, if they hadn't been in mortal fear of their own kind.

Among those who eventually turned state's evidence were Allie Tannenbaum, a Lepke killer, Blue Jaw Magoon of Brownsville, Julie Cantalano, Joe (The Baker) Liberito, Sholem Bernstein, Max Rubin and Paul Berger.

All of this, plus the arrest of Bug Workman in connection with the Dutch Schultz murder, was enough for the syndicate to bring Bugsy Siegel back from the West Coast to head its assassination team. Within days mobsters were either disappearing into hideouts, just "disappearing," or being found dead.

The first men to be charged with murder by the Brooklyn DA's office as a result of Reles and the others' stories were Reles's old associates, Happy Maione and Dasher Abbandando. The accusation was that they had killed George (Whitey) Rudnick, a friend of theirs, whom they suspected of talking to the police. He was found strangled, stabbed 63 times with an ice pick, and with his skull parted by a meat cleaver.

Both Reles and Cantalano testified that they saw Pittsburgh Phil (Big Harry), Dasher Abbandando and Happy Miaone putting Rudnick's body into a car and finishing up the job of killing him. Cantalano's description was particularly vivid. While on the witness stand, he was asked if there was some difficulty in putting Rudnick's body into the car:

I'm telling you, he's too long. Dasher crumples his legs up . . . you know what I mean. That makes the guy shorter. With that, he gives a little cough . . . he goes "hem." And Big Harry says, "This goddamn bum ain't dead yet." They pull the guy out a little bit, with his head leaning out. Big Harry, with an ice pick, he begins punching the guy with the ice pick. The blood comes out. Then Hap and Big Harry pick him up, and they situate him with his head against the back seat, so you couldn't see him from the window while the car is driving. Then Hap says, "Let me hit this son of a bitch for luck." He leans in and hits him with a cleaver . . . one of them butcher things, like you hit bones or meat with. I don't know where he hits him. All I know, I hear a dull noise.

In addition to giving a similar description of the murder, Reles gave a shocked court a little rundown of his credentials. There was this exchange:

Question: "Did you kill one Jake the Painter?"

Answer: "Yes, sir, in 1933 or 1934, I think."

Question: "Did you kill a labor delegate named Greenblatt?"

Answer: "Yes, with somebody else."

Question: "Do you know a man named Rocco who was killed?"

Answer: "I don't recall the name."

Question: "Did you kill a man on Columbia Street?"

Answer: "I was a party to it. There was two of us pulled triggers."

Question: "When Puggy Feinstein was killed, you killed him, didn't you?"

Answer: "I helped, I was part of it."

Question: "Did you shoot any of the Shapiro brothers?"

Answer: "Not alone, I was one of the party."

Maione, when he took the stand, denied everything. He was

asked if he and Abbandando killed Joseph Cooperman in 1934. No. Did he and Pittsburgh Phil kill August Justriano, a tailor, in an argument over women? No. Did he and Gurino kill Harry Schober in 1939? No. Did he, Gurino and Abbandando kill Felice Esposito in 1939? No. Did he and Abbandando take a girl from a bar, force her to go to a hotel and gang-rape her? No. Did he and three other men kidnap a 17-year-old girl and gang-rape her? No.

Squealers had told the DA that Happy Maione had done all those things and more. Eventually Maione and Abbandando were found guilty of murder in the first degree. Then they got a new trial, on a technicality. They were found guilty again, and both finally died in the electric chair on February 19, 1942.

Buggsy Goldstein and Pittsburgh Phil were put on trial for the murder of Irving (Puggy) Feinstein, a gambler. Reles testified that Pittsburgh Phil once told him that the Puggy ''hit'' was a contract job for Albert Anastasia, who was arranging it as a favor for his boss, Vince Mangano.

The killing of Puggy was described by Reles. He said the arrangement was that Dukey Maffetore and Buggsy Goldstein were to bring Puggy to Reles's house late at night on some excuse. Pittsburgh Phil and Reles would do the job there. Reles sent his wife and Buggsy's wife out, and Reles's mother-in-law went to bed. While waiting for the delivery of Puggy, Reles thoughtfully made some preparations. He testified:

So I go into the bedroom where the old lady is sleeping. I ask her, ''Where's the rope we use up at the lake last summer for the washline?'' She says, ''Down in the cellar in the valise.'' I go down and I get the rope. When I come up, I ask the old lady, ''Where's the ice pick?'' She says, ''In the pantry.'' I go look in the pantry and I find it. Big Harry says to the old lady, friendly like, ''Why don't you go back to sleep?''

Then, Reles testified, Pittsburgh Phil said he would sit well down in a big chair that had its back to the door. He would have the ice pick and the rope. Reles would be across the room, with the radio playing. When Puggy came across the room to greet his pal, Reles, Pittsburgh Phil would grab him. While he waited, Pittsburgh Phil sat in the chair calmly drinking a glass of milk.

Buggsy, Dukey and Puggy came in soon thereafter. What happened next was described by Reles:

As soon as Puggy passed the chair, Harry [Pittsburgh Phil] jumps up and puts his arms around him, mugs him, like this. Puggy wiggles around and fights. So, Harry throws him on the couch. Puggy starts hollering, "Don't hit me, don't hit me, I got the money!" [Puggy thought he was being killed over a gambling debt. The real reason was that his small operation had infringed on all-powerful Vince Mangano's territory in Brooklyn.]

Reles: I put the radio on a little louder, because Puggy is making a noise. I go for the rope. I go back over to the couch with it, and Harry is saying, "The bastard bit me in the hand." Harry is like laying over Puggy, so he should not move. Buggsy is hitting him to make him quiet, pounding him. I give Harry one end of the rope and I hold the other end. Puggy is kicking and fighting. He is forcing his head down, so we can't get the rope under his throat [chin]. Buggsy holds his head up, so we can put the rope under. Then me and Harry exchange the ends, cross them, so we can make a knot, a twist. Then we cross them once more. Then we rope around his throat again, to make two loops. Buggsy gets Puggy by the feet, and me and Harry get him by the head. We put him down on the floor. He is kicking. Harry starts finishing tying him up. I am turning him like, and Harry gets his feet tied up with the back of his neck. He ties him up like a little ball. His head is pushed down on his chest. His hands are in between. The rope is around his neck and under his feet. If he moves, the rope will tighten up around his throat more.

Big Harry says, "We'd better burn this bum up, so nobody will know him. Go get some gas."

Puggy was probably dead by the time they put the torch to him at a Brooklyn dump. In any case, police were able to identify the body. The testimony of Reles, Blue Jaw Magoon and Dukey Maffetore was sufficient to convict Buggsy Goldstein and Pittsburgh Phil of murder in the first degree. On being sentenced to death, Buggsy asked for permission to say something. He said to the judge, "Before I die, there is one thing I would like to do. I would like to pee up your leg." Buggsy and Pittsburgh Phil were executed on June 12, 1941.

Blue Jaw Magoon's testimony at the Buggsy-Phil trial was interesting in that, in addition to helping to convict that pair, he mentioned a time that the mob killed the wrong man. It seems that Lepke, in his hideout, remembered that a union official, Philip Orlofsky, "knew too much" about him. Lepke ordered his death, and on the night of July 28, 1939, Blue Jaw Magoon, Louis Capone and Dandy Jack Parisi had waited, guns at the ready, for Orlofsky to come out of his apartment building. A man fitting the intended victim's general appearance finally emerged and the trio gunned him down. He turned out to be one Irving Penn, a well-known music publisher.

The next targets of the Brooklyn DA's office were Louis Capone, Lepke Buchalter and Mendy Weiss. They were charged with the five-year-old murder of Joseph Rosen, a Brooklyn candy store owner. (Actually, there were six men involved in the slaughter. One was Pittsburgh Phil, who was already under a death sentence; another was a citizen named Dizzy Jimmy Feraco, who had already been bumped off by his own kind. There was not enough evidence to convict another, Little Farvel, of murder, but he eventually was put away for eight years on a narcotics rap. When he got out in 1949, he didn't last long. He started a protection racket, with bookies as the potential customers. Unfortunately for him, they objected most strenuously. He was found dead on September 16, 1949, his skull full of lead.)

The motive for Rosen's rubout was that along about 1930, he, having worked hard and saved his money, finally had a thriving legitimate clothing business. Then the Lepke-controlled union threatened a work stoppage, which would ruin Rosen. In exchange for calling off the strike, the mob took control of the firm. Eventually, the customers were siphoned off to other mob-owned factories, and Rosen was out on the street. In 1936 Rosen borrowed money to open a candy store, but grumbled to friends about Lepke and his hoods. Word of this got back to Lepke, who decided that Rosen had better be hit.

One of the things that had puzzled police about the killing was the fact that Rosen had had ten bullets put through him, any one of which might have been fatal, and four of them had apparently been aimed at him while he was lying dead on the floor. To police, this seemed like overdoing it, and they wondered about it.

One of the key witnesses against the three killers was Max Rubin, Lepke's chief union organizer. He'd heard Lepke order Rosen's death, and heard him discuss it with Mendy Weiss.

Rubin came to give testimony against Lepke in a roundabout way. First, he was afraid of being tagged for the Rosen killing. So, in order to square himself with the DA, he agreed to testify against

Lepke, but only about Lepke's rackets. However, hearing that Rubin was talking to the DA about Lepke, Mendy Weiss arranged for his assassination. Weiss got Paul Berger to take Rubin to lunch and finger him for a gunman named Shloime. Two thugs then waylaid Rubin when he came up from the subway and walked along a street ironically named Gun Hill Road, in the Bronx. A gun was pressed against the back of his neck and fired. Rubin fell and the hoodlums ran off. Two months later Rubin walked out of the hospital. The bullet had passed through his skull and out between his eyes. His neck was permanently stiff, but otherwise he was reasonably okay: and that's when he decided to tell the DA anything the law wanted to know about Lepke.

Another Lepke associate, Paul Berger, testified that he pointed out Rosen to Weiss. Sholem Bernstein, the mob's crack car thief, testified that Weiss, Pittsburgh Phil, Louis Capone and Little Farvel told him to steal a car quickly and to get a place to hide it. In the next few days, Louis Capone showed Bernstein where "somebody was gonna be killed," (the candy store), and went over the escape route with him. Bernstein had also listened while Weiss, Capone, Pittsburgh Phil, Little Farvel and Feraco planned the hit.

Allie Tannenbaum, who admitted having done many killings for the mob, testified that he heard Weiss and Lepke talking about the Rosen job, and Weiss said, "I give him [Pittsburgh Phil] strict orders not to do any shooting, but after I shoot Rosen, and he is laying there on the floor, Pep starts shooting him!"

Pittsburgh Phil apparently just liked shooting people, even after they were dead.

Lepke, Weiss and Capone were convicted of first-degree murder on November 31, 1941, but with various appeals and delays, it was to take until March 4, 1944, to get them into the chair.

As for some of the other principals in the trials, Allie Tannenbaum changed his name, disappeared and went straight. In return for his testimony, no charges were pressed against this self-admitted killer. Bug Workman, the syndicate's one-man firing squad, drew a life sentence in New Jersey for the murder of Dutch Schultz.

And then there was Reles. The Brooklyn DA's office had been holding him and three other witnesses at the Half Moon Hotel, in Coney Island. The rooms were on the sixth floor, and the entire floor was guarded at all times by five armed policemen. Nevertheless, on November 12, 1941, during Lepke's trial, the body of Kid Twist was found 42 feet down, under his open window.

There were some knotted bedsheets trailing through the window, which indicated that Reles might have been trying to escape when his makeshift rope parted. This was thought unlikely, though, because Reles was safer inside than he was outside where the mob could get him.

Did Reles fall from the window or was he thrown? If thrown, how did the killers get past the police, who said they saw nothing? A police theory—which some people called farfetched—was that Reles was not trying to escape, nor was he killed. (The escape idea didn't make sense, and killers couldn't have got past the guards.) No, said the police, what Reles was trying to do was simply to play a joke on his guards. He was trying to get into the room below his, which was vacant. Then he was going to walk back upstairs and have the laugh on the cops. Unfortunately his rope gave way.

Nobody ever found out how or why Reles took his fatal plunge. But years afterwards Joe Valachi said "I never met anybody yet who thought Reles went out that window on purpose."

CHAPTER EIGHTEEN
1942-1949

I n New York the mobs quickly moved to cut up Lepke's enterprises, just as they had done those run by Dutch Schultz. The lineup during the war was Vince Mangano, Joseph Bonanno and Joseph Profaci, in Brooklyn, and Frank Costello handling Lucky Luciano's Manhattan outfit while Lucky was in jail, and his lieutenant, Vito Genovese, was hiding in Italy. Albert Anastasia, Vince Mangano's No. 1 boy, was, of all places, in the army. Meyer Lansky supervised various gambling operations. Longy Zwillman ran New Jersey. The mob controlled by Gaetano Gagliano operated in Brooklyn and the Bronx.

The Mafia, as the press called it, or the Cosa Nostra, as the Sicilian-Italian hoods called it, was now the dominant crime force all over the country. The few prominent exceptions were Zwillman, Lansky and Bugsy Siegel.

As for the startling revelations about organized crime that had come to light during the trials of Lepke and the others, as Burton Turkus pointed out in his book, such ordinarily shocking facts were eclipsed constantly by the activities of a much bigger criminal element—the Nazis. Time after time the horrifying details of Murder, Inc.'s activities were pushed to the back pages by the war news. Who was going to worry about organized crime when France was falling, London was being blitzed and/or when the Japs were bombing Pearl Harbor? It wouldn't be until 1950-51 during the hearings conducted by the late Senator Estes Kefauver that the subject of organized crime would be brought to the public's attention again.

In the meantime the mobs made money out of the war. Joe Valachi, the 1960s version of Kid Twist, told how the gas rationing racket worked. Valachi himself made about $200,000 in the gas stamp hustle, and he was just a small-timer. He said he got into it when a gas station operator asked him for some "hot" stamps. It seems that the station owner had been selling more gasoline than he'd been getting stamps for. Gas sold without the proper ration stamps got a high price, of course.

Valachi went to Frank Luciano (no relation to Lucky) and bought stolen stamps. Counterfeit stamps were no good, Valachi said, because they were so easily detected, and the rap for printing them was so heavy. The gang found it much easier to get real ones by breaking into ration stamp offices and/or bribing "bent" Office of Price Administration workers. Used stamps were supposed to be burned, but often weren't. The profit on illegal stamps was about five cents a gallon, and the OPA estimated that 2,500,000 black-market gallons were being sold daily around the country during the war.

The two biggest sellers of stamps to men like Valachi who in turn sold them to the crooked gas station owners, were Carlo Gambino, a lieutenant in Vincent Mangano's outfit, and Settemo Accardi, who ran crime in Newark, New Jersey. (Long after the war, Accardi was finally put away on a narcotics charge.)

The booming new defense industries in California convinced the mobs that there was a lot of money around out there, too, and they urged their representative, Bugsy Siegel, to redouble his efforts to turn some of it their way.

In Florida Frank Costello's associate, Frank Erickson, and John (Boy Mayor) Patton, a pal of Al Capone's, financed Abe Allenberg, a New York lawyer, in the operation of the Wofford Hotel. Other partners in the hotel deal were John Agnersola (also known as John King) of Cleveland, and Anthony Carfano (also known as Little Augie Pisano) of New York. The Wofford, the Kefauver Committee heard, soon became the headquarters for Erickson's bookmaking operations, and his gambling "concessions" at the famous Roney Plaza, Boca Raton and Hollywood Beach hotels.

In 1942 the Kansas City police traced narcotics sold there to Mafia sources in Tampa, and from there to Cuba, and from Cuba to Marseilles.

The Continental Press wire service, meanwhile, was having some trouble. According to estimates the Kefauver Committee made, the business must have been worth a million or so a year. In

240

1942, Arthur B. (Mickey) McBride sold his interest to James Ragen, Jr., of Chicago. James Ragen, Sr. then took over and asked McBride to buy a piece of the business back. It seems that Ragen Sr. thought that McBride's name in the business would help its image. Besides, the elder Ragen had had too much trouble in Chicago with the Capone mob, and he didn't want it, or the government, which was bothering him about his taxes, to look too closely at his wire-service interests. Mickey McBride obligingly bought one-third of Continental back, and put it in his son's name. The Capone gang in Chicago began eyeing Continental with envy at about this time, but decided to wait. It had other things to do.

Toward the end of 1942 there was a fascinating development in the career of Lucky Luciano, who had been languishing in Dannemora prison for 6 years, doing the 35-to-50-year white slavery stretch arranged for him by Tom Dewey. The navy, or so the story goes, became concerned during the war about possible sabotage on New York's waterfront. Then someone in the Navy Department had the brainstorm that waterfront hoods could prevent acts of sabotage, if prevailed upon to do so by someone who mattered to them. It followed that while the mobsters might not be patriotic enough to do this on their own, they might if Lucky Luciano ordered it. Allegedly a deal was worked out: Luciano would pass the word to the docks, and if they were kept relatively sabotage free, he would be released at the end of the war.

That's one version. Another is that Lucky Luciano, in some way, helped the U.S. Army campaign in Sicily. He supposedly passed the word to Mafia associates there that the Americans were the "good guys," and to help them.

In either case, what Luciano did or did not do for his country is still classified information. All that we do know is that a grateful government first transferred Luciano from the bleakness of northernmost Dannemora to a relatively plush cell near Albany, New York. There he patiently awaited an Allied victory.

By 1943 it became known that one of the reasons the Capone gang had postponed taking over Continental Press was that it was busy trying to muscle Hollywood. Unhappily for the hoods involved, Hollywood didn't knuckle under. Paul (The Waiter) Ricca, Louis (Little New York) Campagna and Charles (Cherry Nose) Gioe, with an assortment of other gangsters from Chicago, New York and Los Angeles, were all sentenced to ten years for trying to extort $1,000,000 from the film studios by threatening to have mob-controlled unions go on strike. Willie Bioff, a West Coast union racketeer, was also involved. At the same time, the federal government was after Campagna and Ricca for about $500,000 in unpaid taxes. For the next few years Tony Accardo, left in charge of the Capone outfit, bent every effort to spring his cohorts legally. Accardo had taken over the gang when Frank (The Enforcer) Nitti committed suicide in 1943 when faced with a second jail term, this one for extortion; his first term had been for tax evasion.

In Italy at this time, the exiled Vito Genovese was demonstrating a remarkable ability to land on his feet. He'd fled the United States in 1937 in order to avoid answering some embarrassing questions about his business, and once in Italy he'd become a fast friend of Mussolini's government. In fact, of the $750,000 he took with him on leaving America, he'd donated $250,000 for the building of a new Fascist party headquarters. At one point, he was given the Italian government's highest civilian award.

Things went along pleasantly enough for Genovese until the war had started to go badly for Italy. Then, as the American army swept through Naples, Genovese had immediately switched sides, and became a friend to GI's. His first generous gesture had been to act as an interpreter in American military courts that were restoring law and order in the aftermath of battle. In this way, Genovese was able to put the finger on a number of Neapolitan hoods who might have been his rivals in the upcoming black market. As he'd made friends with his small services and, no doubt, by spreading some of his money around, he'd got a rare document that allowed him unlimited travel throughout Allied-occupied Italy. He'd also got ten letters of recommendation and letters attesting to his honesty from high-ranking officers. Genovese was even praised as a man who had exposed many small black-market operators.

The truth of the matter was that Genovese was probably the biggest black-market operator in Italy. One fine afternoon the U.S. Army caught a bunch of Canadian army deserters and Italian civilians looting an army warehouse. The Italians said they would be quickly freed by "Don Vito," the local Mafia head. A Canadian said that Don Vito was none other than Genovese, and that he was the black market king of Naples. Genovese was tracked down and caught on August 27, 1944, by an army sergeant, Orange C. Dickey, who was with the U.S. Army's Criminal Investigation Division.

Sergeant Dickey then found it incredibly hard to get anyone to care. Many officers, perhaps some of whom Genovese had fooled, just didn't want to know about it. They wanted Genovese, and Dickey, too, to disappear, if possible. Dickey himself had no idea how important a crime figure he had until an informant gave him a book on American crime that had been written years before. Genovese figured prominently in it. Asked about it, Genovese, who assumed there were no American charges against him, readily acknowledged his publicity. Dickey immediately wrote to the FBI in Washington and asked if Genovese was wanted for anything.

While he was waiting for an answer, Dickey found that nobody in the Allied command in Italy was interested in prosecuting Genovese on the black-market charges. Then Dickey was notified by the FBI that Genovese was wanted on an old murder charge. It stemmed from the murder of Ferdinand (The Shadow) Boccia, a con man who'd helped Genovese and Mike Miranda swindle a merchant out of $160,000. When Boccia had demanded his cut of the loot, Genovese had hired William Gallo and Ernest (The Hawk) Rupolo to kill Boccia. Then Genovese and Miranda told Rupolo to kill Gallo after the Boccia job. The mix-up began when Genovese got regular Mafia assassins to do the Boccia job. Rupolo, thinking Phase Two was still called for, tried to kill Gallo, but only wounded him.

After this Gallo told the cops, and Rupolo was given nine to twenty years. He was released in 1944, after ten years, and within a month or so was arrested again, for another attempted killing. Then Rupolo decided to tell everything he knew about crime in order to avoid another long sentence. The first thing he thought of was the old Genovese job. It seemed safe enough to talk about that, with Genovese long gone and overseas. Rupolo had been able to find another witness, Peter LaTempa, who recalled hearing Genovese give orders for the Boccia job. LaTempa, too, had been encouraged to talk because Genovese was out of sight and out of mind.

All this had happened shortly before Dickey picked up Genovese in Italy. When the FBI warrant failed to arrive, Dickey decided to take it on himself to bring Genovese back to the United States to face the murder charges. One day, Genovese offered Dickey $250,000 to forget the whole thing. "Why bother?" he said. "Nobody here cares what you do with me. You're not getting any thanks for this."

About a week later, Genovese stopped offering Dickey money and announced that he would be happy to return to America. What had happened to one of the witnesses against him may have had something to do with his decision. When news of Genovese's arrest had become known in the States, LaTempa had immediately run to the nearest police station and requested sanctuary. On January 15, 1945 he took some of his usual pills for a stomach disorder, and fell over dead. There was enough poison in his body to kill an ox.

Dickey brought Genovese back to Brooklyn, but with LaTempa dead, any chance of prosecuting Genovese had vanished. Genovese was freed on June 10, 1946. He was never even tried for his black market offenses in Italy. Rupolo? He was given "A" for effort by the district attorney's office and freed. No one expected him to live for long, but he managed to elude Mafia gunmen for 18 years. His bullet-filled body finally washed ashore, with a few concrete weights still attached, on August 17, 1964. Four syndicate types were tried for the murder, but were acquitted.

When Genovese returned to his old mob, the one originally run by Luciano, he found Frank Costello in charge. However, with his interests in Florida and New Orleans, Frank was an absentee boss, which gave Genovese a lot of leeway. It was to take 11 years for Genovese really to become insistent about taking control of the mob again. As it was, in the early postwar years, Genovese was content to take the cash and let the credit go. Vito had had enough trouble from the government, and it was nice having someone as famous as Costello to take the heat.

In 1946 Lucky Luciano, killer, extortionist, pimp and drug peddler, was rewarded for his mysterious services to flag and country, and given a parole. He'd served only 10 years of his 35-to-50-year sentence. He was then deported to Italy on the grounds that he'd entered the country illegally.

That same year, the battle for control of Continental Press began. The Capone gang saw the wire service in an expanded form. Not just a relatively small operation serving 24 "publishers" around the country, but a business serving every major bookie in the nation. Instead of grossing $1,000,000, it might gross $10 or $20 million. It would also be a way of employing 8,000 or 9,000 hoods, who between killings, gang wars and strong-arm stuff, were simply kept sitting around, drawing paychecks and doing hardly anything. In addition to all these advantages, the control of the wire service would give the Chicago mob control of all bookmakers in the country. Without race results, the bookies can't operate, and if the Capone gang threatened to cut off the results, well, the opportunity for a little piece of the bookies' profits would protect them from possible losses like that.

Having completed its market research, all the Capone gang had to do was take over Continental Press. This turned out to be more difficult than anticipated. The first effort was diplomatic. Jake Greasy Thumb Guzik, Tony Accardo and Murray the Camel Humphries called on Ragen, Sr., the boss of Continental, and offered to buy part of his firm. He could remain a partner, and the mob would help line up customers. The fatal flaw in this deal, as Ragen, Sr. saw it, was that once he'd taught the mob the business, his value would be greatly diminished, even to the point where he might be found dead in an alley.

Ragen, Sr. then did something almost suicidal: he went to the FBI and told them he was being pestered to sell out to the Capone mob. Shortly afterward a car tried to run him down, but missed. Ragen, Sr. then tried the ploy of writing a 90-page affidavit for the district attorney, telling the latter everything the Capone mob was trying to do to him. He named Guzik, Accardo and Humphries as the men most likely to take him for an unsolicited ride in the country.

The Capone gang resisted resorting to violence, for a while. Instead it started Trans-American Publishing and News Service as a competitor to Continental. Trans-American then pressured customers of Continental to cancel and take the new service. But Ragen, Sr. continued to get new customers, and to fight for business. On June 24, 1946, his prediction came true: he was shotgunned on a Chicago street and died shortly afterwards. The two wire services continued to battle, with Tom Kelly at the helm of Continental, for another year.

Mickey McBride then returned and bought out all the Ragen interests for $370,000, on a ten-year installment plan. Oddly enough, when that happened, the rival Trans-American service folded. Former Capone customers quickly became customers of Continental, and soon it was doing a $10 million business all over the country. The listed owner of Continental at this point was Mickey McBride's son, Edward, a 26-year-old law student.

The wire service continued to prosper long after the Kefauver hearings. It was not stopped until the 1960s, when a new crime law—inspired by Attorney General Robert F. Kennedy—made it illegal for anyone except a legitimate news agency to transmit or receive racing results across state lines. To get around this, the bookies have had to resort to the telephone, elaborate code systems and results "leaked" from legitimate news sources.

Only about a month after the Trans-American wire service closed, Bugsy Siegel was to suffer the fate he'd arranged for so many others. During the Trans-American Continental Press war, Siegel had been muscling in on Las Vegas bookmakers, and as the Nevada representative of the Capone wire service, he'd virtually controlled bookmaking in the state. By forcing bookies to take his service and then threatening to cut it off unless they shared profits with him, Siegel had become a very rich man. He'd done all this while, at the same time, he'd run the Flamingo Hotel for the Costello, Lansky, Adonis and Luciano interests. The $6,000,000 Flamingo, incidentally, was built during the war, when building materials were supposedly hard to come by. But then the mob had been capable of amazing feats during the war. Once in 1942 a plane crashed into a telegraph wire and severed service to an air force field. The mob was able to get its interrupted race results service restored in only 15 minutes. It took the army, which needed the air base ready for instant action in event of a Japanese attack, some three hours to get its communications restored.

When Trans-American folded and word came through for syndicate customers to subscribe to Continental Press, Siegel wasn't pleased. He could see that he would quickly lose control of his bookmaking monopoly once the bookies were no longer his private customers. He decided that he would continue to supply them with racing results, and that they wouldn't subscribe to Continental. It took the mob just two days to get someone out there to "reason" with Siegel.

In June 1947 he was sitting in the Beverly Hills home of his girlfriend, Virginia Hill, and talking to his associate, Allen Smiley (also known as Aaron Smehoff), when someone fired a shotgun through Virginia's lovely plate-glass window. And that was the end of Bugsy. Smiley was so shaken that he quickly sold out his interest in the Flamingo, saying it just wasn't fun anymore.

A minority view of the Siegel murder was that it had nothing to do with the wire-service problem. Instead, it was speculated that the

East Coast crowd, who had set Bugsy up out there, was unhappy at the way he was neglecting the operation of the Flamingo itself. The view was that he had gone soft, and was concentrating too much on having a good time, being a playboy and expanding his own private interests.

The Flamingo's next operator was Sanford Adler, a gambler with a long arrest record. The men who owned the controlling shares in the Flamingo were listed as Moe Sedway, who also operated the wire service in Phoenix, Morris Rosen, and Gus Greenbaum. When Adler quit, or was fired, the three owners operated the hotel themselves, and for a while, tried to maintain Siegel's old wire-service monopoly in Nevada. When a competing wire service began making waves, the state authorities became afraid of another gang war.

In 1949 Nevada decided to preserve the peace, and go into the race results business itself, distributing information to all licensed gambling casinos, a policy that implied that known hoodlums would be turned down. However anyone who'd already had a casino before the act was passed was granted a license. So the law applied only to newcomers.

CHAPTER NINETEEN
1950

The Kefauver Committee's official name was the Senate Special Committee to Investigate Organized Crime in Interstate Commerce. It was formed as a result of a bill introduced in the Senate by Senator Estes Kefauver (D., Tenn.). He became its chairman on May 10, 1950, and held the post for one year. The chief counsel for the committee was Rudolph Halley.

The committee went from city to city, holding hearings, some behind closed dorrs and others televised and seen by upwards of 20 million people. Before each hearing, investigators went out and found out enough about crime in the various locales for the committee to issue subpoenas for witnesses, and know what to ask them when they got there. Often the witnesses merely droned, "I refuse to answer on the ground that it may tend to incriminate me." That, of course, is one of the safeguards of the Fifth Amendment to the U.S. Constitution. It protects a man from being forced to testify against himself.

At times, the hoodlums' sitting there, coolly refusing to answer even the simplest questions, was very frustrating for Kefauver and his fellow senators. The Senate did get some of the most arrogant users of the Fifth Amendment charged with contempt of Congress, but in the very first case the accused was freed on a directed virdict from the judge. While this was irritating to Kefauver and law enforcement officials, because it encouraged other hoods to use the Fifth Amendment, it was altogether proper. The Fifth Amendment was added to the Constitution for good reason, as was pointed out at the time, and not there merely to be cast aside when inconvenient.

Despite the handicaps, however, much information on the Mafia, organized crime, or even the Cosa Nostra, as it is popularly called now, emerged. The hearings, plus the separate pre-hearings investigations, resulted in a Senate report which has for years provided source material for crime historians.

Early on in the hearings it became obvious that few of the people questioned were going to admit any knowledge of the syndicate. Some of the question-answer exchanges were even funny. In Kansas City, one Tony Gizzo was asked, "Do you belong to the Mafia?" His answer: "What is the Mafia? I don't even know what the Mafia is."

Later Gizzo seemed to forget the previous exchange. He was asked, "Do you know Balestrere?"

Gizzo: "Yes, sir."
Question: "He is rather widely known as a prominent man in the Mafia, isn't he?"
Gizzo: "That's what you hear."
Question: "What do you hear?"
Gizzo: "The same thing that you just said there."

Later, at the public hearings on crime in Kansas City, Gizzo was reminded of his conflicting answers at previous sessions. He became excited and yelled, "I wish to hell I know what the Mafia is!"

The widely known Willie Moretti of New Jersey had this exchange with committee counsel Rudolph Halley:

Halley: "Do you know what the Mafia is?"
Moretti: "What?"
Halley: "The Mafia. M-A-F-I-A."
Moretti: "I am sorry, I don't know what you are talking about."
Halley: "You never heard that word before in your life?"
Moretti: "No, sir, I did not."

Jack Dragna, of Los Angeles, was born in Sicily. Nevertheless, he said he didn't know anything about the Mafia, except what he read in the papers. Halley asked him, "Did you ever hear of it in your home?" Dragna said he hadn't. In fact, Dragna said, he never even heard of it when he was a boy, in Sicily.

One who was slightly more informative than the rest was the reasonably articulate Philip D'Andrea, one of the late Al Capone's favorite bodyguards, and a past president of the Chicago Unione

Siciliano. He said he'd heard of the Mafia since he was a child, but he didn't know anything about it. The Unione Siciliano, he said, was merely a cooperative insurance association. He said he didn't know of any racketeer influence in it. D'Andrea had been in California when he'd been hauled back to testify at the Kefauver hearings in Chicago.

Question: "Would you say it would be unusual for any man of your age who was born in Sicily to say that he knew nothing about the Mafia?"

D'Andrea: "Yes, I would think so. If he was born in Sicily, I would think so, because, as I say, years ago it was a byword in every family. People were scared to death of having a little home, for fear somebody would come over and blow it up, or for fear they would get a letter. That was the condition here about 20 years ago, that I recall."

Question: "What would you say were some of the other concepts or principles of the Mafia that you recall from your childhood, having heard talked about in the family?"

D'Andrea: "One of the concepts was that it would be a good idea to keep your mouth closed."

Kefauver's committee visited Chicago three times and built up a report of some 1,400 pages. Shortly before he was to testify before the committee, Police Lieutenant William Drury was killed by parties unknown. The senators could only guess at what he might have told them.

Police Captain Thomas Harrison was asked why nothing had been done about 84 lawbreaking establishments in his district, ones that had been noted in the Chicago Crime Commission's report. Harrison said that the places had never been reported to him. Harrison was asked about policemen who seemed to be living beyond their means and police salaries. Harrison said he didn't know anything about "their private lives." Harrison himself, who earned $5,200 a year, admitted to the committee that he'd bought an $18,500 house, and, between 1933 and 1948, he'd bought stocks in the amount of $57,000. At one point, he said, John J. Lynch, a racing wire service executive, had made him a gift of $30,000.

Another police witness was Captain Daniel A. Gilbert, referred to by the press as "the richest cop in the world." He was the chief investigator for the district attorney, John S. Boyle, who said that Gilbert was "probably the most efficient and hardest working police officer I ever have known." In addition to his dedication to police duties, Gilbert, by dint of brilliant investing, had managed to have a net worth of some $360,000. Gilbert told the committee that he did it this way: in 1921, a politician advised him to buy a certain stock at $18 per share. Gilbert raised all the money he could and bought 200 shares. Eventually the stock hit $45 per share, and by that time, thanks to borrowing, Gilbert had managed to have 1,000 shares. He made other successful speculations in the commodities market, he said.

Before the crash of 1929, he was worth $98,000. After the crash, he had only $5,000. However, thanks to more tips and shrewd buying, he'd managed to build up to the nest egg he had by 1951.

The committee also went into the legendary "springing" of Paul (The Waiter) Ricca, Charles (Cherry Nose) Gioe and Louis (Little New York) Campagna from the pen, where they were serving ten years for trying to extort money from the Hollywood film studios. In 1947, when they'd served but four years, they came up for parole. However they couldn't be paroled until they'd settled a huge tax claim with the government. The IRS said that Ricca owed $141,631 and that Campagna owed $370,583.

The attorney who'd handled their tax problem was Eugene Bernstein. He was a former IRS man himself, and when he'd set up his private practice, his clients had included such notables as Jake Guzik, Tony Accardo, Murray The Camel Humphries and Ralph Capone. Bernstein told the committee that he had taken the case of Ricca and Campagna when their wives had asked him to. But he'd found both of his clients unwilling to talk settlement with the government. They had claimed that they didn't owe the money —period. Bernstein had been about to give up, when Chicago's Tony Accardo had offered to help. During the questioning of Bernstein, Kefauver Committee Counsel Halley asked a question about Accardo, referring to him as a "notorious gangster." Bernstein's answer: "I never knew Mr. Accardo to be a notorious gangster, sir, at that time, nor do I know him to be one now."

Bernstein said that he and Accardo had then made about 12 trips to Leavenworth to see and reason with Ricca and Campagna. Eventually Ricca had settled with the government for $36,146, and Campagna for $90,371. The government, it seems, gave them a discount of $322,000 on their back taxes.

The two hoods then had 60 days to pay the money, which they still said they didn't owe and weren't going to pay. Then a funny thing happened, according to Bernstein. Strange men who didn't give their names had started dropping by his office and leaving bundles of money for Ricca or Campagna. When the correct total was reached, the mysterious, benevolent strangers had stopped coming by. Bernstein paid off the tax claims and Ricca and Campagna were paroled.

When Ricca was questioned by the committee, he was asked who might have put up all that money for him.

"Why, I would be glad to find out who did that for me," he said.

Campagna said he had never even got around to asking Bernstein where the money had come from. "It sounds fantastic," said Campagna, "but it's true!"

While men like Accardo and Guzik simply "took the Fifth" when summoned to testify before the committee, Kefauver's men were still able to learn a lot about them, thanks to a ruling by President Truman that the senators could examine tax returns. Through these it was seen how the Chicago mob had muscled in on numbers rackets all over the country.

One numbers bank had been run by Julius Benvenuti, who had once done a favor for Al Capone and, consequently, had been given a "license" to operate on his own. However, when old Julius died, his sons had found that they did not enjoy the same privilege. In 1947 they reported a net profit of $205,920, on business of $2,317,048. Then their home was bombed. The following year, they had two new partners, Tom Mousey Manno, and Sam Pardy. That year the Benvenutis drew only $100,000 between them, and Manno and Pardy got $307,565 each. In 1949 the split was about the same, except that now there was a new expense: Anthony J. Accardo was paid $278,667 for "special service."

Another interesting witness before the committee was Police Lieutenant George Butler of Dallas, who had managed to record conversations during which Pat Manno and a hoodlum named Paul Jones tried to buy protection for the Capone syndicate's upcoming operations in Texas. Also present during some of the taped conversations had been Dallas County Sheriff-elect Steve Guthrie.

Jones told Butler that the Chicago gang operated "from coast to coast" and in "Canada and Spain." Jones, who obviously wanted to impress Butler with the value of playing along with the mob, said that he (Jones) "could go into any large city in the United States and

253

his syndicate would have some connection there." That's as Butler quoted Jones's remarks from the tapes.

Butler was asked if Jones mentioned any towns in particular, and Butler said, "He named St. Louis, Kansas City, New Orleans, Little Rock." Jones said Jake Guzik was the head of the Chicago syndicate, and Murray the Camel Humphries was his assistant. He said Manno, who was at another of the recorded meetings, was "No. 5."

Jones, according to Butler, said that if the police lieutenant and the sheriff played along, they might share as much as $150,000 a year, just for looking the other way. He said the Chicago syndicate would provide the lawyers and accountants to do the books for Uncle Sam. (Shortly thereafter, Jones was charged with trying to bribe public officials. However, before that came to trial, he was convicted on narcotics charges and was put away.)

Death and violence were ever-present factors to be reckoned with by the Kevauver agents. Sometimes the deaths were natural. Charles Fischetti, one of the leaders of the Capone gang, died of a heart attack in Miami when he and his brother Rocco were served with summonses to appear. One witness, Joseph Fusco, an official of Chicago's Gold Seal Liquors, Inc., a wholesale house, talked to the committee in a closed-door session. Asked how he, a former Capone bootleg liquor driver, worked his way up to running such a successful legitimate business, he had no helpful answers. Nor could he explain the phenomenal growth of Gold Seal. The committee could find no evidence to suggest that muscle was used to convince retail stores to buy from Fusco. Nevertheless the mob somehow got the impression that Fusco was talking—perhaps because the session was closed to the public—and ten days after Fusco's appearance his warehouse was damaged by a black-powder bomb.

In the Miami hearings, one of the people in whom the committee took particular interest was Sheriff Walter Clark of Broward County. He'd been sheriff for some 17 years. There were three well-known gambling spots in his county, the Club Boheme, the Colonial Inn and the Club Greenacres. According to Daniel Sullivan, the director of the Greater Miami Crime Commission, some of the people who had been involved in the running of those places were the following: Meyer and Jake Lansky, Joe Adonis of New York, Vincent Alo of New York, Frank Erickson (in jail at the time of the hearings), Joe Massei and William G. Bischoff (also called Lefty Clark) of Detroit.

Questioned by the committee, Sheriff Clark said he didn't know about any gambling in his area. (The places had recently been closed down.) Later he said, ''I let them have what they want for the tourists down here.'' The sheriff said that his salary was $7,500 a year, but that he made between $15,000 and $35,000, if one counted various other businesses he had. One business that he failed to mention, until it was brought to his attention, was the Broward Novelty Co. The committee discovered that it operated a Cuban numbers lottery and many slot machines. Between 1945 and 1947, the committee's report said, the company had a turnover of $1,135,420.

The sheriff of Dade County, which included Miami, was James A. (Smiling Jimmy) Sullivan. He'd been sheriff since 1945, and he admitted to the committee that his personal fortune had increased from $2,500 to about $70,000 in only five years. His salary had never exceeded $12,000 per year.

One George Patton, a deputy under Sullivan, admitted collecting about $50,000 in bribes in only nine months from Miami Beach gambling joints. He said he was the ''bag man'' for bribes, keeping only $15,000 of the money himself and passing the rest along. It is not recorded to whom he passed it.

Then there was the S&G bookmaking syndicate, run by five Miami men: Harold Salvey, Jules Levitt, Charles Friedman, Sam Cohen and Eddie Rosenbaum. It was started in 1944, and by 1948 it had a working monopoly on bookmaking in Miami, and grossed $26,000,000! In 1949 the Chicago syndicate decided that the S&G boys were being selfish, not sharing their profits with the organization. Using the old ploy of starting a competing business, and then cutting off S&G's race wire service from Continental Press, the Chicago crowd was able to ''buy'' a one-sixth interest in this $26 million business for only $20,000. And it is possible that it didn't cost quite that much, because, at the same time, S&G bought a yacht from Tony Accardo of Chicago for $20,000.

The next stop for the committee was Kansas City, Missouri. Not long before the arrival of Senator Kefauver, a grand jury in Kansas City had found that illegal bookmaking was grossing something like $34 million per year. Some of this money had been used to bribe numerous public officials.

One of the first things that committee investigators learned was that Sheriff J.A. Purdome, of the county police force, had a deputy named Wolf Riman, whose main occupation was running juke boxes and pinball machines. Riman's car even had a siren and a red light. (Neither of these helped, however, when he was murdered for overstepping his territory. Sheriff Purdome later married Riman's widow.)

The committee quickly learned that for years Kansas City's crime, of which there was plenty, had been run by "Five Iron Men," namely Charles Binaggio, Tano Lococo, Tony Gizzo, Charlie Gargotta and Jim Balestrere. Their activities in Kansas City dated all the way back to Prohibition days, and, in a couple of cases, even before. By the time Kefauver's investigation came to town, the Five Iron Men had dwindled to two.

Binaggio and his sidekick, Gargotta, had been blasted to death in their car in 1948. Lococo was in jail on a tax rap.

Binaggio had been "Mr. Politics" for the mob, and was supposed to fix things so that gambling, brothels, and other rackets could go on without hindrance from the law. The Kefauver Committee found an almost unbelievable amount of corruption in Kansas City, some of it extending even up to the State House level. It was speculated that Binaggio and Gargotta, his muscle man, were killed because Binaggio had failed to secure official protection for the rackets. The mobs may have thought that he'd gone soft.

Gargotta, in particular, was small loss to society. He'd been arrested 39 times between 1919 and 1947 for everything from attempted burglary to murder. At one point he was caught killing a man in the street. A bribed policeman confused the murder gun with another, and Gargotta got off. Then the policeman was put away for his part in the episode, and Gargotta was charged with felonious assault. He managed to have his trial postponed 27 times, but was finally sentenced to jail—for three years. He was pardoned before completing his term.

Spectators at the hearings were amused at the description of the operation of the Last Chance Tavern, which was located on the state line between Kansas and Missouri. The gaming room had the state line running right down the center of it. Whenever the Missouri police tried a raid, the players quickly moved across the room into Kansas. It hardly interrupted the game. When the Kansas cops showed up, the reverse happened. Oddly enough, the police from

Kansas and Missouri never seemed able to synchronize their raids so that they arrived at the same time.

Through its control of Continental Press, the Capone gang of Chicago managed to have a piece of Kansas City's bookmaking. The committee also heard how Edward P. Osadchey (also known as Eddie Spitz) and Morris (Snag) Klein of Kansas City managed to buy half of a new $90,000 gambling joint in nearby Council Bluffs, Iowa, for absolutely nothing. Spitz explained to the committee that no "muscle" was involved. He said that he and Klein had simply offered $20,000 for the whole club and that the owners had come back with the offer that they take half of the club for nothing. Spitz said, "It sounds fantastic . . . there are a lot of deals that happen like that . . ."

Another to testify before the committee was Kansas City's leading hoodlum, Tony Gizzo. He had very little to say about crime in Kansas City, but there was one highlight to his testimony. The committee's Senator Alexander Wiley asked Gizzo about his habit of carrying a large bankroll. In an expansive mood, Gizzo said, "Do you want to see it?" He reached in his pocket and counted out $2,500 in hundred-dollar bills.

In St. Louis, the committee was informed that there had been 64 unsolved underworld murders between 1930 and 1950. One of the biggest bookmakers in St. Louis, James Joseph Carroll, admitted that he handled about $20 million per year in bets. He was also the first witness before the committee to object to the TV cameras. He actually claimed that they scared him and gave him such a case of "mike fright" that he was virtually speechless. Considering how little help he was to the committee, he might as well have been.

The questioning of officials of C.J. Rich & Company, run by Charles J. (Kewpie) Rich and Sidney Wyman, revealed that the Western Union telegraph company was, at times, heavily involved in bookmaking operations. Rich and Wyman testified that their business grossed about $4,000,000 to $5,000,000 per year. After being informed that a police raid on Rich Company headquarters had disclosed a list of 100 or more Western Union agents all over the country who acted as secret betting agents for the firm, the Kefauver Committee asked more questions about that.

Prosecuting Attorney Stanley Wallach, of St. Louis County, furnished the committee with a fascinating document. It was a letter written by the Rich firm to a Western Union office manager in far-off Waterville, Maine. It said, "We will be glad to make you what we feel is a good proposition. We will give you 25 percent of the winnings at the end of each month, after deducting the necessary expenses as wire charges and form sheets only." A Western Union official told the committee that Western Union handled about $250,000 per month in money orders and telegrams for Rich in St. Louis. He said that the St. Louis bookmakers had charge accounts in 168 Western Union offices all over America. He said too that Western Union also transmitted money and messages for the J.J. Carroll betting operation.

There were other illegal businesses in the St. Louis area. Prostitution, for instance. Bryan L. Connell, a former district attorney of Pulaski County, Illinois, not too far from St. Louis, said that a sad-funny thing happened a few years back in Cairo, Illinois.

Mr. Connell said: "The good people of one of the churches, I believe it was the Baptist faith, wanted to build a church in the neighborhood. After due deliberation, the city officials decided that the girls had a prior right to the locality, so the church people, if they wished to avoid that [brothel], would have to build somewhere else.

And so it went. The Kefauver Committee listened to a parade of witnesses, heard scores of stories of crime, vice and corruption and eventually had enough testimony to fill a room with bound notes. In a book this size, one can only give the overall picture of the nationwide crime organization uncovered during the Kefauver hearings. Senator Kefauver himself wrote a book about the hearings *(Crime in America)* and even he could merely show the top of the iceberg.

CHAPTER TWENTY
1951

In New Orleans the Kefauver Committee found that Frank Costello, the Lansky brothers and Joe Adonis had a working arrangement with the Mafia boss of the city, Carlos Marcello, whose parents were Sicilian. Marcello himself was born in Tunisia, but came to the United States as a child. The committee learned that Costello & Co. had the slot machine and some gambling casino concessions, and that Marcello was involved in 40 separate businesses, most of them illegal.

Costello's man in New Orleans was Dandy Phil Kastel, a convicted swindler.

The Federal Narcotics Bureau in New Orleans said that the city was an important narcotics port of entry and ranked with Tampa and New York in that respect.

New Orleans Mayor DeLesseps S. Morrison, who apparently had done his best to clean up New Orleans since coming to office in 1946, told the committee that New Orleans was once so wide open that "You could walk down the street, between Canal Street and City Hall, and never miss a race result. They were broadcast from loudspeakers in the bookie joints, and you could hear them through the open doors."

Despite having cracked down on the slots, New Orleans still licensed some 2,000 machines in 1951, the committee heard. In addition, many more illegal machines, casinos, bookmaking parlors and whorehouses operated in the parishes (counties) surrounding New Orleans. In addition to that, you could buy just about any dope you needed in the area if you had the right connections.

The committee listened in amazement to testimony by—or about—various local sheriffs and law enforcement officers. Sheriff

J. (King) Clancy, who had been sheriff of Jefferson Parish for 23 years, admitted that there might be as many as 5,000 illegal slot machines in his bailiwick, plus numerous gambling casinos. His rather novel explanation to the committee was that his tolerance for such things had nothing to do with payoffs. No, indeed. He allowed them to operate because the casinos provided hundreds of jobs to the old and underprivileged!

Though Sheriff Clancy's official salary was never more than $6,000, he admitted making about $20,000 through investments and business ventures and by betting on horses.

Sheriff C.F. (Dutch) Rowley, of St. Bernard Parish, was asked if there were any slots in his parish. (Kefauver investigators had found plenty.) Sheriff Rowley said he didn't know because he "didn't snoop." He was another law officer who earned more from his outside interests than he did through his salary.

The sheriff of New Orleans, John J. Grosch, got a new Cadillac from unnamed businessmen on the day he took office. Grosch's ex-wife told the committee that when her husband was chief of detectives, he'd somehow accumulated $160,000 in cash which he kept in a steel box at home. She said one slot machine operator gave her $39 every week, in an envelope. And that someone who allegedly ran a whorehouse used to come along every Saturday with groceries for a week.

Speaking of prostitution, Sheriff Gilbert Ozenne, of Iberia Parish, told the committee that he didn't know that prostitution was against the law.

In Cleveland the committee learned the background of the 1950 crime picture. Ex-FBI Agent Alvin J. Sutton, Jr., who in 1950 was Cleveland's Public Safety Director, told how, since 1933, Cleveland had gone through the same sort of "organizing" process that other big cities had. He said that following Repeal, the gangs had gone in for gambling in a big way, and that there were many wars over control. By 1950, the committee eventually concluded, this was the situation:

"The Cleveland gambling syndicate consists primarily of the following individuals: Morris Kleinman, Samuel (Gameboy) Miller, Moe Dalitz (alias Davis), Louis Rothkopf (alias Rhody or Zarumba), Samuel Ticker and Thomas J. McGinty. This group has enjoyed close relationships and associations with certain gangsters and muscle men who also participated in enterprises conducted by the gambling syndicate. Included in this latter group are the Polizzis, Alfred and Albert (Chuck), John and George Angersola (alias King), James Licavoli, Jerry Minlano, Joseph DiCarlo, and others."

The gambling in Cleveland was eventually reduced to a large extent by the efforts of Governor Frank Lausche and Cleveland Mayor Harold Burton, who later was to become a Supreme Court Justice. But all the mobs really did was to move out of town, into the counties surrounding Cleveland, and into Kentucky towns across the river from Cincinnati; towns like Coventry and Newport. The Cleveland mob also had its tie-ins with the Detroit mobs, the syndicate that ran Miami, and Mickey Cohen in California. It lent Wilbur Clark $1,000,000 to build his famous Desert Inn Hotel in Las Vegas, and took a 60 percent interest in the casino for doing so.

Governor Lausche tried to close the clubs operating outside the Cleveland city limits. These were the well-known Jungle Inn, Mounds Club, Colony Club and Pettibone Club. When he found himself frequently stymied by reluctant sheriffs and lackadaisical police officials, Lausche resorted to a new weapon. He tied the clubs up in red tape, slapping them with fire, health, building code, tax office and liquor board violations. The casinos eventually gave up and closed.

But it wasn't easy. As an example of what Ohio's governor was up against, there is this story, told to the committee by Anthony A. Rutkowski, who tried to enforce the liquor regulations as part of the governor's "red tape" campaign. Rutkowski showed up one night, along with his party of unarmed raiders, at the Jungle Inn. This was run by Mike and John Farah. Rutkowski called the sheriff and asked him to come over and assist with the arrests. The sheriff got there two and a half hours later. When he arrived, his contribution was to order Rutkowski not to confiscate the slot machines.

Then Mike Farah ran over to the raiders, cursed everyone, and took a punch at one of Rutkowski's men. When they attempted to grab him, Farah dashed into a "pillbox" at one end of the room and yelled, "Kill him, Goon! Kill him! Shoot him!" Happily for Rutkowski, Goon was slow on the trigger, and one of the agents was able to run inside the gun turret and grab the shotgun.

The committee also listened to testimony by Alvin E. Giesey, a former Internal Revenue Service accountant, and the man responsible for catching the then leading Cleveland racketeer, Morris

Kleinman, in a tax fraud. Kleinman got four years. Three years later Giesey went into private practice, and his list of clients for tax advice sounded like a who's who of Cleveland's gambling fraternity.

The Kefauver Committee spent a week holding closed-door hearings in California, many of them lasting from morning until midnight. The feeling among Kefauver investigators was that they might have held hearings in California for two months and still have barely scratched the surface.

The committee found the usual evidence of payoffs to public officials, and one new wrinkle: some Internal Revenue Service men were found to be shaking down vice establishments. One IRS agent demanded money from a brothel madam, and even enclosed a postage-free government envelope for her to use to mail him the money.

After the death of Bugsy Siegel, who was the West Coast representative of the New York-Chicago-Detroit mobs, there appears to have been a battle for control between Mickey Cohen and Jack Dragna. In 1950, the committee heard that the Guarantee Finance Company was, in addition to being a loan agency, the front for a $6,000,000 bookmaking business. The committee was very interested in that, and word of its interest reached one Samuel Rummel, a lawyer for Cohen and other hoods. Shortly thereafter Rummel had a meeting with two police officials, and the next day, he was found dead. Nobody knows who killed Rummel or why, or what he might or might not have told Kefauver.

Cohen himself had survived five assassination attempts up to the time of the Kefauver hearings. The word was that he had fallen out with the Mafia and was now considered not only expendable, but an unnecessary competitor. Apparently his chief rival was Jack Dragna, who had been described by the California Crime Commission as the ''Al Capone of Los Angeles.'' He was also reported to be the Mafia don for California.

Dragna's lieutenant, and heir apparent, was Joe Sica, who had once been indicted on narcotics charges. This case fell apart when one of the witnesses, Abraham Davidian, was slaughtered. Mickey Cohen, who had worked with Dragna during the Continental Press ''sales campaign'' in California, was charged with murder one, but got off on self-defense. It seems that one Max Shaman came into Mickey's paint shop with a gun and threatened to kill him. Cohen, too, had a gun and used it first, he told the committee.

Cohen told the committee that he was virtually broke, and living on borrowed money. Luckily for him, he was able to borrow some $300,000 in four years. Since the Kefauver hearings, Cohen has either been on the lam from rival mobsters, or in jail on one charge or another.

The highlight of the public hearings regarding California involved Arthur H. Samish, a lobbyist. A tall, heavy man, with a shock of gray hair, Samish remained completely calm and cool, despite relentless pursuit by Kefauver questioners. And if any one of the hundreds of witnesses before the committee can be said to have "won," Samish was that man.

Asked a question he didn't want to answer, Samish would often reply in a long, roundabout way, complete with totally boring details, and in the end, be found not to have shed any light at all. He also was gifted with a failing memory and a complete innocence of bookkeeping and approved business practices.

Samish's chief client was the California State Brewers Institute, which gave him $36,000 per year, plus use of a $153,000 per year slush fund. His chief occupation seemed to be contributing to election campaigns and looking out for brewers' interests when it came to legislation. In particular he was against any community passing "dry" laws.

The Brewers Institute was a tax-free enterprise that had, among its other lofty aims, the ambition to "educate and elevate the minds of men." To this end, the brewers arranged that for every barrel of beer produced, five cents went into a special fund for Samish to use as he thought best. In six years, between 1944 and 1950, that came to almost $1,000,000. Samish said that checks against the account were drawn at his request and signed by three officials of the institute. One of them said he signed anything he was asked to and never questioned it. Another signer whom the Kefauver people would have interviewed was sick and ordered not to leave his house by his doctor. The president of the institute simply could not be found.

This left Samish to do the explaining. Since the institute didn't have to pay taxes, the senators thought that perhaps Samish should, since he spent the money, or at least had the money spent. What had he done with it? Samish said he had great difficulty remembering. The committee asked Samish's accountant for records concerning the $1,000,000 fund. The accountant said he'd never seen any records of it. He was asked about the canceled checks. He said that Mr. Samish always destroyed the canceled checks after they came in. What about the check stubs? The accountant said that he didn't know anything about them. The accountant brought gasps of astonishment from his questioners when he said that because Mr. Samish used the $1,000,000 for institute business, there was no need for him to keep track of it.

Next the committee tried to interview Samish's two secretaries. One was on vacation and the other was "off" for a weekend. The bookkeeper for the institute was "out of town." The secretary of the institute said he knew nothing whatsoever about the Samish account.

Back to Samish. Senator Kefauver said to him, "It seems fantastic that there are no check stubs for checks written on this account. Also I can't understand why the canceled checks were thrown away . . . the Internal Revenue Service requires it, Mr. Samish."

Samish said, in effect, that this was just the way he did things. He could see no point in keeping track of a fund on which the taxes were already paid. Eventually the committee got a partial accounting of the fund for about two years. It showed that checks for as much as $40,000 were made out to either "cash" or "contributions." In the end, the Kefauver Committee never did find out what Samish did with the money.

The Kefauver Committee held many closed-door hearings in New York, but it was the eight days of televised hearings featuring New York figures that caused the sensation. The public hearings brought out many of the details of New York crime discussed earlier in this book.

Albert Anastasia was questioned by the committee, but he refused to incriminate himself. It is possible that Albert had other things on his mind than answering irksome questions from nosey senators. Only a month after the Kefauver hearings in New York, Albert's boss, Vincent Mangano, disappeared, never to be seen again. The underworld grapevine said that Anastasia wanted control of the mob because Mangano was getting old and losing his eagerness for new business.

Frank Costello, then 60, turned out to be the star witness of the Kefauver hearings. He insisted that the TV cameras caused him discomfort and, for that reason, the nation was treated to the perplexing picture of the gangster's hands as he answered questions. As the author recalls those sessions, Costello's hands were not all that expressive, but much was made of it at the time.

As it turned out, Costello was not nearly as bright as had been imagined before he'd appeared. Numerous times he trapped himself in lies. For instance, after admitting that he'd been put out of the slot-machine business in New York by Mayor LaGuardia, he said he'd gone to Louisiana at the invitation of Governor Huey Long. Actually, though, said Costello, he had nothing to do with the slot-machine business in New Orleans. At the same time he was hard put to explain why, then, he took a share in the profits. In 1944 this share had amounted to $70,000. Nor could Costello explain why Salvatore Moretti, a New Jersey gangster, referred to him in a tapped telephone conversation as "Chief."

Costello admitted that he was a partner in a New Orleans gambling joint called the Beverly Country Club with Dandy Phil Kastel and Carlos Marcello. He said that they paid him $1,000 per month to be a "goodwill man." As if to demonstrate his worth, Costello took the opportunity while on TV to recommend the place to anyone going to Louisiana.

The groundwork for the denaturalization and deportation of Costello back to Italy—though the case was to take years—was laid by the committee when it established that Costello had lied about his criminal record when he'd applied for citizenship in 1923. He'd neglected to mention a gun-carrying conviction in 1915, when he was using the name Saverio.

In his book about the hearings, Senator Kefauver made these points in summing up the hearings:

1. A nationwide crime syndicate does exist in the United States of America, despite the protestations of a strangely assorted company of criminals, self-serving politicians, plain blind fools and others who may be honestly misguided, that there is no such combine.

2. Behind the local mobs which make up the national crime syndicate is a shadowy international criminal organization known as the Mafia, so fantastic that most Americans find it hard to believe that it really exists.

Joe Valachi, a smallfry Mafia soldier who achieved fame by squealing to the FBI and the Senate.

Frank Erickson, reputedly the gambling boss of Florida.

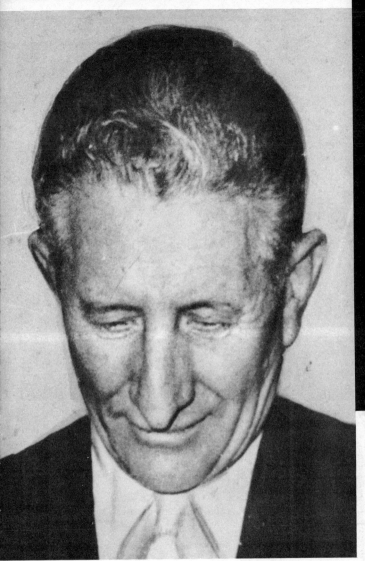

Carlo Gambino, New York's most powerful Mafia figure in the 1970s.

West Coast crime figure, Jack Dragna.

Mickey Cohen. For awhile, Dragna and Cohen disputed territory, but Cohen went to prison and Dragna had no other serious challengers.

One of the leading witnessses at the Kefauver hearings of 1951 was Frank Costello. Costello is talking to his attorney, George Wolf.

Costello is telling the Senators that he usually kept $50,000 in his apartment for his betting operations.

Jake Guzik, the Chicago hood, had nothing to say to the Senate Crime Committee except that anything he said might tend to incriminate him.

A face from the past was Waxey Gordon, who told a Senate Committee that he had nothing to do with crooked U.S. surplus property deals.

Not long after this picture was taken of a smiling Laurence "Dago" Mangano, in 1944, he and his companion, Michael Pantillo, were gunned to death in their car.

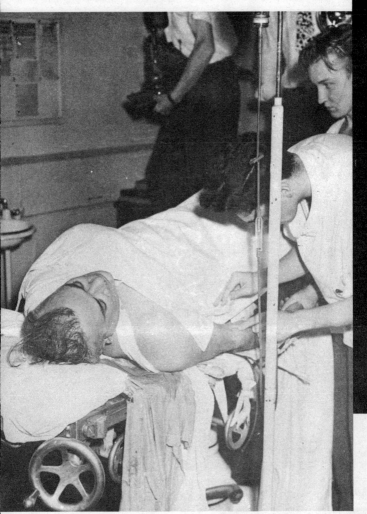

Doctors trying in vain to save Mangano's life.

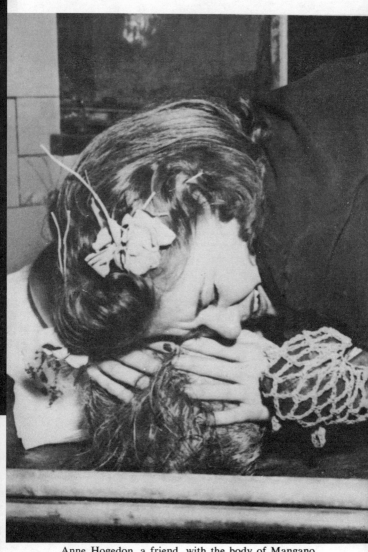

Anne Hogedon, a friend, with the body of Mangano.

Rita Reyes, who was in the car at the time of the shooting, sits in a police station, still wearing her blood-splattered clothes.

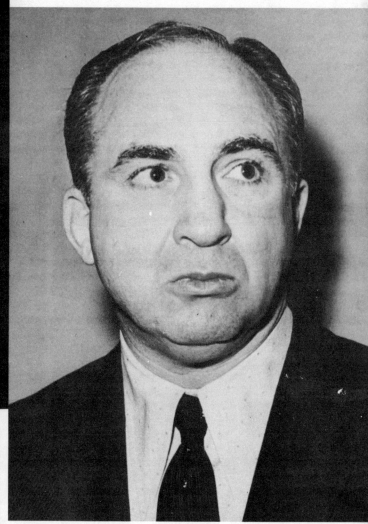

West Coast hoodlum Mickey Cohen is shown after being arrested in New York for consorting with known criminals. He was simply told by police to leave town.

Cohen is frisked after being arrested on suspicion of murdering bookie Jack OHara Whalen in Los Angeles in 1959.

These five men are questioned by Police in connection with a bomb being thrown at Cohen's house. They are, from left to right, Louis Dragna, Tom Dragna, Frank Dragna, Guillermo Adamo and Paul Dragma. The boss Dragna, Jack, could not be found.

When one of Cohen's friends, for whom he'd posted bail, skipped, Cohen had to auction his gun collection to get the necessary $50,000.

In 1959, he's shown just after being released from jail after being held temporarily on suspicion of murder.

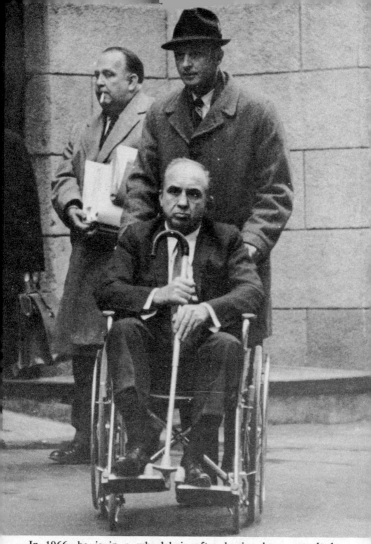

In 1966, he is in a wheelchair after having been assaulted three years earlier by another prisoner in Atlanta pen.

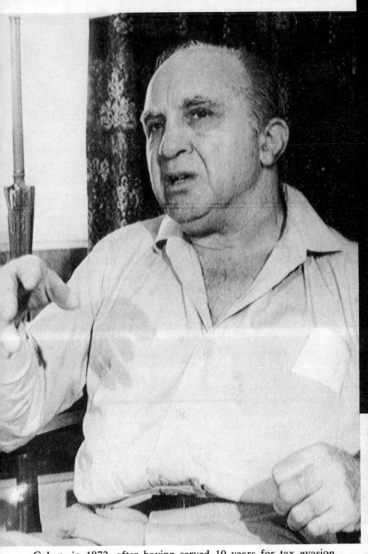

Cohen, in 1972, after having served 10 years for tax evasion.

An interesting look into the affairs of organized crime was provided in 1963 when Joseph Valachi, a former Mafioso, decided to rat. Here he's being escorted into a Senate hearing by a posse of Federal bodyguards.

Here he's testifying.

One of the stories that Valachi told was particularly chilling. It seems that in 1952, Arnold Schuster, a shoe salesman, happened to see Willie Sutton, a wanted bank robber, in the street in New York. Schuster told a policeman and Sutton was caught.

According to Valachi, Albert Anastasia saw this photo of hero Schuster in The New York Daily News, and, even though Anastasia had never even met Willie Sutton, ordered Schuster's death. Valachi said, "It was just that Albert hated squealers." When Schuster was shot and killed, police were completely baffled, as Sutton had no known connection with killers or mobs and was known as a loner.

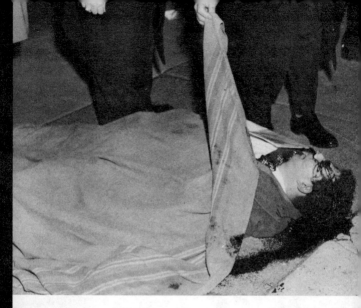

The body of Arnold Schuster lies where he was shot, just outside his home in Brooklyn. An unknown gunman had fired four bullets into his head and body.

The man who gave the contract on Schuster, Albert Anastasia.

Frank Costello was walking into his New York apartment building one night in 1957 when an unidentified gunman fired a shot at his head. The bullet only creased his scalp, but Frank got the message: The mob wanted him to retire, so he did.

Costello lived until 1973, when he died of natural causes at the age of 70.

Above is Joseph Magliocco, who, along with Carlo Gambino, at right, was suspected by police of having attended the Mafia convention in Apalachin, N.Y. Both were questioned.

Two pictures of Albert Anastasia, the reputed head of "Murder, Inc.," the enforcement arm of the Mafia, taken shortly before the syndicate put out a contract on Albert himself.

The barbershop of the Park Sheraton Hotel in New York, where Anastasia was having a shave when two masked men came in and blasted him where he sat. His assailants were never caught.

Anastasia's body being carried out.

Bill Bonanno is the son of Joseph Bonanno.

The elder Bonanno, a deposed Mafia boss in Brooklyn, is shown here talking to his lawyer, Albert J. Krieger. The younger Bonanno, who once tried to run his father's gang, went to prison for misuse of a credit card.

Sam Decavalcante, a New Jersey racketeer, whose phone was tapped by police. Here, he's trying to ward off reporters after being charged with gambling violations.

Meyer Lansky, seen shortly before pleading not guilty to charges of tax evasion.

Patsy Fuca, facing a New York police desk sergeant with lowered head, was one of those arrested in the famous "French Connection" dope case of 1964.

Sam Decavalcante is once again trying to elude the press outside of a courthouse where he has been charged, along with 54 other persons, with running a $20 million per year gambling operation in New Jersey.

In the summer of 1971, Joseph Colombo did an unprecedented thing for a Mafia don. He actually courted publicity. He formed the Italian-American Civil Rights League, made speeches and demonstrated in front of the FBI building in New York. Colombo's beef was that the FBI was singling out Italians for special attention. Here he's making a speech, while being watched by Rabbi Meir Kahane.

305

Colombo poses in front of the monument at Columbus Circle, where he is to conduct "Unity Day" the following morning.

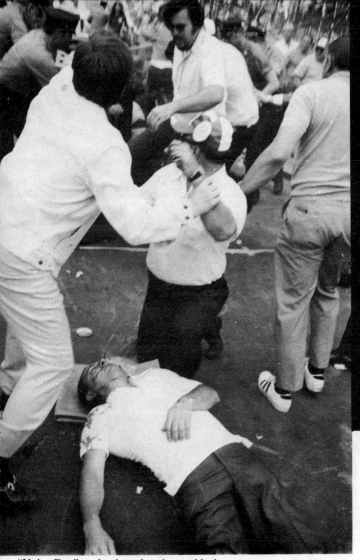

"Unity Day" ends abruptly when a black gunman comes out of the crowd and shoots Colombo in the head. The assailant is killed by Colombo's guards.

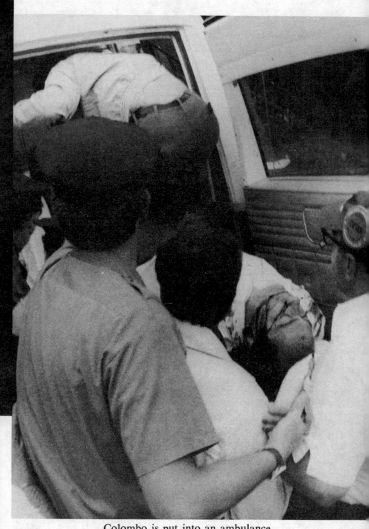

Colombo is put into an ambulance.

Brooklyn hoods Joey and Larry Gallo (l. to r.) are escorted out of their warehouse "fortress" after being rescued from the Profaci mob by police intervention. The dispute was over gambling takings in Brooklyn.

This is Umberto's Clam House, where, in 1972, Joey Gallo was eating dinner when a gunman walked in and shot him in the chest. Gallo chased the man outside, but dropped dead on the sidewalk. He was the third such New York gangster to die in similar fashion in as many days.

Tommy Eboli, at left, seen with his lawyer, Wilford L. Davis, took over the Vito Genovese mob while the latter was in prison. Eboli was shot dead in 1972.

CHAPTER TWENTY-ONE
1952-1956

After the Kefauver hearings, organized crime did its best to "cool it." Public pressure aroused by the televised hearings inspired, even forced some local authorities to close down bookie joints, if only temporarily. And there were a number of indictments and, in a few cases, convictions, of known criminals, as a result of the Kefauver investigations, and/or the testimony the hearings developed.

The next change in major gang leadership came in 1953, when Gaetano Gagliano died of natural causes. His mob was then taken over by Tommy (Three-Finger Brown) Lucchese. With Albert Anastasia running the Mangano outfit, due to the sudden and strange disappearance of Vincent Mangano, there had been two changes in the five-man rule of New York's underworld in two years. Frank Costello continued to be the titular head of the Luciano outfit, with Vito Genovese as executive vice president. The other two bosses, Joseph Bonanno and Joseph Profaci, seemed secure.

Another reason for the gangsters to keep their heads down was that shortly after the Kefauver hearings there soon was another committee breathing down their necks: the McClellan Committee, with its determined, gangster-hating counsel, Robert F. Kennedy. The proper name of the McClellan Committee, which was chaired by Senator John L. McClellan (D., Ark.), was the Subcommittee on Investigations of the Senate Committee on Government Operations.

While the Kefauver Committee had seemed particularly interested in gambling, and how this funded all manner of other criminal activities, the McClellan Committee delved more into union racketeering. Still, the heat wasn't on organized crime as it had been during the Kefauver hearings. When the McClellan hearings did come to the public's attention, it was usually because somebody like Jimmy Hoffa was in the hot seat. It was not to be until the early 1960s, when the McClellan Committee came face to face with Joe Valachi, that the television audience was again to be held rapt.

In the early 1950s, though, Valachi, a third-rater in the Genovese mob, was merely trying to stay out of the way as his bosses struggled for power. Valachi worked under Anthony (Tony Bender) Strollo, who in turn, worked under Vito Genovese. And Genovese's boss, in theory at least, was Frank Costello. Genovese was somewhat reluctant to debate the point with Costello because Costello was Lucky Luciano's "appointee," and Lucky, whether he was in Italy or not, was a force to be reckoned with. As a matter of fact, Luciano was not always in Italy. In the early fifties he quietly took up residence in Cuba, and commenced to run his New York-Florida gang from "offshore." Frank Costello had visited him there on one occasion.

The United States government was understandably upset by the nearness of Luciano. It hadn't deported him to Italy only to have him set himself up just 90 miles from Miami. For a while, it looked as though Cuba might ignore United States suggestions that it kick Luciano out. The Batista government was susceptible to bribes, and it was making quite a bit of money in partnership with United States gambler-controlled casinos. (The author and another newspaper reporter had dinner with Mr. Lefty Clark, alias William G. Bischoff, one night in October of 1959, at the famous Tropicana Hotel in Havana. Unfortunately there were no great revelations or insights into gambling or anything else that evening. The conversation was chiefly about the impending arrival of Fidel Castro, and how he might close all the casinos and hotels for a while. As it turned out, Castro closed the casinos for good, and the American gamblers had to give up and come home.)

Eventually, by threatening to cut off all aid to Cuba, including its support for the price of sugar, the United States was able to convince Cuba that it could get along without the presence of Charlie Lucky. He went back to Naples.

In 1952 Vito Genovese began making moves to solidify his position. The first was the killing of Eugenio Giannini, a hood who worked for Tommy Lucchese. The word had come down to

Vito Genovese from Luciano in Italy that Giannini was an informer for the Federal Bureau of Narcotics. The important thing to Genovese was that *he* had been told to handle it, and not Costello. For that reason, Vito told Tony Bender to put somebody good onto the extermination job.

Bender called in Joe Valachi and said that Giannini had to be hit. This annoyed the little hoodlum, because, at the time, Giannini owed him money. However, he knew better than to refuse the contract on those grounds. In any case, the gang was dead right about Giannini; he was an informer, and he had been dispatched to Italy by the government to make a dope buy, and then to reveal the details of it. Giannini had been a busy man in Italy. Too busy, in fact. While negotiating with Lucky for drugs and informing on him, he was also passing counterfeit United States money. The Italian cops caught him for that, and while he was in an Italian jail, trying to get the United States to get him out on some excuse, Lucky found out that he was a squealer.

As luck or perhaps diplomacy would have it, the Italian counterfeiting case against Giannini collapsed and he was allowed to return home. It was at this point that Valachi began arranging the hit. In most cases like this, an informer is killed by his own gang. However, Genovese wanted to show his connection with Luciano, so he didn't give Three-Finger Brown the opportunity.

The plan was for Valachi to hire the gunmen who would actually do the job. The murder orders therefore went from Luciano to Genovese to Bender to Valachi to three unknown gunmen, who had no idea why they were scrubbing Giannini, or even who he was. It's setups like this that make the solution of a gangland killing so difficult for the police. Valachi lined up three East Harlem youths, who were apprentice members of the Genovese outfit. They were Joseph and Pat Pagano and Valachi's nephew, Fiore Siano.

The first couple of times that Valachi tried to meet with his old friend, Giannini "to discuss the money" that Giannini owed him, he noticed that Giannini was being tailed, probably by the law. Finally though, he found out that Giannini was going to a crap game run by the Lucchese gang. Valachi got permission to do the job there. He took his killers through a few rehearsals, and then they were all set for the big night. Valachi went to dinner with friends.

About 4 A.M. his nephew called and said it was all over.

313

Valachi, happy in his work, went home to sleep.

There was one odd development. Giannini was rubbed out in front of the gambling joint on Second Avenue at East 112th Street. But his body was found in the gutter at 282 West 234th Street. It seems that the gamblers, in an effort to protect the location of the game, scooped the body up after the shooting and dumped it elsewhere.

This was only one of many mysteries that Valachi cleared up for authorities when he began his marathon talk-in some 10 years later. To date no one has been charged with the Giannini job. The late Valachi's testimony alone was not enough. Siano has disappeared and is believed dead, and the Pagano brothers have since been in and out of prison on various other charges.

Another crime of the period that Valachi knew something about was the murder of Willie Moretti. Genovese wanted him out of the way for two reasons. The most urgent one was that Moretti was suffering from brain damage, due to syphilis, and was talking more and more to just anybody who came along. In addition, he had a private army of some 40 thugs who were loyal to him and Frank Costello. The decision to "get" Moretti was taken between the gangs, without consulting Costello, who would have been against it. Valachi said it was an "open" contract, meaning that the first syndicate member who had a chance at Moretti should take it.

Moretti was found shot dead in a New Jersey restaurant.

In 1953 Genovese was in for some embarrassment. His wife Anna sued him for divorce, and in asking for settlement, not only said that her husband was a murderous gang leader, but that he was also a man who had immense wealth stashed away in safety deposit boxes in the United States and Europe. She also talked quite a bit in open court about his income from loan sharking, gambling, labor racketeering and the Italian lottery, from which, she said, he garnered some $30,000 per week. All of this seemed to be particularly ungrateful behavior to Genovese, considering how much trouble he'd gone to to get her. Readers will recall that Joe Valachi once said that Genovese had arranged to have Anna's previous husband strangled.

Nobody in gangland could understand why Genovese didn't arrange a similar accident for Anna, but the fact seems to be that the old villain still loved her and couldn't bear to do it. However, he did the next best thing, according to Valachi; he ordered the death of Steve Franse, who'd helped Anna run several of Genovese's nightclubs in Greenwich Village. Genovese apparently decided that Franse had failed to keep Anna in line during the time that Genovese was hiding out in Italy and letting his wife watch over his interests.

Valachi said that he was told by Tony Bender to expect Franse to drop by Valachi's restaurant late one night with a couple of the boys, and that Valachi was to take care of the problem. Eventually Pat Pagano and Fiore Siano brought Franse by to see Joe's swell new joint after hours. Valachi said that Pagano and Siano killed Franse in the kitchen, choking him with a chain. Then Franse was driven off in his own car, and police found the body in the Bronx on June 19, 1953.

The next Genovese contract was for Valachi's old friend, Dominick (The Gap) Petrilli, who had helped Valachi get into the Mafia in the first place. The Gap had been deported to Italy years before and while there he had made the mistake of becoming an informer on the narcotics traffic. The Gap came back to the States with a phony story that he'd sneaked in by jumping ship and that he was onto a good narcotics buy.

As soon as The Gap contacted Valachi, Valachi told Bender. Petrilli was shot and killed on December 9, 1953, by three men wearing dark glasses who found him playing cards at the restaurant owned by Albert Mauriello, a brother of the former heavyweight contender, Tami Mauriello.

For the next couple of years throughout the United States, the controversy that raged among the gangs was whether or not to get into the hard-dope hustle. Most of the gang leaders, who made plenty of money with all their other enterprises, simply didn't want to chance it. The risks were too great and the sentences, if caught, were too long. The Mafia was not very interested in the marijuana traffic, since too many amateurs were into it.

Heroin smuggling and selling, however, was very tempting to Mafia members on the lower levels, who saw it as a quick way to easy money. Sometimes they did it despite the orders of their bosses. Costello, for instance, was absolutely against the narcotics scene, and said so. Genovese, though, only pretended to be against it. He allowed his underlings to try their hands at it, just so long as he got his cut and wasn't otherwise involved.

Tony Accardo in Chicago was said to have paid an extra $200 a week to any of his men who had been in narcotics to make them stay out of it. He did this after he decided that the game was just too dangerous. Other gang leaders told their men that if they wanted to handle drugs they could, but not to involve the whole gang, and not to expect any gang help with lawyers if they got caught.

Frank Costello was convicted of evading taxes over a two-year period, and sentenced to five years in 1954. However, with appeals, he avoided going to prison to begin his sentence until May 1956. While he was gone, Vito Genovese was to be in complete command of the Luciano-Costello family.

The major social event of 1956, so far as the Mafia was concerned, was the wedding of Bill Bonanno, son of Mafia don Joseph Bonanno, to Rosalie Profaci, a niece of another New York Mafia don, Joseph Profaci. Since the Bonanno and Profaci families were two of the most powerful in New York's underworld, the uniting of the two families was cause for celebration or concern, depending on where you sat.

It was not all that unusual, of course, for the children of mobsters to intermarry. The Mafia is a closed society in more ways than one. The wife of Joseph Bonanno was the sister of Frank Labruzzo, a top man in the Bonanno outfit. Joseph Profaci was married to the sister of his No. 1 man, Joseph Magliocco. Stefano Magaddino was a cousin of Joseph Bonanno. Bonanno's No. 3 man, Gaspar DiGregorio, and Stefano Magaddino were brothers-in-law. Peter Magaddino, a Bonanno sidekick, was a nephew of Stefano Magaddino. Carlo Gambino and Tommy Three-Finger Brown Lucchese had children who married. Joe Valachi was married to the daughter of Tony Reina, a Masseria lieutenant who'd been killed in the Castellammarese War. A family tree of the Mafia would show that across the United States the gangs are tied up not only in a business way, but by blood or marriage relationships. *Life* magazine did such a chart in the early 1960s and it showed, for instance, that the Profacis in New York were related by marriage to the Zerillis and Toccos in Detroit. The chart covered two full pages.

The wedding reception for Bonanno and his bride in New York on August 18, 1956, was a gangland fiesta. There were probably as many of the top hoods from around the country there as later attended the famous meeting in Apalachin, New York, yet nobody seemed to take much notice of it. The party was held at the Astor Hotel, the ballroom, of course, and more than 3,000 guests attended. Entertainment was by the Four Lads and Tony Bennett.

Among those present: Vito Genovese, Albert Anastasia, Joseph Barbara (who owned a soon-to-be famous house in Apalachin), all of the Bonannos and Profacis, Stefano Magaddino of Buffalo, Joseph Zerilli, the new boss in Detroit, Tony Accardo and Sam Giancana from Chicago. In Gay Talese's book about the Bonanno family, *Honor Thy Father*, he says that all 24 Mafia families around the United States were represented there, and that the delegation from Los Angeles alone numbered 80. Bill Bonanno told Talese that he'd often wondered what the FBI would have done if it had got its hands on his guest list. As it happened, the guest list was written in code, and was under the personal protection of Frank Labruzzo, who also had many heavy gentlemen stationed at the doors of the ballroom. They escorted all guests to their tables. There were no gate crashers that night.

The party was a success in a number of other ways. A little business was discussed here and there, and the bridal couple received lots of small white envelopes. When opened, they contained about $100,000. Cash.

A footnote to the 1950s was the 1952 rub-out of one Arnold Schuster, salesman and good citizen. Mr. Schuster was walking down the street when he saw a face that was being displayed in all post offices, namely that of Willie Sutton, a notorious bank robber. Schuster followed him and then told police, who arrested Sutton. Schuster became a hero of the *New York Daily News* and was featured on television. Unfortunately for him, Albert Anastasia happened to be watching the show and he growled to one of his men, "I hate squealers. Hit dat guy!" Schuster was mowed down on the sidewalk about a month later. At the time, the cops couldn't figure it out, as Sutton had always been a loner, with no known mob connections. Joe Valachi, explaining the killing some ten years later, said it was just Albert's way of doing a favor for a fellow crook, even though he'd never met Sutton in his life.

CHAPTER TWENTY-TWO

1957-1960

1957 was not to be a banner year for the mobs in New York or elsewhere in the country. There were three major events, though: Frank Costello was wounded, Albert Anastasia was killed and the police raided the Mafia's convention in Apalachin, New York.

Genovese made the first move in a series of events which culminated in the Mafia's greatest disaster. He decided to "get" Costello before the latter went back to the relative safety of prison. So long as Costello lived, Genovese felt that nobody would recognize him as Lucky Luciano's heir.

On the evening of May 2, 1957, Costello dined at the swank L'Aiglon restaurant in Manhattan and then returned to his apartment house on Central Park West. As he left the cab and walked into the lobby, a large man followed him inside and yelled, "This is for you, Frank!"

Costello whirled around just in time to have a bullet crease his scalp. As Costello tumbled onto a sofa in the lobby, the gunman ran out, jumped into a car and made his escape. Costello took himself to the emergency room at Roosevelt Hospital, thinking that the bullet might still be in his skull. As it turned out, it wasn't, and he wasn't badly hurt. Unhappily for him, though, the police found a slip showing "wins" of more than a million dollars at his gambling casinos in his pocket. The only thing it didn't show was how long a period it covered. This didn't help Costello's tax appeal.

From police file photos the doorman at Costello's apartment house picked out Vincent (The Chin) Gigante as the assailant. Unfortunately, the doorman became uncertain about his identification in court, and Gigante got off. Years later, Joe Valachi was scornful of the marksmanship of Costello's assailant: "He wasted a whole month practicing!"

Genovese began to get nervous. He worried about Costello's reaction. In the old days, such an incident would have caused a major war among rival factions of the gang. It would remain to be seen whether Frank had gotten soft. In the meantime, Genovese was taking no chances.

According to Valachi, Tony Bender's entire crew was called in to protect Genovese. At least 40 gunmen were stationed day and night at Genovese's home. Then, when Costello continued to show no signs of retaliating, Genovese proclaimed himself head of the "family" and he appointed Gerardo (Jerry) Catena to the late Moretti's job as underboss.

Then the Genovese gang heard that Albert Anastasia and Frank Costello were having secret meetings. It was well known that Albert and Frank were close friends, although of different philosophies. Costello tried to "work things out"; Albert just killed anyone who got in his way.

While Genovese and Co. were wondering what to do, one of Anastasia's lieutenants received four bullets in the head on June 17, 1957 as he shopped for peaches at a Bronx fruit stand. The victim was Frank (Don Cheech) Scalice and the killers were two men who escaped by auto.

At first police thought it might be another Genovese job, a sort of warning to Anastasia not to interfere in the Genovese-Costello argument. Then they thought perhaps Anastasia had Scalice killed because the latter was making a fortune in narcotics and not sharing with his boss. The real reason for the killing wasn't learned until Joe Valachi talked some five years later.

It seems that membership in the Mafia had been closed since 1954. New people could go to work for the mobs, but they weren't to be allowed on the "inside" of what was happening. In 1954, new members were being accepted again, and Scalice had nominated all sorts of recruits. It turned out he was selling Mafia memberships for as much as $50,000.

Anastasia, on orders from the National Commission, was told to get rid of Scalice, which he did. Scalice's brother Joseph then rashly started talking about revenging himself against Anastasia. Reasonably enough he did this from a hideout. Albert sent word that he would let bygones be bygones if Scalice would.

Joseph Scalice foolishly went back to work for the Anastasia gang on or about the first of September. He disappeared from the face of the earth on September 7.

All these developments played into Genovese's hands. He knew that Albert was in trouble with the National Commission for overstepping his territory, and it wasn't happy with him for having killed his old boss, Vincent Mangano, in 1951. In addition the commission wasn't completely sure that Albert wasn't in on the sale of Mafia memberships with Scalice.

During the months of September and October 1957, police were aware of meetings between Genovese and Lucchese, still one of New York's five major gang leaders. Later both these men got together with Carlo Gambino, one of Albert Anastasia's lieutenants, a man of great ambition. Another meeting of note was taking place simultaneously in Sicily: Joseph Bonanno was meeting with Lucky Luciano.

According to Valachi, Gambino and another Anastasia aide, Joseph (Joe Bandy) Biondo, finally agreed to set Anastasia up for the slaughter.

On the morning of October 25, 1957, Albert was seated in a barber's chair in the Park-Sheraton Hotel in midtown Manhattan. His bodyguard was off on an errand. Anastasia's face was covered with hot towels, so he didn't see two gunmen walk in and stop in front of his chair.

While goggle-eyed barbers and customers watched, they riddled Anastasia with bullets. It's doubtful if gangdom's leading killer even knew what hit him. The gunmen walked quickly away, tossing their guns aside in a hotel corridor, and then lost themselves in the crowds on New York's busy sidewalks.

Gambino then became head of the Anastasia gang and, as of this writing, has remained so. Frank Costello announced his "retirement," although exactly from what he didn't say.

However, both Genovese and Gambino needed to be confirmed as new bosses by the National Commission and the sale of Mafia memberships indicated that some new rules needed to be laid down. There was other business for the syndicate to talk over as well.

Some of the new soldiers brought into the organization since 1954 simply hadn't worked out. According to Valachi, the mobs were concerned that there had been 27 recent "contracts" that were either botched completely or badly done.

A decision needed to be made whether to go into the dope business in a big way or leave it alone.

A number of the hoods from around the country wanted the conclave to be held in Chicago, where there were lots of hotel rooms, nice restaurants, and the protection of the Capone gang if the cops got too nosy. But Stefano Magaddino, the boss of Buffalo, and a senior member of the National Commission, argued for the home of one of his aides, Joseph Barbara, in Apalachin, New York. The Buffalo boss said that at 66 he was too old to travel, and besides, Barbara's home had been used before for smaller Mafia meetings.

Magaddino said the gang leaders could have lots of nice, fresh country air and plenty of privacy. He was right about the air, as some of the nation's leading hoods discovered when they had to scamper through the woods in order to escape police on the day they arrived.

It is now known that every one of the 24 major gangs around the country was represented at Apalachin. Police managed to pull at least 60 of the men in for questioning, and it is speculated that at least that many got away.

The day of the meeting was November 14, 1957, and for a day or so preceding it, big cars, some of them rented, arrived in the small town of Apalachin. The occupants filled almost every motel facility in the area.

Among the many Apalachin folks who noticed the sudden influx of mysterious strangers was New York State Police Sergeant Edgar D. Crosswell. Those men in the flashy silk suits didn't look like nature lovers. Just for kicks, he tailed one of the cars and found that it led him to the remote home of Barbara, about whom the cops had their suspicions.

Crosswell then set up a roadblock, with only three men helping him, to see what would happen. All he wanted to do was learn the identity of some of the men attending the ''party.'' Quite unexpectedly, the Mafia panicked. Most of the guests had already arrived when one of Barbara's men said that the cops had a roadblock operating about a mile away. Drinks were dropped and the rush for the doors was on. Had the mobsters simply sat tight and waited, the police might merely have stopped one or two, decided that they couldn't find anything illegal going on, and gone away. But when the participants ran, the cops knew they were on to something big.

Vito Genovese was one of those who elected to try to bluff his way out in his car. He was stopped and arrested. Many others tried to elude the police by running through the woods. New York's Joseph Bonanno tried that, along with Chicago's Sam Giancana, and was caught as police reinforcements were rushed in. Giancana got away and now claims that he was never there at all.

Others who were caught were Frank DeSimone, Joe Dragna's successor as boss of California; James Civello, the boss of Dallas; James Colletti of Denver; Joseph Profaci of New York; John Scalish of Cleveland; Joseph Ida of Philadelphia; John Montana of Buffalo; Louis Trafficante of Florida and Joseph Magliocco of New York.

The 60 men who were arrested were found to have $300,000 between them, in cash, in their pockets. Police said more money and a couple of guns were found tossed away in the woods. Once caught, the men were charged with obstructing justice by refusing to state the purpose of their meeting. The defendants claimed that they were at Apalachin simply to cheer up Barbara, who had recently recovered from a heart attack. The men were convicted, fined and sentenced. However, as one might expect, all of the cases were later reversed, on the ground that a meeting is not necessarily a crime. Unless the law can prove that there is some nefarious purpose for a meeting, i.e., a conspiracy to commit a crime, the Constitution safeguards the right of citizens to congregate peacefully.

Investigators exploring the backgrounds of the arrested men found that 9 were in the vending machine business; 11 were in olive oil and cheese importing; 17 owned bars or restaurants; 10 owned grocery stores. Many of them owned, or had large pieces of, other legitimate businesses.

One of the results of the Mafia's embarrassment in Apalachin was the publicity, which proved once again to anyone who cared that there was a nationwide crime organization. In addition, Apalachin made it easier for the Justice Department to wring more money out of Congress for the battle against organized crime. And it became easier in the courts to get permission to tap phones.

Senator McClellan, whose committee looked long and hard at the implications of the Apalachin meeting, said, "The telephone communications among these men just before the meeting gave conclusive evidence of the national scope and significance of this surreptitious conclave of the high and mighty in the underworld's secret domain."

In November 1957 police listened in on a telephone conversation about the Apalachin bust between Stefano Magaddino, the boss of Buffalo, and Sam Giancana, the boss of Chicago.

Magaddino: "It never would've happened in your place."

Giancana: "You're f———right, it wouldn't. This is the safest territory in the world for a big meet. . . . We've got three towns just outside Chicago with the police chiefs in our pocket. We got this territory locked up tight."

Following the Mafia's disaster at Apalachin, the Justice Department learned that there were a number of similar, but smaller meetings held by hoods here and there around the country. The interrupted business still had to be discussed, and certain decisions still had to be made.

Vito Genovese ended the year having accomplished his lifelong goal. At last, he was the commission-approved head of the old Luciano mob. Vito's joy, however, was to be short lived.

There were two postscripts to the year 1957: Johnny Torrio, the ancient warrior of both Chicago and New York, finally died of a heart attack at the ripe old age of 75. And Bugs Moran expired of lung cancer while still in prison for bank robbery.

In 1958 things started to go wrong for many people. In the former Anastasia outfit, now run by Carlo Gambino, there was some tidying up to do. For a start, John (Johnny Roberts) Robilotto, was knocked off.

Johnny Roberts was one of numerous soldiers who were always trying to work their way up. He was said to have been the finger man for the extermination of Willie Moretti by Genovese's forces in 1952. That was when Genovese was still trying to muscle Frank Costello. Roberts was then working for Tony Bender, Genovese's chief aide. Charges against Roberts were dropped for lack of evidence. Roberts was also a partner with Bender in several nightclub ventures and a partner with Joe Valachi in a small loansharking operation.

In the middle fifties, Roberts had joined Albert Anastasia's family. When Albert was killed, Tony Bender and Genovese, Roberts' old associates, warned him not to try to take revenge against Gambino, his new boss. Apparently, according to Valachi, Roberts didn't listen, and was getting a gang together for a war with

Gambino, when he was killed, on September 7, 1958. It was probably a contract job, since Gambino was the "approved" head of a mob, and bumping off mob leaders was frowned on by the National Commission.

That same year, Vito Genovese was charged with narcotics violations. The police were using evidence furnished by Nelson Cantellops, a Puerto Rican. He had turned informer after drawing a sentence for dope peddling, and deciding that the mob had not tried hard enough to spring him. He told all he knew—which was a lot—about New York's dope operations.

At this point, according to Valachi, Tony Bender said that the word was out on "Cantaloupes," and that anybody who saw him should kill him. Since Cantellops was in jail, the assignment wasn't carried out immediately. In fact, Cantellops was to survive until 1965, when he was released from prison and shortly thereafter killed in a never-explained bar fight.

The grand jury returned indictments against Genovese and 23 other men as a result of Cantellops's testimony. Among those charged with narcotics violations were members of three separate New York families, including Big John Ormento, of Tommy (Three-Finger Brown) Lucchese's mob, Joe Valachi of Genovese's gang, and Carmine Galante of the Joseph Bonanno crowd.

While awaiting developments, Vito Genovese had Little Augie Pisano killed on suspicion of disloyalty. The aging and sick gangster had been a longtime friend of Frank Costello.

In 1959, Genovese and 14 others were brought to trial, and, much to everyone's amazement, Genovese was convicted and sentenced to 15 years. It was a terrible comedown for Genovese, who had gone to so much trouble to take over the mob, only to enjoy his power for slightly more than a year. Others were convicted with him. The trial of Valachi and associates came up the following year, and Valachi drew 15 years too.

In his absence, Genovese appointed two new favorites to run the gang: Tommy Ryan Eboli, and Gerardo (Jerry) Catena. This bypassing of Tony Bender should have told Bender something, but the message seems to have escaped him at the time. Genovese, according to Valachi, thought Bender had been holding back money on him, in the expectation that Genovese was going away for a long time and was through as a mob leader.

While being sought for trial, Valachi had hidden out in Canada, where he'd met several members of the Magaddino family, among them the brothers Albert and Vito Agueci. They were later in jail with Valachi, and Albert Agueci wasn't happy about it. He, like Cantellops, felt that the mob wasn't doing enough to get him out.

Valachi said that Albert then started sending threatening messages to Magaddino, saying that if he weren't sprung on bail pretty quickly he would implicate Magaddino himself in the narcotics case.

This turned out to be another case of gangland suicide. Agueci did, in fact, get released on bail. While he was out, a police wire tap listened to a conversation between two Magaddino aides. They were laughing about what was going to happen to Agueci. His body was found on November 23, 1961, on a farm near Rochester, New York. Police said that about 30 pounds of flesh had been sliced from his body while he was still alive, and that then he'd been strangled with a clothesline, soaked with gasoline and set on fire. Throughout all this, his hands had been tightly wired behind his back.

While they'd been in prison together, Valachi said later, he had once warned Agueci about sending ultimatums to Magaddino, but Agueci wouldn't listen. Joe had asked him one day how old he was. Agueci said he was 38.

Joe privately guessed he wouldn't live to be 39, and he was right.

CHAPTER TWENTY-THREE
1961-1964

In 1960 the Chicago Police Superintendent, Orlando W. Wilson, estimated that between that year and 1919 there had been 976 gangland killings in Chicago alone.

But Chicago in the 1960s was mild compared to what was happening in New York. The Gallo brothers' revolt began in 1960. It was to bring even more unwanted headlines to the Mafia and leave 20 dead and 35 wounded. It was also the inspiration for newspaperman Jimmy Breslin's funny book, *The Gang That Couldn't Shoot Straight*.

Until the outbreak of hostilities, the Gallos had seemed content to run their own vending machine business, albeit with force and violence. You installed their machines—or else. But one thing they never did was try to put the muscle on a mob-controlled bar or restaurant. If they wanted machines in a gang-run joint, they would simply let a mob man in as a partner. Joe Valachi had a share in a string of Gallo machines.

Eventually, through diligence and dirty work, the Gallos were accepted into the Profaci family as minor partners in 1954, when Mafia membership was opened briefly. By 1960, however, the Gallos and other "young tigers" in the Profaci gang weren't too happy at how things were carved up.

According to Raymond V. Martin, the Assistant Chief of Brooklyn (South) Detectives, the Gallo brothers got annoyed when it became apparent that any good things that came along were given by Profaci to his relatives and old friends. Martin told his theory to the McClellan Committee, when it was looking into the history of New York's organized crime.

Another McClellan witness on the subject of the Gallo-Profaci war was Ralph Salerno, a former New York police official. He said the opening gun had been sounded as far back as 1959, when a Profaci lieutenant, Frank Abbatemarco, had been killed by parties unknown, presumably for overstepping his territory. The Gallos, Carmine Persico, Jr., and Joseph Giorelli, all of whom had worked for Abbatemarco, thought that they would be given a piece of Abbatemarco's operation. Profaci, however, had ignored them, and kept those rackets for his "close friends."

For a year or so, the Gallo side bided its time, thinking that perhaps Profaci and his chief aide, Magliocco, would be sent to prison for a short term as a result of their conviction for "obstructing justice" at Apalachin. While the two big shots were away, the Gallos had thought they might move in and run things. When Profaci got out, he might find, as did Costello, that he didn't run the gang anymore. The Gallos were also friendly with two other usurpers of power: Vito Genovese, who'd overthrown Costello, and Carlo Gambino, who'd taken over the Anastasia gang.

When the Apalachin conviction had been set aside and it had become apparent that Profaci and Magliocco weren't going anywhere, the Gallos had decided that drastic action was called for.

In 1961, the Gallos suddenly kidnapped old Magliocco and three other Profaci men. The ransom they demanded was that they should get a bigger share in all rackets that Profaci had going. Otherwise, they said, Magliocco and the others would be found dead.

Profaci was thoroughly embarrassed by the whole thing. It looked as though he'd lost control of his troops. His first move was to appeal to the National Commission to "let contracts" on the Gallos and everyone else who was "breaking bad." Then Profaci asked for help from the other families.

The National Commission at that time was composed of Sam Giancana of Chicago, Stefano Magaddino of Buffalo, Angelo Bruno of Philadelphia, Carlo Gambino of New York, Tommy Lucchese of New York, Vito Genovese of New York (in jail), and Profaci himself.

The vote went against Profaci for a number of reasons. Gambino and Lucchese saw the possible fall of Profaci as a means of increasing their own power in New York. Genovese, in jail, but still wanting to be the boss of bosses in New York, was also jealous of Profaci. Magaddino in Buffalo distrusted the closeness between Profaci and Bonanno and he didn't like Bonanno's recent intrusions into Canadian rackets. Magadinno considered Canada all his.

Giancana and Bruno could see that a wild shooting spree was shaping up, and they elected to stay out of it. The result of the National Commission's consultations, therefore, was that Profaci's problems with the Gallos were "internal," and he'd just have to deal with them himself.

Profaci immediately went into hiding in Florida, and left his lieutenant Joseph Colombo, Sr. to work out a deal with the Gallos. All Colombo could do, however, was to agree to everything the Gallos asked for in exchange for the live bodies of the four Profaci men.

Eventually Magliocco and his cohorts were freed, and the Gallos celebrated their great victory. Within a few days, however, it became clear to them that Profaci was going to honor none of the things to which Colombo had agreed. He also sent word to the Gallos that if they gave him any more trouble there would be a lot of black ties worn in Brooklyn.

There followed an uneasy six-month truce, during which the Gallos continued to smolder and threaten. Finally Profaci, possibly helped by some of Bonanno's men, launched his long-expected counterattack. His first move was to get three former Gallo men to switch sides. They were Carmine Persico, Jr., Nicholas (Jiggs) Forlano and John Scimone. Then, to demonstrate that the Gallos were really loners, he set this trio against them.

Very soon thereafter, Joseph (Joe Jelly) Giorelli disappeared for good. A number of shots were fired at Larry Gallo. In the next 18 months, 9 other men, mostly Gallo allies, were killed, 3 Gallo hoodlums disappeared and 15 were wounded. There were numerous other shooting incidents.

The whole thing became too hairy even for the Gallos, and they eventually holed up in a Brooklyn warehouse with their diminished forces. The windows were barred, shooting holes were cut into the walls and nobody got in or out without an elaborate security check. The newspapers at the time referred to the Gallo hideout as a fortress.

Profaci, himself, though, did not live to see the Gallos brought to bay. He'd died of natural causes in 1963, leaving his old sidekick, Magliocco, in command. The war finally ended when, to prevent further bloodshed and the mass slaughtering of the Gallos, the police and the FBI surrounded the building and actually protected the Gallo gang.

Magliocco then died of a heart attack, while he was allowing Bill

Bonanno, son of Joseph, to hide out in his home. The Bonanno gang at the time was having internal problems of its own, in what was the start of the "Banana War."

With the death of Magliocco, Joseph Colombo, Sr. took over the gang and he was able to make peace with the Gallos who, by now thoroughly shaken, were willing to scale down their demands.

Colombo was not immediately made a National Commission member. The old Profaci seat on the commission was taken by Joseph Zerilli of Detroit.

The other major crime event of 1963 was the TV "talk-in" staged by Joe Valachi. It will be recalled that in 1960 Valachi had been dispatched to the federal pen in Atlanta, on a 15-year sentence for dealing in heroin. There, he'd met some 90 other Mafia types, including his old boss, Vito Genovese. The two had become cellmates, although Genovese had acted strangely, as though he thought that Joe had talked.

In 1961 Valachi had been taken out of the pen and brought back to New York to be tried along with 11 others on still more dope charges. Among the defendants were the Agueci brothers. It was while out on bail, awaiting this trial, that Albert Agueci had been so horribly killed. Valachi had been convicted again, and given a 20-year sentence, to be served concurrently with his 15-year one. He had then been sent back to Atlanta. It was Valachi's opinion that the second trial was the one which caused him so much trouble with Genovese. The old don had become even more sure that Valachi was talking, probably because the narcotics agents had spent so much time with him.

Genovese also implied to Valachi that he was suspicious of Valachi's old boss, Tony Bender Strollo. Genovese thought that Bender was holding out profits on him because he was in jail, and that Bender may even have helped the feds to convict Genovese so that he could take over the mob. For these reasons, Genovese had let it be known that Tommy Ryan Eboli and Jerry Catena were running his mob for him while he was away.

Tony Bender disappeared on the evening of April 8, 1962. His wife said that his last words to her, on being advised by her to wear his overcoat, were, "I'm only going out for a few minutes. Besides, I'm wearing thermal underwear." Police think that wherever Bender went, he probably got another overcoat—of concrete.

The apparent murder of Bender made Valachi a very nervous little man. In May of 1962, Valachi had seen John (Johnnie Dio) Dioguardi, Vito Agueci and Joseph (Joe Beck) DiPalermo conferring in the prison yard. After that, all the Mafia crowd had begun ignoring Valachi. When Joe Beck had suddenly offered Valachi a sandwich, the latter decided they were trying to poison him. He'd thrown the sandwich away, and had tried to subsist on packaged foods he'd been able to buy in the prison commissary. Then Dio had tried to trick Valachi into going into the shower room alone. There had been a few more such incidents, and finally, in order to stay alive, Valachi had requested solitary confinement. He then refused to eat and demanded to see George Gaffney of New York's Narcotics Bureau.

This failed, and Valachi was forcefully released from solitary on June 22, 1962. He had then resolved that if he was "gonna go," he'd take the assassin with him. An hour after his release from solitary, Valachi was crossing the prison yard when he noticed three convicts watching him. Then a man whom he thought was Joe Beck walked past him. Thinking that he was about to be attacked, Valachi had rushed up behind "Beck" and hit him with an iron pipe. Then he'd run at the three others, only to see one of them pull a knife. Retreating to "Beck," Valachi slammed the prostrate man's head twice more. Valachi had then been disarmed by guards and taken to the warden's office, where he later learned that the man he'd hit, and who had later died, wasn't Joe Beck at all, but a non-Mafia forger named John Saupp, whom Valachi hadn't even known.

Valachi had then decided to tell all, and he suddenly became the prize in a tug-of-war between the FBI and the Federal Narcotics Bureau. The narcotics bureau finally won, and Valachi started talking in September, 1962. He had continued to talk all through 1963, mostly to the FBI by then, and in September of that year, he'd been brought to Washington to face the McClellan Committee.

It was then that the public became aware of Valachi for the first time. His appearances before the McClellan Committee, while sensational and helpful in stimulating support for anticrime bills and appropriations in Congress, contributed little new knowledge of organized crime. The hoodlum had already been thoroughly pumped on that subject by expert interrogators in private.

In his book *The Valachi Papers,* author Peter Maas lists several examples of the silliness connected with the McClellan Committee episode. Maas says that Senator McClellan himself visited Valachi in the Washington jail, and according to Valachi, the senator asked him not to mention Hot Springs, Arkansas, in his testimony. Arkansas is McClellan's home state. Whether Valachi was telling the truth or not, we don't know, but we do know that the well-known gangster spa of Hot Springs was not mentioned once at the hearings.

On another occasion, Maas writes, Senator Carl Curtis of Nebraska asked Valachi about crime in Omaha. Valachi was seen to confer with a Justice Department man sitting next to him. Valachi then said he didn't know anything about it. And what had Valachi asked the Justice Department man after Curtis's penetrating question? "Where the hell is Omaha?"

Valachi was to remain a source of information to law officials until April 1971, when he was to die, still in jail, of natural causes. He wouldn't have been eligible for parole until 1980, but it is doubtful that even then he would willingly have walked outside. The Mafia contract for the killing of Valachi was worth $100,000.

As it was, Valachi was to outlive his nemesis, Vito Genovese, who was to die of natural causes in 1969 at the age of 70, while still in prison.

Meanwhile, as Valachi was appearing on TV and as the Profaci-Gallo war was drawing to a close in 1963, the Banana War was just heating up.

This had begun in 1962, when the National Commission, under the influence of Buffalo don Stefano Magaddino, began to express annoyance about Joseph Bonanno's habit of either ignoring commission meetings or sending his lieutenants to them. By early 1963 the National Commission was threatening to suspend Bonanno from membership. Part of his trouble was, of course, that in addition to the animosity of Magaddino in Buffalo, he was not getting along with Tommy Lucchese (head of the old Gagliano mob), Tommy Eboli (who was running Genovese's outfit) and Carlo Gambino (who'd taken over from Albert Anastasia).

All of these men were aware that Bonanno was applying for Canadian citizenship and moving into certain Canadian rackets. Also he was "the man" in Arizona, and was known to have several interests in the Caribbean and in Florida. Magaddino is quoted as saying, "He's planting flags everywhere!" And it certainly did appear that Bonanno was trying to be the boss of bosses nationally, internationally and in New York, all at the same time. His son Bill was known to have been living with Joseph Magliocco, Profaci's successor, and Bill was married to Profaci's niece. While Magliocco lived, a combined Profaci-Bonanno mob had seemed quite likely. This in turn had given the shivers to Lucchese, Eboli and Gambino, whose mobs, if taken on individually, would have been outnumbered.

In the summer of 1963 Magliocco had virtually proved to everyone that the New York takeover was on when he had tried to kill Gambino and Lucchese at the same time. Bill Bonanno had been implicated in this, at least to the satisfaction of Lucchese and Gambino, thanks to an incident in Magliocco's car at a train station on Long Island. Magliocco had told Bill Bonanno to bring a gun with him when they'd gone to meet someone on the train. Magliocco had armed himself with a shotgun; Bonanno had taken a pistol.

As recorded in Gay Talese's book, Bonanno had been sitting in the car with Magliocco when a man got off the train, walked over to the car, smiled at Bill, and assured Magliocco, ''Everything is being taken care of.''

Later Bonanno had decided that Magliocco had brought him along to assure somebody that the Bonanno mob was behind the operation with the Profaci mob. As it turned out, the operation, which had been the rub-out of Lucchese and Gambino, had failed. Bill Bonanno later claimed that he had known nothing about it. Magliocco had immediately been called before the National Commission and fined $40,000 for attempting to erase his fellow bosses. Magliocco's excuse to the commission was that Gambino and Lucchese had helped the Gallos in their insurrection. He later confided to Bonanno that he'd been lucky to come away from that meeting alive. Bonanno had his own complaint against Magliocco, for having involved the Bonanno gang without telling him what was going on. Then Magliocco died and Joseph Colombo, Sr. took over.

Colombo was no particular friend of the Bonanno crowd, so by 1963 the merger of the two gangs, if it had ever been on, was off. The other major gang leaders in New York then relaxed a bit. But not so Magadinno in Buffalo. He was still vexed about Bonanno's international expansion plan, and also about the promotion of young Bill Bonanno to the No. 3 position in the mob. This put Bill, only

31, over Gaspar DiGregorio, a long-time Bonanno captain and a brother-in-law of Magaddino.

Magaddino urged DiGregorio to form his own gang, and to take as many Bonanno men with him as he could. Magaddino was as anxious to remove Bonanno as a competitor as he was to see DiGregorio get ahead.

During 1964 the elder Bonanno laid low in Canada and ignored all summonses from the commission. Since Magaddino was the major influence at commission meetings, Bonanno saw no point in appearing.

Several times Bonanno was contacted by Sam DeCavalcante of New Jersey, who said he had been asked by the commission to reason with Bonanno. Unknown to DeCavalcante, the FBI was listening to his every word. In 1969 the FBI revealed that DeCavalcante's office had been bugged between 1961 and 1965.

In 1964 Joseph Bonanno was booted out of Canada and forced to return to the States, where he had to appear before a grand jury. That year Joseph Colombo, much to some mob leaders' surprise (according to the DeCavalcante tapes), was elevated to the National Commission.

Another newsworthy item in 1964 was the famous "French Connection" case. Two New York detectives became curious when they saw a hood named Patsy Fuca tossing money around like a drunken sailor in the Copacabana nightclub in New York. They quickly learned that he was an underling of a mobster named Little Angie Tuminaro, a lieutenant in the Gambino gang.

Thanks to a year's brilliant detective work, the two detectives, aided by federal officers, were able to grab Fuca, several other Brooklyn hoods and three Frenchmen, including a well-known (in France) TV singing star. All were convicted of arranging the sale and delivery of 116 pounds of raw heroin, the largest shipment ever seized up to that time.

The dope had come into New York concealed in the body of an automobile. The detectives also learned that similar shipments had been made that way in Canada, most of the dope coming from Turkey by way of Marseilles. The salesmen on the other end were Corsicans. The chief intermediary, one Jean Jehan, now dead of natural causes, barely escaped. The sad postscript to this story was to come some seven years later, when it was revealed that all this confiscated heroin, plus more, was eventually stolen from the New

York police property office and presumably put back on the streets of New York!

In October 1964, when Joseph Bonanno had already appeared before one grand jury without saying much, and was scheduled to testify before another, the mob boss was "kidnaped!" Both the police and some other mob leaders thought that Bonanno had arranged the thing himself, as a means of ducking either the grand jury, the syndicate, or both.

The so-called snatch, according to Bonanno's lawyer who was with him at the time, occurred in front of an apartment house at Park Avenue and 36th Street. Bonanno and the lawyer, William P. Maloney, had just stepped out of a cab, and were going across the sidewalk when two men came out of the shadows and grabbed Bonanno by the arms. One of them said, "C'mon, Joe, my boss wants to see you." As they dragged Bonanno away, the lawyer rushed after them and yelled "Hey, what's going on? That's my client!"

One of the men warned the lawyer back and when he continued to chase them, the hood whipped around and fired a shot into the sidewalk. That, at last, discouraged the attorney, and he ran into the lobby to call the police. Bonanno was whisked away in a car.

The younger Bonanno was not to hear any news of his father for two months, and to this day he says that he doesn't know exactly where the old man was. At first some Bonanno members thought that DiGregorio was behind it, but this was ruled out on the grounds that DiGregorio wouldn't have dared. Besides the two men, despite their differences, were very old friends, and Bonanno had resisted every argument by his lieutenants that he should take care of DiGregorio.

It was finally concluded by the Bonanno gang that their boss was either dead, hiding out on his own, or being held by Magaddino. If the last was the case, then it was thought that Bonanno was reasonably safe, simply because he and Magaddino were not only old associates, but distantly related. The gang now being run by Bill Bonanno, Frank Labruzzo and Joseph Notaro, decided to wait and see.

And in the meantime they resolved to hide out as much as possible. "If they got Joe, then we're next," one of them speculated, without really knowing who "they" were.

CHAPTER TWENTY-FOUR
1965-71

Early in 1965 there was a meeting at the Cedarhurst Restaurant in Long Island. Among the participants were Sam Giancana of Chicago, Thomas Eboli (Genovese's heir) and Carmine Tramunti, a Lucchese representative. Among the subjects discussed were Bonanno's disappearance and his possible expulsion from the hierarchy of organized crime.

The gang leaders were also concerned about the crackdown on vice that was taking place all over the country. More than 600 men had been arrested nationally, on charges ranging from bookmaking and loan sharking to gambling and prostitution. There were raids in Tampa, Columbus, Nashville, St. Paul, Denver and St. Louis.

Meanwhile the United States had prevailed upon police in Sicily to search for Bonanno in Castellammare del Golfo, and Interpol was asked to watch for him in North Africa.

In 1965 *The New York Times* estimated that the Genovese gang had 27 millionaires among its members.

In New York United States Attorney Robert M. Morgenthau had asked three separate grand juries to question organized crime figures. If ever there was a time for a top Mafia official to keep out of sight, this was it. There is no doubt that many of the syndicate bosses secretly envied Joseph Bonanno and his disappearing ways.

For the entire time that the elder Bonanno was missing, his son maintained a vigil at a certain pay telephone booth. The summer before he'd been kidnapped, the older Bonanno had told his son that if he ever got "lost" again, Bill was to sit at that phone booth every Thursday night, at 8 P.M.

On Thursday, December 17, 1964, the phone had rung, and Bill had answered it. A voice, not his father's, had said that the old man was okay, and that Bill would be seeing him soon. Bill told Maloney, the lawyer, and Maloney inexplicably told the press. The lawyer also said that Bonanno would finally appear before the grand jury on the following Monday.

Two weeks passed, and still there was no Bonanno. The newspapers were having a ball with the story, using headlines such as "Yes, We Have No Bonannos." Bill decided to rest in Arizona, where he was promptly arrested and brought back to New York for a grand jury appearance. The grand jury asked him what had happened to his father, and he—probably truthfully—said he knew no more than the police about the Great Disappearance. He had to say that at 21 separate appearances before the grand jury gave up on it. Bonanno was then sentenced to jail for refusing to say what he'd told his father's lawyer about the latter's return. He was released from jail on June 5, 1965 after serving three months.

In January 1966, with the elder Bonanno still missing, DiGregorio let it be known that he was thinking of retiring at 63, and that he wanted to talk peace. Both young Bonanno and his aide, Frank Labruzzo, suspected that DiGregorio might be about to make his big move and was setting them up to be killed. In any case, they agreed to meet and talk with DiGregorio at a Bonanno relative's house on Troutman Street, in Brooklyn. The Bonanno gang arrived at 11 P.M., and as they walked slowly down the street in the freezing cold, they were suddenly blasted at by shotguns sticking out of the windows of several houses.

The Bonanno men fled in every direction, hurling a few shots back as they ran. No one was killed or wounded on either side. The National Commission then urged DiGregorio to go ahead and really retire, namely because he'd failed so miserably, and because he'd drawn more heat on the mobs. DiGregorio's replacement was to be Paul Sciacca.

On May 17, Joseph Bonanno finally turned up, in a Manhattan courthouse, along with a new lawyer. He didn't say where he'd been, and after a long court argument, he was freed the same day on $150,000 bail. He also was allowed to visit his wife in Arizona, though he was subject to be called whenever necessary by a grand jury.

That same day, the Bonanno gang gathered at the La Scala restaurant to celebrate his return. During the party Bonanno lieutenant and long-time friend Joseph Notaro collapsed and died of a heart attack. The FBI turned up to photograph his funeral.

The elder Bonanno then departed for Arizona, taking with him one bodyguard, Peter Magaddino, a nephew of Stefano Magaddino, the Buffalo boss who was backing DiGregorio. The reason for Peter Magaddino's loyalty to Bonanno seems to have been that he didn't get on too well with his uncle, and, in addition, he'd never cared for DiGregorio.

During the summer of 1966, the police in Queens, New York, discovered a "Little Apalachin Meeting" at the La Stella Restaurant in Forest Hills. There were 13 Mafia figures there from various parts of the United States. Among them were gang leaders such as Carlos Marcello of New Orleans, Santo Trafficante of Tampa, and Joseph Colombo, Tommy Eboli and Mike Miranda, all of New York.

They had a number of things to discuss. First on the agenda was what to do about Bonanno and his continuing defiance of the National Commission. (Shortly after the La Stella meeting, the Bonanno gang discovered that the council, through unions it influenced, had ordered all Bonanno soldiers off the union payrolls unless they went over to DiGregorio.) Another commission problem was finding a reliable man to head the Lucchese organization, since Lucchese himself was dying of a brain tumor. The commission was also concerned about Bonanno's expected reply to the Troutman Street ambush. Despite the heat being put on both Bonannos by the government, it was unlikely that the Bonanno crowd was going to take DiGregorio's treachery lying down.

The Bonanno gang, however, was going through a period of doubt and reorganization. Joseph Notaro and then Frank Labruzzo, two top aides, had died, Notaro from a heart attack and Labruzzo of cancer. John Morale, Bonanno's second in command, was acting as though he wanted to change sides. Then there was the pressure of money. With the commission cutting many of Bonanno's soldiers off from their featherbed jobs in the union, the gang needed extra cash to support them. When the "war" had begun, the Bonanno army had numbered some 300 men. Now about 60 had gone over to DiGregorio, and others had simply gone away, rather than be pressured to pick one side or another. The Bonanno gang, at this point, had a hard-core following of perhaps 175 loyalists.

Then the counterattack began. Frank Mari, whom police thought probably had been the leader of DiGregorio's forces at the Troutman Street ambush, was shot and severely wounded in Brooklyn.

In October 1966 Bill Bonanno was clapped into jail again, this time for refusing to tell a grand jury what he knew of the Troutman Street shooting the previous January. Bonanno served a month, and then joined his father in Arizona for a family Christmas.

In January 1967 Bill Bonanno and five of his men were found in Montreal, and arrested for carrying guns. They drew suspended sentences and were kicked out of the country. The police theory was that they'd been there to confer with their Canadian associates and to look at the elder Bonanno's new interests there.

Then in October 1967, two Bonanno men, Vincent Cassese and Vincent Garofalo, were wounded.

Bonanno's reply came only two weeks later. Three DiGregorio men, Thomas Di Angelo, James Di Angelo and Frank Telleri, all of whom had been with Bonanno before defecting to DiGregorio, were dining at the Cypress Gardens Restaurant in Queens. A lone man, carrying a machine gun under his raincoat, walked in, and before the eyes of some 20 other customers, shot and killed all three men.

The main suspect, according to police, was Gaspare Magaddino, the younger brother of Peter, who, police thought, might have been imported from Sicily to do the job; they were, however, unable to find him. (When he did turn up one year later in a Brooklyn gutter, he was dead of shotgun wounds.)

In March 1968, while both Bonannos were in Arizona, one of their most trusted lieutenants, Sam Perrone, was riddled with bullets as he crossed the street in front of his Brooklyn warehouse. The police suspected Frank Mari, DiGregorio's ace assassin, who had apparently recovered from his own wounds.

The slaying of Perrone infuriated the Bonanno mob, and it was at this time that the elder Bonanno was quoted as saying, "The next time they hit one of my men, they lose two, first in one family, then in another."

This apparently was a reference to Bonanno's suspicions that the Colombo gang was being entirely too helpful to DiGregorio. In April young Bonanno was summoned to court in Brooklyn, where along with other men, he was to be questioned once again on the Troutman Street incident. In court he chanced to see one Mike Consolo, a former Bonanno man who'd gone over to DiGregorio.

That very night Consolo was found dead in the street, shot six times. Young Bonanno told Gay Talese that Consolo must have been killed by his own men, who, seeing him laughing with Bonanno, had mistakenly thought he was switching sides again.

A week later one of Perrone's men was wounded. Then a Di-Gregorio man was wounded. At the end of April, Charles LoCicero, a member of the Colombo family, was shot and killed as he munched a hamburger in a Brooklyn diner. If one coupled the Colombo man's murder with that of DiGregorio's man Consolo, one might have got the idea that this constituted "first in one family, then in another."

Along about here, DiGregorio, whose health was failing, decided to take the commission's advice and retire. In the war so far, most of the wounded were his, and in killings, he was losing by a score of 5-1.

DiGregorio's replacement, Paul Sciacca, proved equally inept.

During the summer, Bonanno's home in Tucson, and that of one of his aides were bombed. At first DiGregorio was suspected, but it later turned out that the bombings were the work of zealous amateurs who were trying to alarm the Tucson public and cause a demand that the gangster elements get out of town.

The last major incident in the Banana War came in September 1968, when Frank Mari and two other DiGregorio-Sciacca men mysteriously disappeared. All three were presumed dead and have not been seen to this day. The score was then 8-1, in favor of Bonanno.

The war finally ended shortly after February 6, 1969, when Thomas Zummo, 29, a DiGregorio-Sciacca man, was cut down in a hail of lead as he walked toward his girlfriend's apartment house in Queens. At this point, both factions of the Bonanno gang agreed that there had to be a truce. There was too much public pressure, too many court appearances and too much press and police attention for the war to continue. It had gotten so that a hood couldn't even walk down the street with a machine gun without being pestered by the law or reporters.

Another reason for the truce was that most of the leaders of the gangs were ill. DiGregorio was lingering near death; his brother had just died. Joseph Bonanno had had a heart attack, as had Paul Sciacca. Tommy Lucchese had just died. Carlo Gambino had heart trouble. Tommy Eboli had collapsed from "overwork" at a restaurant. Vito Genovese had died in prison. What the Mafia in New

341

York needed in 1969 was a health clinic, not a gang war.

On June 10, 1969 the syndicate was to be revealed once again as a nationwide crime cartel. It was on this date that the FBI chose to reveal the existence of the DeCavalcante tapes. Sam Rizzo De-Cavalcante was a New Jersey crime figure who had been used as a go-between by the National Commission and its members in New York. It was DeCavalcante who, at the urging of the commission, had been trying to get Bonanno to listen to reason in the mid-1960s. For at least four years, between 1961 and 1965, the FBI had had his office bugged, and it turned over to the court 2,500 pages of recording transcripts.

In those pages DeCavalcante talked about the syndicate, the commission, his own gang and other people's. Unfortunately for some he mentioned, he was prone to brag about his connections, both in gangland and in lawful society. Not everyone was grateful to be mentioned in the DeCavalcante tapes, especially some politicians who, to be fair, probably were innocent victims of DeCavalcante's name dropping.

As usual in cases like this, there was much publicity, many shocked utterances in Congress and sturdy editorials saying that something should be done about organized crime. Books were hastily written using the 13 volumes of FBI transcripts as material, and there was even a long-playing record, "The Voice of the Mafia."

DeCavalcante himself, charged with extortion and conspiracy, was found guilty and sentenced to 15 years.

On March 9, 1970, having been found guilty of using someone else's credit card during a trip between New York and Arizona, Bill Bonanno was sentenced to four years in prison. His sidekick Peter Notaro was given a year.

Lots of Mafia figures were threatened with prison or actually put there that year. Carlo Gambino himself was charged with conspiracy to hijack Chase Manhattan Bank armored trucks carrying up to $5,000,000 in cash. Jerry Catena, the co-director of the Genovese mob, was tossed inside for refusing to answer questions about the Mafia. Meyer Lansky was grabbed in Miami for having drugs in his suitcase when he returned from Mexico. The drugs were for his stomach disorder, but he didn't have a prescription for them. Angelo Bruno, the Mafia leader of Philadelphia, was imprisoned for refusing to talk about the syndicate.

Angelo DeCarlo, a New Jersey crime potentate, was sent to prison for two years on extortion charges. And then there was Joseph Colombo who, unlike the other syndicate figures, refused to go quietly to jail, if he had to go.

In 1970 Colombo was indicted by a grand jury for evading his taxes. Almost simultaneously, one of his sons, Joseph Jr., was charged, with several other men, with melting down U.S. coins for their precious metal content. (He later beat this rap.)

This double blow made Colombo see red. The first thing he did was to organize pickets to protest the FBI's "discrimination" against Italian-Americans. He claimed that the use of words such as "Cosa Nostra" (which was given to the world not by the FBI, but by Joe Valachi) and "Mafia" (which had been known centuries before there even *was* an FBI) were a slur on the good name of Italian-Americans everywhere.

The author recalls walking past FBI headquarters in Manhattan during the summer of 1970 and seeing the protesters with their signs, "FBI Unfair to Italian-Americans," and thinking to himself that the whole affair was simply ridiculous, especially when one knew that the man behind it all was one of the biggest gangsters of our time. Despite that, Colombo was able to get all sorts of innocent and perhaps none-too-bright people to join in this silly tableau. The author, then a news reporter, tried to talk to some protesters one afternoon, while bemused police stood by and listened.

"How can you possibly confuse the arrests of known killers and gangsters with discrimination against Italians in general?"

The replies were almost hysterical, but they boiled down to the fact that the author should mind his own business. The author then advanced the theory that it was men like Colombo who were giving Italian-Americans a bad name, not the FBI, and that if Italian-Americans wanted to do some real good, they'd protest in front of the offices of Colombo, Bonanno, Gambino and the rest, and not in front of the FBI. A brief scuffle followed that remark, but the author was rescued by police before any harm was done.

One of the people taken in by Colombo's public relations campaign was Dick Cavett, the well-known TV personality. He actually had Colombo on his late-night talk show and let the gangster expound his daffy views. Cavett was of course skeptical, and even biting in his sarcasm, but it would have shown far better taste not to have had Colombo on at all.

There were Colombo-inspired newspaper advertisements, too, and even speeches supporting Colombo's position.

Not everyone was impressed, least of all some newspapers. They were quick to point out that Colombo had been a lieutenant in the old Profaci mob, that he had negotiated the peace with the Gallos, that he had "saved" Lucchese and Gambino from being scragged by Magliocco, that he had supplied hoods to DiGregorio in the Banana War, that he had been arrested at La Stella with 12 other leading Mafia figures from around the country, and that he was up on tax charges himself.

The apex of Colombo's career as a crusader came on June 29, 1970, when 40,000 people attended Italian-American Unity Day at Columbus Circle, in New York. One of the last speakers to say his piece was Joseph Colombo, Sr., and he got one of the biggest hands of the afternoon.

Another segment of society that was not overly impressed by Colombo's campaign was the Mafia itself, and Carlo Gambino, in particular. It struck him that Colombo was not exactly going along with *omerta*, the well-known code of silence. Other Mafia figures were also known to be wishing that Joseph Colombo would shut up.

Colombo's efforts to make himself beloved continued through the winter of 1970 and into the spring of 1971. During this time he was charged with "mediating" an argument between the participants in a huge jewel robbery. He was also charged with operating a $5,000,000-a-year gambling business.

In June 1971, at yet another Italian-American Unity Day rally at Columbus Circle, Joseph Colombo, Sr. was shot in the head by a black gunman, who in turn was quickly shot and killed by a white man. The second gunman got away.

Colombo went into a coma from which he never emerged. The man who shot him was identified as Jerome A. Johnson, who had been at the rally posing as a photographer. The police had no record on him. Theories about the shooting included these: that Johnson was hired by the Mafia to silence Colombo, and then killed by the Mafia because, if caught, he might talk. If it was a Mafia setup, it was speculated that Johnson may have been in one of the Harlem gangs affiliated with Mafia-run numbers rackets. If that was the case, then Carlo Gambino could have been the man behind Colombo's shooting.

The Colombo gang itself maintained that Johnson must simply

have been a Lee Harvey Oswald-type "nut." Police thought that this theory by the Colombo gang could contain a certain amount of self-protective guile. If, for example, they had said that they thought Gambino did it, or the Gallos, they would immediately have been blamed if anything sudden had happened to either party. Also there was no point in forewarning one's enemies, particularly enemies who might operate on the first-strike principle.

Another police theory was that the man who killed Johnson was in any case a Mafia man. He was either a Colombo bodyguard or part of a Mafia assassination team.

A final theory involved the Gallos, long humiliated over their defeat by Profaci. Colombo was the leader of the old Profaci mob—the man who'd promised them everything and, at the urging of Profaci, gone back on his word. It was known that the Gallos were still yearning for a bigger piece of the Profaci-Colombo pie and, even more interesting, they were known to have many black "soldiers" doing routine strong-arm stuff for them in Brooklyn.

CHAPTER TWENTY-FIVE
1972-1973

A year passed before the next headline incident in New York's almost continuous crime war. In April 1972 Joey Gallo, family, friends and bodyguards were dining in a restaurant in New York's Little Italy.

Gallo looked up from his spaghetti just in time to see a man approaching his table, holding a gun before him. It was the classic scene in what has become, in gangland, almost a set piece: the victim half rises from his seat, the gunman blasts away, the victim falls back and the killer fades away into the crowd, or escapes by way of a waiting car.

Gallo varied the script only slightly; instead of slumping to the floor, he took three bullets in the chest and then chased the killer out onto the pavement, screaming curses all the way. There he keeled over and died. The gunman got away, after wounding Gallo's bodyguard in the hand.

At the funeral Joey's sister was heard to yell, "They'll be sorry for this! Blood will flow in the streets!"

And so it has.

The police are still not sure who got Gallo. It might have been Carlo Gambino, who was still trying to be New York's boss of bosses at the age of 73, or it might have been the Colombo gang, who may have blamed Gallo for the shooting of their leader.

Police didn't have long to dwell on that, though, because the 21st killing in the war that began in 1970 for control of New York's mobs, took place in July 1972. This one claimed Tommy Ryan Eboli, 61, the leader of the old Genovese gang. And this hit was definitely put down to Gambino.

Eboli, it is generally conceded, had nothing to do with the

shooting of Colombo or Gallo. His problem was that he failed to acknowledge Carlo Gambino as his superior. Significantly enough, on the demise of Eboli, his gang members immediately recognized Gambino as their new father figure. Eboli had had a charmed life, though, up until that night in a Brooklyn carpark.

He had begun as a soldier helping to supervise the late Vito Genovese's joints in Greenwich Village. Then, once he'd had a little money, he'd taken over the contracts of a few prizefighters, and is best remembered for jumping into the ring and punching a referee who called a decision against his gladiator. This ended Eboli's boxing career, but it had brought him to the attention of Lucky Luciano, who was exiled in Italy. Lucky apparently liked his spirit and had recommended Eboli's promotion to Genovese. When Genovese had gone to prison in 1959 for 15 years, he had entrusted the running of his gang to Eboli and Gerry Catena, passing over Tony Bender Strollo to do so.

Strollo had objected to this, but only briefly. He disappeared one evening, and the consensus in gangland is that Bender was crushed to death in an automobile scrap machine located in a Brooklyn junk yard. Then, when Gerry Catena had gone to jail, Eboli had been left in sole command.

To this day, no one knows exactly who or what lured Eboli, alone, to a Brooklyn car lot at 1 A.M. All that is known is that he was found a few feet from his new blue Cadillac with five bullets in him, most of them in his head.

The following month, Carmine Tramunti, boss of the old Lucchese family, was willing to tell anyone who cared that Carlo Gambino was the boss of all New York—or even the world, as far as he was concerned.

The Brooklyn DA's office has a pretty good idea of what Tramunti was saying at this time, thanks to a bug it had managed to place in a trailer parked in a Brooklyn junk yard. The trailer was the headquarters of one Paul Vario, a captain in the Lucchese-Tramunti family.

In addition to the tapes, the DA's men had made 54,000 telephoto pictures of people who went in and out of the trailer. Along with this, there were 36,000 feet of color movie film.

Together these things documented the fact that members of all five of New York's major crime mobs had visited the trailer frequently. And so had politicians, businessmen, more than 100 policemen and several judges. The 1,622,600 feet of recording tape revealed that the mobs were involved in the running of 200 legitimate businesses in and around New York. The tapes also gave inside information—in the hoodlums' own words—about gambling, prostitution, counterfeiting, hijacking, insurance swindles, cigarette smuggling, dope pushing and labor rackets.

The DA's office issued summonses for 667 men in October 1972 as a result of the information immediately gleaned, but some experts say that it may take years to run down every lead contained in those tapes. There seems little doubt though, as the President's Commission on Law Enforcement argued in its 1967 Task Force Report on Organized Crime, that the "bug" and the wiretap are the law's best, and perhaps only really effective weapons against the secret society.

Despite some of the Mafia's recent setbacks, however, organized crime marches on.

In Chicago Sam Giancana has been rushed into retirement due to hounding by the law. His place has been taken by Tony Accardo, who is less well known to the nightclub set in Las Vegas and the press. Al Capone's old headquarters, the Hawthorne Inn, in Cicero, remained in gangster control until as recently as 1970, when it burned down.

The Hawthorne, which was renamed the Towne Hotel, was owned by Rossmar Realty, Inc., the president of which was Joseph Aiuppa. He will be remembered as a onetime gunman for Capone. State officials once questioned Aiuppa about the ownership of the hotel, but he pleaded the Fifth Amendment some 60 times. Aiuppa is the gang boss of Cicero.

In 1964 the police made a rather surprising discovery at the Towne. They had raided a coffee shop in Cicero, and in the basement found nothing. Yet they'd seen lots of people go in, and few come out. After tapping walls awhile, the police found a secret door. This had led them to another empty room. But in the floor of the room, they found a steel trapdoor, bolted and strapped on the underside. Sledgehammering their way through, the police then found themselves in an underground passageway that led to another steel door. They battered that down too, and then finally found a gambling game and four chagrined dealers. Leading from the gaming room there had been other underground passageways; one of them had led to the adjacent Towne Hotel. In the other passageways there had been 11 men who could hardly have said they were waiting for a bus.

If in this book it has seemed that most of the attention has been on the Mafia in New York and Chicago, it is because these two cities have always been the axis of organized crime in the United States. New York and Chicago provided the men and the money for the organizations of Florida, Nevada, California, Arizona and other places. Of the 5,000 or so hoodlums who compose the Mafia today, at least 2,000 of them are in the New York, New Jersey and Philadelphia area.

There are at least another 1,500 syndicate men in Chicago. Of the remainder elsewhere in the country, many, as stated, are transplanted New Yorkers or Chicagoans. It would, of course, be possible to write volumes on the crime organizations of every big city in the United States, but that would simply drown the reader in details. Even the Kefauver Committee, which went from city to city and gathered many thousands of pages of testimony, was unable to give more than the broad picture.

This book has described, or at least mentioned, a total of 140 gangland killings. It has been, at times, a monotonous diary showing only stupid men killing each other, often for inconsequential reasons and sometimes even by mistake. Yet the 140 murders mentioned are only a fraction of the 3,500 or so gangland killings that have taken place in the United States since 1920, the year crime really began to get organized. This organizing, of course, is still going on. In Chicago 46 men have been killed in the last two years as various factions of the Capone mob have sought to straighten out their differences. In New York at this writing Carlo Gambino has almost achieved the goal of many ill-fated gang leaders before him: he is within one step of being the boss of bosses.

The gangs he has now under his command are his own, the former Mangano-Anastasia outfit, the old Luciano-Genovese-Eboli gang the former Profaci-Colombo mob, and the former Gagliano-Lucchese gang.

The only holdout, as we go to press, is Phil Rastelli, the new boss of the Bonanno gang. Rastelli took over on the retirement of Joseph Bonanno, who has had a series of heart attacks. Rastelli has an army of some 400 men, against Gambino's estimated 1,500. Still nobody is willing to bet on a Gambino victory. The Bonanno crowd has been outnumbered before.

In addition, Gambino was 74 in 1974, and Rastelli may be banking on that. There is also the historic fact that trying to be boss of bosses has proved difficult or fatal for everyone who has tried it in New York.

Morello, Masseria, Maranzano and Anastasia were all killed trying for the title. Luciano, who came closest, probably survived by virtue of being in jail or in exile most of the time. Genovese was thrown in jail for the rest of his life just as he was claiming to be all-powerful in New York. Joseph Bonanno was kidnaped and driven into retirement.

There are today those who say that the Mafia is an anachronism, that it is dying out and that once the last of the old dons in various cities around the country die off, the gangs will split up, the syndicate will be disbanded and that the organization will never be the same again. The younger Italian-Sicilian generations aren't interested in crime, the thinking goes; they aren't hungry enough.

Some mobologists point out that more and more of the strong-arm stuff, the dope peddling and the gambling is handled by ghetto dwellers who are no longer poor Italians and Sicilians, but blacks and Puerto Ricans, and that they will compose the big gangs of the future.

Perhaps so, but one wouldn't like to bet on it.

As recently as October 1972, New York police had to admit that the 112 pounds of dope, plus more, that was seized in the "French Connection" case, had vanished from the police property room. It was worth approximately $100 million on the street, and there is little doubt that this is exactly where it went. Some of those young men and women found lying dead from overdoses in doorways in New York can be laid to this shameful bit of malfeasance.

In November 1972, the police of New York were revealed in even a more sorry light. During a series of hearings, some police admitted that almost every cop they knew was "on the take" from petty criminals and major crime figures. In some precincts, the corruption went from the captains on down.

In January 1973, the blanket-wrapped body of Emanuel Gambino, 29, was found on a New Jersey garbage dump. This may or may not have been the opening shot in a Gambino-Rastelli war. Or perhaps it was some other gang's message to Gambino. Whatever it was, it is a sign that, in gangland at least, nothing seems to change. Just the faces, not the methods. As you read these last pages, somewhere out there—in the dumps of Brooklyn, in the streets of Chicago, in the alleys of Detroit—a gang figure probably is getting shot through the head, strangled or set on fire and cut up into small pieces.

As the woman at Tommy Eboli's funeral said, "That's the kind of life they seem to want." And the kind of death.

WHO'S WHO and WHO WAS WHO

ABBANDANDO, Frank (Dasher). Gangster in New York in the 1920s. He ran loan and bookmaking rackets in association with Happy Maione and later joined Kid Twist Reles. He got his nickname because of his dashing baseball game as infielder of the Elmira Reformatory team. He was executed for the murder of Puggy Feinstein in 1942.

ABBATEMARCO, Frank. New York gangster. A Profaci lieutenant, his death in 1959 was said to have been a cause of the Gallo-Profaci war.

ACCARDI, Settemo. New Jersey gangster and racketeer. He was in gas-stamp black marketeering during World War II. After the war he was jailed on narcotics charges.

ACCARDO, Tony (Joe Batters). Chicago gang leader and laundry racketeer. In 1931 he was listed by the Chicago Crime Commission as a public enemy. In 1945 he was suspected of kidnaping Jake (Greasy Thumb) Guzik, who reputedly paid $75,000 for his freedom, but nevertheless, in 1950 Guzik and Rocco Fischetti were teamed with Accardo in what the Kefauver Commission named as one of the strongest organizations in the nation's underworld. He was subpoenaed by the Kefauver Commission in 1951.

ADONIS, Joe. Brooklyn gangster. He was on Joe (The Boss) Masseria's side in the Castellammarese War of 1930. He was named in the Kefauver Report in 1950 as a gambling-club operator.

JOE ADONIS

354

AGUECI, Albert and Vito. Gangsters. They were associated with the Magaddino gang, and when serving a jail sentence on narcotics offenses, Albert felt nothing was being done to release them. He threatened to implicate Magaddino, and was very promptly let out on bail and brutally murdered in 1961. Vito was still in jail when Joe Valachi was sentenced in 1962.

AIELLO, Andrew, Antonio, Dominick, Joseph. Sicilian family. They went into bootlegging, and took over the Genna gang in 1925. Two Aiellos were shot dead in an attempt to oust Tony Lombardo from the presidency of the Chicago Unione Siciliano in 1926. Also in 1926, six gang members were killed by Capone as a warning not to continue to attempt to dislodge him from power. An Aiello setup intended to kill Capone and Lombardo was foiled by the police. Joseph and Dominick were both killed in separate shooting incidents in 1930.

AIUPPA, Joseph. Chicago gangster and gunman for Al Capone. He was president of Rossmar Realty, Inc., which owned the old Hawthorne Inn in Chicago. When questioned about this company he pleaded the Fifth Amendment. He is a Cicero gang boss.

ALO, Vincent (Jimmy Blue Eyes). New York gangster, named in the Kefauver Report.

ALPERT, Alex (Red). Small-time gangster who operated in Brooklyn. He tried to sell Pittsburgh Phil some hot jewelry, but refused the low price he was offered, so Phil ordered his death. This was carried out by choking by three "contract" men in 1934, though it was not until Harry Rudolph and others talked in 1940 that the facts of his murder were known to the police.

ALTERIE, Louis (Two-Gun). Chicago gangster. He was a gunman for Dion O'Bannion in the 1920s, and one of the guests at O'Bannion's party at the Webster Hotel in 1924. They were arrested in the police raid on the Sieben Brewery. O'Bannion

ALBERT ANASTASIA

was killed almost immediately after, and Alterie issued a public challenge to shoot it out with the killer. He also supervised the vengeance killing of the horse which threw and fatally injured his friend Nails Morton.

ANASTASIA, Albert. Italian. Smuggled into the United States in 1917, he fought on the Masseria side in the Castellammarese War. According to Kid Twist Reles, he was the big boss of Murder, Inc. activities during the thirties in New York. No one could be killed, no killer hired, without his permission. He became one of the five New York dons after Vincent Mangano's disappearance in 1951, for which he was thought to be responsible. He was associated with Bugsy Siegel. During Reles's disclosures he went into hiding until Reles was dead. He was an influential member of the Unione, a labor boss, unchallenged in waterfront affairs in Brooklyn. He had spent 18 months under sentence of death for the murder of Joe Turino in 1920, but gained a retrial and was freed, and in spite of his undoubted responsibility for very many more murders, and many more arrests, he always managed to get acquittals. His Unione colleagues found him inclined to overstep his territory, and he was shot dead in a barber shop in New York in 1957.

ANGERISKA, John. Cleveland gambling racketeer.

ANGERSOLA, John (alias King). Cleveland gambler. He became one of the partners in the Miami Wofford Hotel operation in 1941.

ANNENBERG, Moe. He operated a nationwide news service until 1939. He was then about to be charged with tax fraud, so he retired. The service was taken over by Arthur McBride, and later by James Ragen, and became known as the Continental Press.

ANSELMI, Albert. Sicilian. Chicago gangster and bootlegger. He operated with the Genna brothers, and was with Mike Genna and John Scalise in a gunfight with the police in 1925, during which Genna was fatally wounded. He and Scalise were

ANTHONY ACCARDO

charged with the murder of the two policemen who had been killed, but after two years' delay, during which chief witnesses were threatened, the case was dropped. He and his partners, Scalise and Joseph (Hop Toad) Giunta, were known as the Homicide Squad, and were suspected of many ruthless murders. When it was reported to Al Capone in 1929 that these three were plotting to gain control of the Chicago Unione Siciliano and overthrow him, Capone arranged a Sicilian-style dinner party for them. All three were invited to dinner and lavishly entertained with food and drink, after which they were all shot dead.

ARMATO, Dominic. Chicago bootlegger. He was killed in reprisal for the death of Thomas Keane in 1923.

ARNSTEIN, Nicky. Transatlantic gambler, racketeer. A dandy, he married Fanny Brice, the Broadway star. He was jailed in 1928 for bond forgery. As late as 1962, when Barbra Streisand was starring in *Funny Girl,* the musical based on Fanny Brice's life, he was alive and well, living in California, 84 years old.

BAGDONOWITZ, John. New Jersey racketeer. He tried to drop out of the gangs and go straight, but Murder, Inc. was put on his trail. He was followed to his mother's house and shot there on the doorstep, in 1933. The gunmen were Vito Gurino, Joe Mercaldo and Julie Catalino.

BAKER, George (Red). Chicago gangster of the 1920s. He was listed as a public enemy by the Chicago Crime Commission in 1923.

BALDELLI, Eddie. Chicago gangster. He was a collector for the Anselmi-Scalise "legal defense fund." He was killed in 1926 in revenge for the deaths of Henry Spingola and Antonio and Augustino Moreci.

BALESTRERE, Jim. Member of the Kansas City Mafia. He was named in the Kefauver Report as one of the "Five Iron Men" of Kansas City.

JOE BARBARA

BARBARA, Joseph. New York gang boss. His house at Apalachin, New York, was used for the famous Mafia meeting in 1957.

BARKO, Louis. Chicago gangster and gunman, he was associated with Al Capone, and wounded in a gang fight in 1926.

BARRESE, Michael. New York gangster. He was said by Joe Valachi to have killed (on Vito Genovese's orders) the husband of the lady whom Vito then married himself. He disappeared shortly after fulfilling the contract.

BASCONE, Vito. Chicago gangster. He was a collector for the Anselmi-Scalise "legal defense" fund, and was killed in 1926 in revenge for the deaths of Henry Spingola and Antonio and Augustino Moreci.

BATTAGLIA, Charles. One of Joseph Bonanno's top aides in Tucson. In 1969, the FBI charged Joseph Bonanno and Peter Notaro with conspiring to bring about Battaglia's release from Leavenworth Prison where he was serving a ten-year sentence. They were acquitted.

BECKER, Charles. New York detective, who in 1912 hired Lefty Louis and Gyp the Blood to kill gambler Herman Rosenthal. He was afraid Rosenthal was about to inform on him for having accepted bribes.

BELCASTRO, James. Chicago gangster and gunman. He was listed by the Chicago Crime Commission as a public enemy in 1923. In 1931 he was suspected of being responsible for the murder of Johnny Genaro, Al Capone's henchman.

BENDER, Tony. *See* Strollo, Anthony.

BENVENUTI, Julius, Leo and Caesar. Chicago numbers racketeers. Julius had once done Al Capone a favor, so the brothers operated under Capone's protection until 1950 when Julius died, and other racketeers including Tony Accardo muscled in on them.

JOSEPH BONANNO

BERGER, Paul. Brooklyn gangster and racketeer who turned state's evidence when arrested in 1940.

BERMAN, Abbadabba. A mathematician with phenomenally quick brain for computing race odds. Dutch Schultz used his abilities to help him beat the odds on Schultz's numbers rackets.

BERNSTEIN, Eugene. An Internal Revenue Service accountant who left the service and set up his own private practice. His clients included many well-known gangsters. He acted for Paul (The Waiter) Ricca and Louis (Little New York) Campagna.

BERNSTEIN, Sholem. Gangster operating in Brooklyn in the 1920s and 1930s. He was an inveterate and unsuccessful gambler and at 16 was hopelessly in debt. He went to the local shylocks, and soon decided to become a loan shark himself. He was involved in many varied felonies, but his specialty was stealing cars for gang contracts. He later confessed to at least 100 car thefts, but was arrested only once and never convicted. He was not a member of a gang, operating mostly alone, and in 1940 the idea gained credence that he knew too much. He ran for his life, followed cross-country by mobsters. He finally decided to seek protection in the law and turned informer.

BINAGGIO, Charlie. He was named in the Kefauver Report as one of the "Five Iron Men" of Kansas City. He had been killed in 1949.

BINION, Lester (Benny). Dallas racketeer operating numbers rackets. In 1936 he was run out of Dallas by other hoods, and he started operating legally in Las Vegas, but keeping a hand in Dallas from a distance.

BIOFF, Willie (The Squealer). A Capone man, he was principally involved in "organizing" the movie industry in the 1930s. After conviction for extortion and conspiracy, he informed on his Mafia bosses. Upon his release from prison, he went

BILL BONANNO

to live in Arizona as "Bill Nelson, cattle dealer." In 1955, at the age of 55, he was blown to bits by a car bomb. No one was ever arrested.

BIONDO, Joseph (Joe Bandy). New York gangster and an aide of Albert Anastasia's, possibly involved in Albert's death.

BOCCIA, Ferdinand (The Shadow). New York gangster. He was implicated with Lucky Luciano and others in a "money-machine" fraud. He demanded a share in the deal and was consequently killed in 1931.

BONANNO, Joseph (Joe Bananas). Born 1905 in Castellammare del Golfo, Sicily. He escaped from a fascist purge of the Sicilian Mafia, and was smuggled into the United States in 1924. He became a top boss of the Mafia in New York. In 1964 he was wanted for questioning about some murders, and disappeared until 1966. On his return he attempted to reinstate himself as boss, and a good deal of shooting ensued. His home in Tucson was bombed in 1966.

BONANNO, Salvatore (Bill). Son of Joseph, born 1932. He was nominated by Joseph to succeed him, but this was not acceptable to other members of the Commission. In 1966 an opposition gang, headed by DiGregorio, organized a big gunfight against Bonanno's men on Troutman Street in Brooklyn. There were no casualties, however. Bill was jailed for four years in 1970.

BONVENTRE, John. Sicilian. Veteran Mafia boss and cousin of Joseph Bonanno. He retired to Sicily in 1950, and was cited as a Mafia leader in an Italian government anti-Mafia drive in 1971 and exiled to a small island off the coast of Sicily.

BROOKS, Joe (Dynamite). Chicago gangster and alky peddler. He was killed in 1925.

BUCHALTER, Louis (Lepke). New York racketeer. He was also a bootlegger and top labor extortionist, and a member of

LOUIS BUCHALTER

Murder, Inc. In 1939 J. Edgar Hoover named him "the most dangerous criminal in America" and Thomas E. Dewey "the worst industrial racketeer in the United States." He was convicted of murder on Kid Twist Reles's information, and executed in 1944.

BUCHALSKY, Izzy (The Rat). Chicago labor racketeer.

BUCHER, George (Spot). Bootlegger. He was a member of the O'Donnell gang in Chicago, and was killed in a gang revenge murder in 1923.

BUFFA, Thomas. St. Louis Mafia chief. He operated in narcotics in association with Tony Lapiparo. After he had testified for the government in 1943 there was an unsuccessful attempt to assassinate him. He was finally shot dead in California in 1946.

BURKE, Fred. St. Louis gangster and gunman. He was to have been one of the gunmen in the St. Valentine's Day massacre in 1929 in Chicago. He vanished afterwards.

BUSTER FROM CHICAGO. Gunman whose real identity was never known to Joe Valachi. He was responsible for the death of Peter Morello and his bodyguard in New York in 1930. He was described as young looking, and carried his gun in a violin case. He was also known to have been a gunman in several other killings.

CALABRIESE, Joseph (Little Joe). Chicago gangster. He was a collector for the Genna brothers and was shot dead in a revenge killing in 1925.

CAMPAGNA, Louis (Little New York). Chicago gangster. He was a gunman for Capone. In 1940 he was indicted for tax evasion, but released. In 1943 he was charged with extortion from the Hollywood movie industry, and jailed for ten years. In 1947 he and others on the same charge were paroled, in what Kefauver called a "shocking misuse of parole powers." He died of a heart attack in 1963, age 57.

AL CAPONE

CAMPAGNA, Tony. An independent purveyor of alky in Chicago. He was killed in 1925.

CANTELLOPS, Nelson. Puerto Rican dope peddler who operated in Manhattan. Sentenced to a five-year term on dope charges in 1959, he felt the organization should have protected him from this, and in revenge turned informer. He was very small fry, but his information led directly to the successful charges subsequently brought against many important men in the Bonanno and Lucchese families, including Joseph Valachi and Vito Genovese himself.

CAPEZIO, Anthony (Tough Tony). Chicago gangster who operated with Capone.

CAPONE, Alphonse (Scarface). Born in New York in 1899. He joined the Five Points Gang in New York in 1915. One of Chicago's gang leaders, Johnny Torrio, invited Al to join him there in 1919, and by degrees he became the big boss of Chicago, eliminating all opposition by terror, murder, extortion or any other means. He also gained immense political influence, and was therefore able to escape every sort of legal charge. In 1922 he was elected a deputy sheriff of Cook County. He was finally jailed for tax evasion in 1931, and sentenced to 11 years. He died of a brain hemorrhage in Miami in 1947, the result of untreated tertiary syphilis.

CAPONE, Frank. Brother of Al. He worked for his brother and was killed in an election fight with the police in 1924.

CAPONE, Louis. No relation to Al, he was active much later in New York. He owned a coffee shop where many prominent gang bosses used to meet. He encouraged youngsters to come there to meet the bosses, and perhaps emulate them. His proteges included Kid Twist Reles, Pittsburgh Phil and Dasher Abbandando. He was appointed liaison man between the Brownsville and Ocean Hill gangs in 1931. He was convicted of the murder of Joseph Rosen in 1941 and executed in 1944.

CAPONE, Ralph (Bottles). Older brother of Al. He was treasurer

LOUIS CAPONE

for the Capone mob, and later led it when Al was jailed. Ralph himself was jailed on tax charges in 1924 and again in 1929. He was named as a Chicago gang leader in the Kefauver Report. He died of natural causes.

CAPUZZI, Nick (The Thief). New York gangster. He operated with the mob on Joe (the Boss) Masseria's side in the Castellammarese War.

CARBO, Frankie. He was charged with implication in the murder of Harry Greenberg in 1938 but got off. He became known as a fight promoter in the 1940s.

CARFANO, Anthony (Little Augie Pisano). New York gangster and union racketeer. He was one of the bosses of the gang while Lucky Luciano was in prison from 1936. In 1941 he was one of the partners in the Miami Wofford Hotel operation. He was shot dead in his car in 1958, together with his girlfriend, a former Miss New Jersey.

CARUSO, Angelo. He was a lifelong aide to Joseph Bonanno, and also closely associated with Salvatore Maranzano. He strongly supported Bill Bonanno as his father's successor in 1962.

CASSESE, Vincent. A soldier in the Bonanno family. He was wounded in the Banana War in 1967.

CATALANO, Julie. Brooklyn gangster and member of Murder, Inc. He testified before the Turkus commission in 1940.

CATANIA, Joseph (Joe the Baker). New York gangster. He was a Masseria aide in the Castellammarese War, and was shot dead as he kissed his wife good-bye one morning in 1931.

CATENA, Gerardo (Jerry). New York gangster. He was one of Vito Genovese's successors in 1969. At 68 years of age he was jailed for an indefinite period for refusing to answer questions about organized crime.

JOE COLOMBO

CIVELLO, James. Dallas gang boss. He was taken into custody at the Apalachin meeting in 1957.

CLARK, James (Car). Chicago gangster. He was Bugs Moran's brother-in-law and chief bodyguard, and was killed in the St. Valentine's Day massacre in 1929.

CLEMENTS, Hilary. Chicago gangster and gunman in the Sheldon gang. He was shot dead in 1926, his death being the first to break the 70-day armistice imposed by Capone after Hymie Weiss's death.

COHEN, Lou. New York gangster and gunman for Li'l Augie Orgen. He was charged with the murder of Kid Dropper in 1925 and jailed. Soon after his release in 1939 he was killed by Lepke Buchalter's men.

COHEN, Mickey (The Louse). Cleveland gangster and gambler. He worked with gangs in Los Angeles, and survived five assassination attempts. He was jailed in Texas on drug charges.

COHEN, Sam. He was a founder-partner in 1944 of the S&G bookmaking syndicate in Miami.

COLOMBO, Anthony. Son of Joseph. In 1970 he was accused of melting silver coins by the FBI, but the charge was dropped when the chief witness said he had been bribed by that organization. He was an enthusiastic supporter of his father's ideas and vice-president of his father's Italian-American Civil Rights League.

COLOMBO, Joseph. Boss of a New York family. He took over Profaci's old gang from Joseph Magliocco and organized peace after the Gallo brothers' revolt in 1960. He was a leading member of the commission, and present at the 1966 gang meeting in the La Stella Restaurant in Queens. In 1970, charges of tax evasion and contempt were dropped. Also in 1970 he started the Italian-American Civil Rights League.

JIM COLOSIMO

He organized protests in New York against "slurs" on Italian-Americans. He also appeared on TV. He was shot and crippled by a black gunman at a rally in 1971. This was possibly arranged by Gambino and other members of the commission, who disapproved of all the publicity.

COLOSIMO, James (Big Jim). Early Chicago gang boss in prostitution and protection rackets. He appointed both Johnny Torrio, his nephew, and Al Capone as his lieutenants. He was shot dead in his own restaurant in 1920, and Torrio was suspected of arranging the murder. He was given a lavish funeral.

CONLON, Frank. Chicago gangster. He was killed in 1926.

CONSOLO, Mike. New York gangster. He was one of Joseph Bonanno's lieutenants, but later worked for DiGregorio. In 1968 he was killed by DiGregorio men who may have thought he meant to switch again.

COPPOLA, Mike (Trigger). New York gangster. He was one of Lucky Luciano's mob who shared the leadership when Lucky was in jail in 1936.

CORALLO, Antonio (Tony Ducks). A member of Thomas Lucchese's organization. He was implicated in a New York scandal in 1967, involving the misappropriation of funds in a contract for a city reservoir.

COSMANO, Sunny Jim. A Chicago gangster who ran the Black Hand in the early 1900s.

COSTELLO, Frank (Francesco Castiglia). New York racketeer. He fought on the Masseria side in the Castellammarese War and gained considerable political influence as a diplomat and peacemaker. In 1929, after the St. Valentine's Day massacre, he attended a conference of fifty national gang bosses in Atlantic City. While Vito Genovese was in exile, Costello was acting boss of the Luciano family, and on Genovese's return to the United States in 1945, there was a great deal of

FRANK COSTELLO

friction. He was summoned to give evidence before the Kefauver Committee in 1951 and was jailed 18 months for contempt. Further charges of tax evasion were squashed until 1956, when he was sentenced on tax charges, and released on appeal after a year in jail. An unsuccessful attempt was made on his life by Vincent (the Chin) Gigante, one of Genovese's men, in 1957. He was denaturalized and deported to Italy, and died there of natural causes in February 1973, aged 70.

COUGHLIN, John (The Bathhouse). Alderman of a Chicago ward in the early 1900s, voted in largely on Jim Colosimo's influence. He was a great reader and writer of poetry.

CRUTCHFIELD, William. Negro porter in Don O'Bannion's flower shop who witnessed O'Bannion's murder.

CUTTY, Tommy. Gangster who operated gambling rackets for the Cleveland mob in Nevada and Florida.

DALITZ, Moe (alias Davis). Member of a Cleveland gambling syndicate. He was named in the Kefauver Report.

D'ANDREA, Anthony. One of three brothers (see below). Italian immigrant. He was a lawyer, and also a bank robber and counterfeiter, and was alleged to have been a defrocked priest. He ran for aldermanic election in Chicago in 1916, his candidacy being supported by guns. In 1919, he ran for the Democratic nomination, and again in 1921, he ran for alderman. There were gunfights and bombs at all these elections, but he was never elected to office. When he was shot dead in 1921, 8,000 mourners attended his funeral.

D'ANDREA, Joseph (Joey). He was a forger and a Chicago gang boss. He became president of the Sewer Diggers & Tunnel Miners' Union, and was killed in a labor dispute.

D'ANDREA, Phil. Gunman. He was Capone's financial manager. He became president of the Unione Siciliano.

DE AMATO, James. Chicago racketeer. He acted as spy for Al

377

LEGS DIAMOND

Capone who sent him to get information on New York liquor hijacking. He was shot dead in 1927.

De CARLO, Angelo (The Gyp). New Jersey gang boss. He was charged with extortion in 1970 and jailed for two years.

DeCAVALCANTE, Simone Rizzo (Sam the Plumber). Mafia boss in New Jersey, and member of the commission, for whom he served as go-between with different factions in the Banana War. His offices were bugged by the FBI, and his conversations with Mafia mates in 1964-65 formed a 2,300-page log, which the FBI gave national circulation. He was charged with conspiracy and enforcement in 1969, and received a 15-year sentence.

DECKMAN, Alfred. Chicago bootlegger. He was shot dead in 1924. Walter O'Donnell was charged with his murder, but acquitted.

DEFEO, George. Gangster and gunman for Kid Twist Reles. He was shot dead in an ambush by the Shapiro brothers, in 1930.

DEJOHN, Nick. Chicago and San Francisco racketeer. He was found garrotted in 1950.

DE LAURENTIS, Frank. Chicago bootlegger who worked with the Sheldon gang. He became too independent, and when he seemed to threaten McErlane in 1926, he was killed.

DE LUCA, Joe and Frank. Members of the Mafia in Kansas City. They were named in the Kefauver Report.

DeQUATRO, Dominick (Dom the Sailor). New York gangster. One of Lucky Luciano's men, he shared the leadership when Luciano was jailed in 1936.

DeSIMONE, Frank. Californian gang boss. He was taken into custody at the Apalachin gang meeting in 1957.

DIAMOND, Eddie and Legs. Gunmen and beer hijackers. Legs

JOHNNY DIO

was a New York stickup man and labor racketeer. He was killed in 1934 trying to muscle in on mob rackets.

DIAMOND, Frank (Maritote). Gangster and extortionist in Chicago. He was a gunman for Al Capone and was said to be implicated in the killing of McSwiggin.

Di ANGELO, Thomas and James. New York gangsters. They were DiGregorio aides, and were both shot dead while dining out in 1967. Their deaths were reprisal shootings in the Banana War. They both had defected earlier from the Bonanno forces.

DI CARLO, Joseph. Cleveland gangster. He was named in the Kefauver Report.

DICKMAN, William. Chicago bootlegger. He was a member of the Saltis-McErlane gang. He was with George (Big Bates) Karl when Karl was killed in 1925. Dickman was then killed for knowing too much.

DI GIOVANNO, Pete and Joseph. Members of the Kansas City Mafia. They were both named in the Kefauver Report.

DI GREGORIO, Gasperino (Gasper). Born 1905 in Castellammare del Golfo, Sicily, and closely associated with Joseph Bonanno. He was also Stefano Magaddino's brother-in-law. He was a New York gang leader, and owned garment factories. On the disappearance of Joseph Bonanno in 1964, he took over the family in opposition to Bonanno's wishes that his son Salvatore (Bill) should succeed him. This started the Banana War. His followers and Salvatore's had a gun battle on Troutman Street in Brooklyn in 1966, but there were no casualties. In 1966 Joseph came out of hiding and reclaimed the leadership. DiGregorio was already ailing, and when summoned to give evidence before a New York grand jury, he suffered a heart attack. He was deposed from his seat on the National Commission.

DIOGUARDI, John (Johnny Dio). Gangster. He was in jail with Joe Valachi in 1962.

VINCENT DRUCCI

DIPALERMO, Joseph (Joe Beck). Gangster. He also was in jail with Joe Valachi in 1962.

DOHERTY, James. Chicago gangster. One of Torrio's gunmen. He was one of Eddie Tancl's killers. In 1926, he was shot dead while with Assistant District Attorney McSwiggin.

DRAGNA, Jack (alias Antonio Rizzoti). Sicilian. Los Angeles gangster. He was known as the "Al Capone of Los Angeles." He testified before the Kefauver Committee in 1951 and denied all knowledge of the Mafia.

DROPPER, Kid. New York gangster. When he tried to extend his operations beyond his bit of Manhattan in 1925, he was killed by Lou Cohen, one of Li'l Augie Orgen's gunmen.

DRUCCI, Vincent (The Schemer). Chicago gangster. He was a gunman in the Bugs Moran-Weiss gang. He gunned down Angelo Genna and Amatuna in 1926. He was wounded in one gang fight, but emerged from many others unscathed. He was shot dead by a policeman while being arrested during the elections of 1927.

DRUGGAN, Terry. Irish. Chicago hoodlum who became a gang leader. He was associated with Frank Lake in the beer wars. He amassed a large fortune, and eventually retired to New York State. At one time he rivaled Al Capone as boss. He died of natural causes in 1950.

DUFFY, Thomas (The Goat). Chicago gangster. He was a Colosimo henchman. He was charged with killing Isaac Hengow, a police stool pigeon, but got off. In 1926 he was killed while with Assistant District Attorney McSwiggin.

EASTMAN, Monk. New York hoodlum who acted as "heavy" for loan shark Arnold Rothstein.

EBOLI, Thomas (Tommy Ryan). New York gangster. A former prizefighter, while Vito Genovese was in prison in 1959, he became acting boss of the family. He was present at the

JACK DRAGNA

meeting of gang bosses in Long Island in 1965, and again at the La Stella meeting in 1966 in Queens. He was shot dead in 1972.

EISEN, Maxie. Chicago gangster. He was associated with the Saltis-McErlane gang and represented them at Capone's peace talks in Chicago in 1926.

ELLISON, James (Biff). Irish. He was a member of the Five Points Gang of New York in the early 1900s.

ENRIGHT, Maurice (Mossy). He was a pioneer in the Chicago labor rackets, and was killed in 1920.

ERICKSON, Frank. Gang leader in Florida. He operated booze and gambling rackets in association with Frank Costello.

ESPOSITO, Diamond Joe. Italian. Gangster and labor racketeer. He ran Esposito's Bella Napoli Café in Chicago (where Al Capone liked to go for his spaghetti) until 1920, but later became a powerful gang leader in Illinois. He exercised considerable power in the Unione Siciliano, and with Mike Merlo, held feuding gangsters in some restraint whenever possible. He achieved political power and influence. Although surrounded by his own bodyguards, he was shot dead with garlic-poisoned slugs in Chicago's 1928 "pineapple election," so called because of all the bombs thrown.

EVOLA, Natale. Friend and associate of Joseph Bonanno, he was an usher at the Bonanno wedding.

FANELLI, Rocco. Chicago gangster. He was a gunman for Al Capone. He was one of the suspects arrested after the St. Valentine's Day massacre in 1929, and also appeared on the list of public enemies in 1923.

FARAH, Mike and John. Owners of a gambling operation in Ohio.

FARVEL, "Little." Brooklyn gangster and gunman, he associated with Lepke Buchalter and others in the murder of

ROCCO FISCHETTI

Joseph Rosen in 1936, but escaped conviction. He was jailed for eight years on narcotics offenses. On his release he tried to start his own protection racket, and was found shot dead in 1949.

FEINSTEIN, Irving (Puggy). New York gangster and gambler. He crossed Albert Anastasia in some way, and Albert gave out the contract for his death in 1940. It was a particularly brutal and cold-blooded murder, for which both Happy Maione and Dasher Abbandando were executed.

FERACO, Jimmy (Dizzy). Brooklyn gangster. He was wanted for murder but was killed by the gangs between 1940 and 1941.

FERRIGNO, Steven (Fennuci). New York gangster. He was one of Joe the Boss Masseria's lieutenants, and was killed in an ambush by Joe Valachi and his mob in 1930.

FERRO, Vito Cascio. Sicilian. He emigrated to the United States as a young man and joined the Black Hand. Later he returned to Sicily and for many years was undisputed and much respected Don of the island Mafia. Although he adhered rigidly to ancient Mafia rituals, he was a reformer and quite progressive. He flew in the first hot-air balloon over Sicily. Even in prison he organized an extensive welfare system. He undoubtedly committed numerous crimes, but was never brought to trial until eventually Prefect Mori had to resort to a trumped-up charge of smuggling to get him into court, in 1920. Don Vito had only this to say at the trial: "Gentlemen, as you have been unable to obtain proof of any of my numerous crimes, you have been reduced to condemning me for the only one I have never committed." He died of heart failure soon after starting his prison sentence. He admitted one killing, that of Joseph Petrosino.

FINALLI, Tony. Chicago gangster. He was a collector for the Anselmi-Scalise gang funds. He was killed in 1926 in revenge for the deaths of Henry Spingola and Antonio and Augustino Moreci.

CARLO GAMBINO

FINCH, Homer. Chicago gangster and roadhouse owner. He was killed by the O'Donnell gang in 1924.

FISCHETTI, Rocco, Joseph and Charles. Cousins of Al Capone and lieutenants in his Chicago gang. They were gunmen and gamblers. Charles was implicated in the murder of a policeman. He died of a heart attack in 1951 while he and Rocco were in custody. Rocco and Joseph were subpoenaed by the Kefauver Committee, but fled to Brazil.

FITZPATRICK, Mac. Chicago gangster of the early days. He was a triggerman for Johnny Torrio.

FLORIO, Jimmy. New York gangster. He was accused with Albert Anastasia of killing longshoreman Joe Turino in 1925, but although convicted, the case was later retried and then dismissed.

FOLEY, John (Mitters). Chicago bootlegger. He was much involved in gang killings in the beer wars, and was a member of the Sheldon gang. He was eliminated in 1926 in a revenge killing by the Saltis gang.

FORLANO, Nicholas (Jiggs). New York gangster. He was in the Gallo gang, but switched to Profaci during the gang feud.

FRANSE, Steve. New York gangster. He was deputized by Vito Genovese to look after the nightclubs run by Anna Genovese, but didn't do it well enough, so he was choked to death by Genovese henchmen in 1953.

FRANZESE, John (Sonny). An officer in the Profaci organization. Much was known about his activities, as the FBI had been able to install a bugging system in his Long Island home during its construction.

FRESINA, Carmelo. Sicilian. Chicago gangster. He was once shot in the buttock and always carried a pillow to sit on, so his gang became known as the Pillow gang. He was eventually shot in the head.

JOEY GALLO

FRIEDMAN, Charles. He was a founder-partner in 1944 of the S&G bookmaking syndicate in Miami, and was subpoenaed to testify before the Kefauver Committee in Chicago in 1950.

FUCA, Patsy. Brooklyn gangster. He was a henchman of Little Angie Tuminaro. He was convicted on narcotics charges after the "French Connection" smuggling case.

FUSCO, Joseph Charles (Joe). He graduated from driving bootleg liquor in Chicago for Al Capone to managing a large legitimate wholesale liquor business, and gave evidence before the Kefauver Committee in 1950. Ten days later his warehouse was bombed.

GAGLIANO, Gaetano (Joseph). New York hoodlum. Although not from Castellammare del Golfo, he was Maranzano's deputy in the Castellammarese War. He preferred to be thought a peacemaker, and recruited unknown gunmen to do his killings, but was nevertheless responsible for the assassination of Joseph Pinzola and many others. He was appointed boss by Maranzano, and rewarded for his services with a five-day fund-raising banquet. He died of natural causes in 1953.

GALANTE, Carmine. Top aide of Joseph Bonanno. Against the boss's express orders he got involved in narcotics deals, was caught, and sentenced to 20 years.

GALLO, Albert, Lawrence and Joey. Soldiers in the Cosa Nostra organization of New York. They were racketeers in labor and enforcement. During the 1960s they led a revolt against the boss, Albert Profaci, during which many were killed. In 1961 the brothers kidnaped Joseph Magliocco and three other Profaci men, demanding bigger shares in rackets as the ransom. Joey was killed in April 1972.

GAMBINO, Carlo. New York gangster. He fought on the Masseria side in the Castellammarese War. He became boss of a New York family, and was present at the La Stella, New

ANGELO GENNA

York meeting in 1966. During the 1970s he has been suspected of complicity in many Mafia assassinations in a bid to remain the boss, although he is already over 70 years old.

GAMBINO, Emanuel. Nephew of Carlo. He was found dead in New Jersey in 1973.

GARGOTTA, Charlie. Gangster. He was one of the "Five Iron Men" of Kansas City named in the Kefauver Report. He escaped a murder charge, committed before witnesses, because he was able to bribe police to confuse the bullets. He had been a henchman of Charlie Binaggio, and both were killed in 1948.

GAROFALO, Frank. Sicilian, born in Castellammare del Golfo. He was an officer in the Bonanno New York gang, and also a business manager in legitimate business. He left the United States for Sicily in 1957, and died of natural causes there.

GENARO, John. Chicago gangster. He was one of Capone's gunmen, and had convictions for robbery. In 1931 he was killed in typical gangland style—gunned down from a moving car.

GENERO, Joseph (Peppy). Chicago gangster. He was listed as a public enemy in 1926.

GENNA, Angelo, Michael (Mike), Tony (the Gentleman), Sam, Peter and Jim. Sicilian family. They were some of Chicago's leading gangsters, known as the "Terrible Gennas." They settled in the United States in 1910, and were allied to the Torrio-Capone factions. They were also powerful in the Unione Siciliano. Five of the brothers were particularly brutal, but Tony (the Gentleman) was never known to kill. He educated himself, and acted only in an advisory capacity in the family conflicts. The family ran a $5,000,000 business in thousands of tenement distilleries. They were identified as killers in many instances, in particular in the aldermanic wars, but had sufficient influence to give them complete immunity from the law. The family had a long and

SAM GIANCANA

bitter feud with the O'Bannion gang, but this was finally resolved by Capone's henchmen in 1926, after which the family power was also lost. In that year Angelo was shot dead in May, Mike was shot in a fight with police in June (though he lived long enough to kick the ambulance attendant in the face before dying), and Tony was ambushed and shot dead. Sam and Pete went into hiding and Jim fled back to Sicily, where he was jailed for five years.

GENOVESE, Vito. Sicilian. Boss of a powerful New York Mafia family. He had been prominent in the Castellammarese Wars in 1930 and arranged the killing of Maranzano in 1931. He had to flee the country in 1934 to avoid a murder charge, but returned in 1945 to New York. In 1959 he was jailed for 15 years for narcotics offenses. He continued to exert a strong influence from jail, though Thomas Eboli was acting boss in his absence. He was a leading member of the commission an old-style boss, living very simply, although he was a millionaire. He died of heart disease in 1969, while still in prison.

GENTILE, Nicole. Sicilian. He was a New York racketeer in narcotics, and an agent for the International Mafia. In 1937 he jumped bail and fled back to Sicily.

GENTLEMEN, Peter. He was the son of a policeman, but he turned gunman in Chicago, and was killed by Walter Stevens in the beer wars.

GIANCANA, Salvatore (Sam Mooney). Chicago racketeer. He was boss of the laundry syndicate in the 1950s. He refused to testify before a grand jury in 1954. In 1962 he became a member of the National Commission, and was at the Long Island meeting of gangsters in 1965. He is now retired.

GIANNINI, Eugenio. Gangster. He worked for Lucchese, but was later suspected of informing to the Federal Bureau of Narcotics. He was killed on orders from Vito Genovese in 1953.

GIESEY, Alvin E. Agent for the Internal Revenue Service who, in

CHARLIE GIOE

1933, quit the service and set up his own tax advice office. His clients included the Polizzis, Morris Kleinman, and many other known gambling racketeers.

GIGANTE, Vincent (the Chin). New York hood and gunman. He was hired to kill Costello in 1957, but missed.

GIOE, Charles (Cherry Nose). Chicago gangster, and member of the syndicate. He was found guilty of extorting money from the Hollywood film industry in 1943, and given a ten-year sentence. He was paroled in 1947, with others on the same charge, in what Senator Kefauver called "a shocking misuse of parole powers." He was shot dead in 1954.

GIORELLI, Joseph. New York gangster and aide of the Gallo gang. He disappeared permanently during the Gallo-Profaci war in 1962.

GIUNTA, Joseph (Hop Toad). Sicilian, born 1907. He was a gunman and a persuader. He loved dancing, which game him his nickname, and was a very slick dresser. He was one of John Scalise's aides, and so was killed with him and Albert Anselmi in a ritual Sicilian dinner-party murder arranged by Al Capone in 1929.

GIZZO, Tony. He was a member of the Mafia in Kansas City, and was named in the Kefauver Report as one of the "Five Iron Men" of Kansas City.

GIUNTA, Joseph (Hop Toad). Sicilian, born 1907. He was a gunman and a persuader. He loved dancing, which gave him his nickname, and was a very slick dresser. He was one of John Scalise's aides, and so was killed with him and Albert Anselmi in a ritual Sicilian dinner-party murder arranged by Al Capone in 1929.

GOLDSTEIN, Buggsy. Gangster in Brooklyn. He was one of Kid Twist Reles's aides and was wounded by the Shapiro gang. Later he joined Reles and Pittsburgh Phil in the takeover of homicide and protection rackets in Brownsville and East New York.

WAXEY GORDON

GOLDSTEIN, Bunny. Chicago hoodlum. He was associated with Sam Amatuna, and was killed shortly after Sam in 1925—probably by the same killers who may have feared vengeance.

GORDON, Waxey. New York gang leader, he was associated with Jake Shapiro in the 1920s. He was a bootlegger and specialized in raiding government liquor held for those with medical liquor permits. He was on Masseria's side in the Castellammarese War. After 1951, when he was given a long jail sentence for dope offenses he faded out.

GRABINER, Joseph (Jew Kid). Chicago gang boss. He owned brothels and gaming houses.

GREENBERG, Alec Louis. Gangster. He was Capone's accountant and was shot dead in a Chicago café in 1955.

GREENBERG, Harry (Big Greenie). Gangster who was at one time associated with Lepke Buchalter. Bugsy Siegel contracted to kill him in 1938 for Lepke, when he came under suspicion of being an informer.

GUILFOYLE, Martin. Chicago gangster. He was a partner in a syndicate with Al Winge and Matt Kolb, running a very profitable bootlegging racket, which he kept intact against rivals with guns, and finally, in 1927, with a well aimed bomb on the rival headquarters on Milwaukee Avenue. He was replaced as boss in 1931.

GURINO, Vito. Gangster who operated in Brooklyn in the 1920s. He was associated with Kid Twist Reles in the takeover of the Shapiro gang in 1930-31. He was an expert shot and kept in practice shooting off chickens' heads as they ran round the yard. He owned bakeries and was influential in the bakers' union.

GUSENBERG, Frank and Pete. Chicago gunmen in Bugs Moran's gang, they were both killed in the St. Valentine's Day massacre, 1929.

JAKE GUZIK

GUZIK, Jake (Greasy Thumb). Born 1886. He was a Chicago bootlegger with interests in prostitution, one of Al Capone's lieutenants, and was in charge of payoffs for Capone, hence his nickname. Capone valued his services so highly that he had permanent guards stationed at his hospital bedside when he was ill in 1924. He had a long run. He was already active in 1916, and still going strong when the Kefauver Committee investigated crime in 1950. In 1930 he was jailed for five years for tax evasion. He died in bed of natural causes in 1956.

GYP THE BLOOD. New York hoodlum called in to kill Herman Rosenthal in 1912.

HASMILLER, Henry (Harry). New York gunman. He was hired by the Chicago South Side O'Donnell gang during the beer wars. He was shot dead in 1924.

HEITLER, Michael (Mike the Pike). Chicago gangster, gunman and extortionist of the early 1900s. He was a "levee king," twice sentenced for white-slave trafficking. He became one of Johnny Torrio's captains.

HEYER, Adam. Chicago gangster, he was associated with Bugs Moran and owned the garage where the St. Valentine's Day massacre took place in 1929, in which he was killed.

HOFF, Max. Philadelphia gang leader. He attended the Mafia meeting in Atlantic City.

HOLTZ, Curly. New York gangster. He was a lieutenant in Li'l Augie Orgen's gang.

HOWARD, Joseph. He was an unattached Chicago hoodlum who beat up Jake Guzik in 1923. He also hijacked Capone beer trucks. He was shot dead by Al Capone in 1923.

HRUBEC, Charles (Big Hayes). Chicago gangster. He was killed in 1927.

HUMPHRIES, Murray (The Camel). Chicago gangster and gambler. He tried to oppose Al Capone as Big Boss in the 1930s, but later came to terms with him. In 1940 he was head of the Chicago syndicate's labor rackets and in that year was indicted on charges of conspiracy.

HUNT, Sam (Golf Bag). Chicago gangster. He was a gunman for Al Capone, and later became his financial secretary. He gained his nickname after once being arrested with a shotgun hidden in the golf bag he was carrying. He died of natural causes in 1955.

IDA, Joseph. Gang boss of Philadelphia. He was taken into custody at Apalachin in 1957.

IMPOSTATO, Nicolo. Chicago gangster. He went to Kansas City in 1929 to work for John Lazia, and was killed.

JOHNSON, Enoch J. (Nucky). Atlantic City gang leader. He was a numbers racketeer, and attended the Atlantic City Mafia meeting.

JOHNSON, Jerome A. The gunman who wounded Joseph Colombo at an Italian-American Unity Day Rally in New York in 1971. He was immediately shot dead by an unknown gunman, and little has ever been learned about his background.

JONES, Paul. Dallas hoodlum. Conversations taped by the police were heard at the Kefauver Committee inquiry in 1950, in which he was negotiating for protection for Al Capone's syndicate in Texas.

KARL, George (Big Bates.) Chicago bootlegger. He was a member of the Saltis-McErlane gang, but in 1925 he was killed by them for the money he carried.

KASTEL, Philip (Dandy). Member of the New Orleans Mafia. He was overseer of slot machines there for Frank Costello.

KEANE, Thomas (Morris). Chicago gangster. He was a driver for various bootlegging gangs. He was killed in 1923 in a "take 'em for a ride" murder.

KELLY, Paul (Paolo Antonini Vaccarelli). Italian. He was a leader of the New York Five Points gang in the early 1900s.

KENNA, Michael (Hinky Dink). Alderman of a Chicago ward in early 1900s. He was voted into office largely on rigged votes and was chief fix-it man for Jim Colosimo.

KILMAS, Leo. Waiter in Eddie Tancl's Hawthorne Inn in Chicago. He was killed by O'Donnell gunmen in the same attack as Tancl in 1924.

KLEIN, Morris (Snag). Kansas City gangster and gambler. He gave evidence before the Kefauver Committee in 1950.

KLEINMAN, Morris. Gambling racketeer whose influence started in the 1920s in Cleveland, where he was a member of the syndicate. He was named in the Kefauver Report.

KOLB, Matt. Gangster and bootlegger in Chicago. He was a Capone man at first, but in 1926 he became a partner with Roger (Terrible) Touhy in a very successful enterprise in Cook County. Capone had him kidnaped in 1931, in a campaign to enforce cooperation from the Touhy-Kolb gang. A ransom was paid, he was released, and then killed by Capone's men.

KONCIL, Lefty, Chicago gangster. He was killed in 1927.

KONIGSBERG, Harold (Kayo). Loan shark who operated in New Jersey. He was jailed in 1966.

LABRUZZO, Frank. Sicilian. In the early 1920s he was a New York hoodlum. He was a brother-in-law of Joseph Bonanno, who named him as leader of his gang when Bonanno went into hiding. The National Commission would not accept his nomination as leader. He died of cancer in 1968.

MEYER LANSKY

LA FONTAINE, Jimmy. Gambling club operator in Washington. He was kidnaped by Philadelphia hoods in 1932, and forced to pay $100,000 for his release.

LAKE, Frank. Irish. He was a Chicago gang leader associated with Terry Druggan. He started as a fireman, became an operator in the beer wars, then a brewery owner, and ended up a millionaire racehorse owner. He had once been in charge of Chicago's pickpockets, but his only conviction was for contempt, for which he was sentenced to one year.

LANSKY, Meyer and Jake. Russian immigrants. New York gangsters. They were active in the beer wars, and in the 1934 "treaty" were assigned territory in Florida. Owing to his outstanding ability as an organizer, and loyalty to Vito Genovese and others, Meyer was at one time the only non-Italian/Sicilian member allowed in the Cosa Nostra.

LANZA, Joseph (Socks). A labor hoodlum. In 1942 he cooperated with the government in preventing wartime sabotage and keeping the Manhattan piers operational.

LAPIPARO, Tony. Mafia chief in St. Louis. He operated in narcotics.

LARASSO, Louis. A minor Mafia member who obtained some prominence in 1965 when some of his conversations with other Mafiosi were taped by the FBI.

LaTEMPA, Peter. Brooklyn gangster and racketeer. He was prepared to testify against Vito Genovese about the murder of Ferdinand Boccia, and in 1945, when Vito Genovese was about to return to the States from Sicily, sought police protection in jail. His sanctuary proved unsuccessful. On arriving in jail he took some of his usual stomach pills and fell dead from poisoning.

LATTYAK, Ed. Chicago gangster and bootlegger. He was a member of the Sheldon gang, and was killed in 1925.

LUCKY LUCIANO

LAVENUTO, Sam. Chicago gangster. He was an independent alky producer who operated in Capone territory. He was killed in 1925.

LAZAR, Sam. Philadelphia gang leader. He attended the Mafia meeting in Atlantic City in 1929.

LEATHERS, Bill. Chicago gunman who operated for Dion O'Bannion.

LECICERO, Charles. New York gangster. He was a Colombo man, and was killed in 1966.

LEFTY LOUIE. New York hoodlum called in by Charles Becker to kill Herman Rosenthal in 1912.

LEVINE, Sam (Pretty, Red). Brooklyn gangster and gun for hire. He was arrested in 1940 and joined with Kid Twist Reles and others then in jail in giving information about gang affairs.

LEVITT, Jules. He was a founder-partner in 1944 of the S&G bookmaking syndicate in Miami, and was subpoenaed to testify before the Kefauver Committee in Washington in 1950.

LIBERITO, Joe (The Baker). Gangster who operated in association with Lepke Buchalter. He eventually turned state's evidence along with Kid Twist Reles and others.

LICAVOLI, Peter. Gangster with interests in Detroit and Tucson. He was a close friend of Joseph Bonanno. His son and Joseph Bonanno, Jr. were charged with car theft together in 1967. His ranch in Tucson was damaged by a bomb blast in 1968.

LIVORSI, Frank. New York gangster. He started the Castellammarese War on Masseria's side, but later switched to Maranzano, and was implicated in Masseria's killing in 1931.

LOCOCO, Tano. He was one of the Five Iron Men of Kansas City named in the Kefauver Report.

JOE MAGLIOCCO

LOLORDO, Joseph. Sicilian. He was thought to have been one of the killers in the St. Valentine's Day massacre in 1929. He was said to have operated the tommy gun, and to have regarded the massacre as revenge for the death of his brother Pasquale the previous month.

LOLORDO, Pasquale (Patsy). Sicilian. Chicago gangster. He represented Al Capone at the National Crime Syndicate in Cleveland, and in 1928, under Capone's auspices, he was voted president of the Unione Siciliano. He was killed with Sicilian ritual by the Aiello brothers in January 1929. They wined and dined him generously, and on the toast ''Here's to Pasqualino,'' gunned him down.

LOMBARDO, Antonio (Tony). Italian. He immigrated to the United States in 1906, and became a Chicago racketeer and gang leader, Al Capone used him as mediator at the gangster treaty of 1926. He became president of the Unione Siciliano in 1927, under Capone's patronage. Although he had accrued considerable influence, he was gunned down in the street in 1928.

LUCCHESE, Thomas Gaetano (Three-Finger Brown). He succeeded Gaetano Gagliano, on his death in 1953, as boss of a New York family. He died in 1967 after a long illness.

LUCIANO, Charles (Lucky). (Salvatore Luciana) Born in Naples, he came to the United States and was a member of the Five Points gang in New York, and also prominent in prostitution and heroin smuggling. He helped to organize the National Crime Syndicate with Al Capone in 1929, at meetings held in Atlantic City. He started the Castellammarese War as chief aide to Masseria, then plotted Masseria's murder with Maranzano's regime, and hired assassins to shoot him dead in 1931. He set up the five-boss network to control New York, and to do away with a boss of bosses. In 1936 he was jailed by Thomas E. Dewey, and was serving his sentence in World War II when the U.S. War Department enlisted his help to prevent war sabotage on the New York docks. He organized this war work from his cell. In 1946 he

STEFANO MAGADDINO

was deported to Italy. While in exile he kept his hand in, smuggling dope to the United States from the Mediterranean area. He died in his bed some 20 years later.

LUPO, Joseph (The Wolf) (alias Ignazio Saietta). New York gang leader and hired gunman. He was charged so often with murder that he claimed he was being "hounded" by the police. He was given a sentence of 30 years on a counterfeiting charge in 1925.

MADDEN, Owney. Thug and onetime pal of Al Capone, he was a New York bootlegger who was later transferred to Hot Springs, Arkansas, to run mob-controlled gambling casinos.

MADDOX, Claude (Screwy). He was a syndicate boss in Cicero, and an executive for Al Capone. He also owned gambling houses. He died of natural causes in 1958.

MAFFATORE, Dukey. Gangster who operated widely in Brooklyn and was associated with Kid Twist Reles, and arrested with him in 1940. He also turned informer.

MAGADDINO, Gaspare. Brother of Peter. He was suspected of a triple murder in 1967, for which he would have been hired especially and brought over from Sicily. He was found shot dead in Brooklyn in 1968.

MAGADDINO, Peter. Born in 1902, in Castellammare del Golfo, Sicily. He was Stefano Magaddino's nephew, and a boyhood friend of Joseph Bonanno. He was smuggled into the United States with Bonanno in 1924. He joined Magaddino's Buffalo gang, and later acted as Bonanno's bodyguard.

MAGADDINO, Stefano. Born 1891 in Castellammare del Golfo, Sicily. He was a Mafia boss in Buffalo and Ohio. He was involved in, and helped finance the Castellammarese War in 1929. He was DeGregorio's brother-in-law, and a cousin of Joseph Bonanno, but after the 1960s became Bonanno's enemy. He was an influential member of the National Commission, which he joined in 1962. In 1966, he was subpoenaed to appear before a government inquiry, but was

DAGO MANGANO

excused on the grounds of ill health. He died of heart disease in 1974.

MAGLIOCCO, Joseph (Giuseppe). Born in Sicily. He was Joseph Profaci's lieutenant, whom he succeeded as boss of the New York gang on Profaci's death in 1962. He married Profaci's sister. In 1960 he was kidnaped by members of the Gallo gang. In 1963 he became a member of the National Commission. He died of a heart attack shortly thereafter.

MAGOON, Blue Jaw. Mobster in Brooklyn in the 1930s. He was a huge, slow-moving, slow-talking, fearless man. He kept his hair close cropped, and his chin unshaved. He had been involved in two shootings by 1933, and many other felonies, and was soon affiliated with the gangs. He was used as the wheelman in many mob killings, and he and his partner, Bobby Burns, an ex-prizefighter, were strong-arm men in union rackets. He later turned informer about Murder, Inc.

MAIONE, Happy. Brooklyn gangster who operated loan and bookie rackets. He was associated with Dasher Abbandando, and later joined Kid Twist Reles in ousting the Shapiro brothers. He was executed in 1942 for the murder of Puggy Feinstein.

MAJURI, Frank. Gangster. He was a member of the Bonanno gang.

MANGANO, Lawrence (Dago Lawrence). Chicago gangster. His first recorded prosecution was in 1912 for pandering, after which he had a long record of charges and imprisonments for vice, gambling, larceny, etc. In 1923, he was listed by the Chicago Crime Commission as a public enemy. In 1928 he was implicated in the bombing of a policeman's house in Chicago. The incident took place after one of Mangano's establishments had been raided by the officer.

MANGANO, Vincent. Mafia boss in New York. He disappeared in 1951, and it was rumored that Albert Anastasia had him killed, then buried in the concrete foundations of a housing project.

BUGS MORAN

MANNO, Patrick, Tom (Mousey) and Nick (Jeff) (alias Manning). Chicago gangsters. They were numbers racketeers who ran the Roman Silver Wheel racket with Peter Tremont. They were all named in the Kefauver Report. Patrick was one of the policy makers in the Chicago syndicate.

MARANZANO, Salvatore. Born near Castellammarese del Golfo, Sicily. He was a Mafia boss in Sicily. Later, in the United States, he was one of the leaders in the Castellammarese War, 1928-31. He organized the Sicilian element versus the Italian. His death was plotted and effected by Luciano in 1931.

MARCELLO, Carlos (Little Big Man). Born in Africa of Sicilian parents. He was a New Orleans Mafia leader. He was one of a mob of gangsters with a great diversity of interests, hardly any of them legal. In 1938 he was convicted of peddling narcotics. In 1950 he was cited for contempt, after refusing to give evidence before the Kefauver Committee. He was present at the Mafia meeting at La Stella in 1966.

MARI, Frank. New York gangster. He left Joseph Bonanno's gang and joined DeGregorio, and was wounded in a gang fight in 1966, during the Banana War. He disappeared in 1967 and is presumed dead.

MARKS, Willie. Chicago gangster. He was Bugs Moran's lieutenant.

MARQUEZ, Raymond (Spanish Raymond). New York gambler. His father had been one of Vito Genovese's aides. In 1965 he was the boss of a Puerto Rican numbers game.

MASSERIA, Joseph (Joe the Boss). Italian. He had a long criminal record starting in 1907. He announced himself as boss of Italian rackets, and proceeded to make good the claim. His insistence on retaining domination over Brooklyn rackets led to the Castellammarese War in 1928-31, during which 60 or more soldiers died on both sides. At one time his army numbered about 600. He was eventually outmaneuvered by Salvatore Maranzano, who led the opposing faction, and two of his own top lieutenants, Lucky Luciano and Frank Costello, who changed their allegiance. They arranged his death in a Coney Island restaurant in 1931.

MAY, John. Chicago gangster. He was a professional safecracker and operated in the Bugs Moran gang. He was killed in the St. Valentine's Day massacre in 1929.

McBRIDE, Arthur B. Cleveland sportsman. He became a millionaire with real estate holdings, a football club, and taxi service, and in 1939 took over Continental Press from Moe Annenberg.

McCULLOUGH, Robert (Big Bob). Chicago gangster. He was implicated in the McSwiggin killing in 1926. He was questioned by the Kefauver Committee in 1950.

McERLANE, Frank. Chicago gangster. He was a bootlegger, and was accused of various killings in the beer wars, and suspected of even more. He operated a South Side Chicago gang with Polack Joe Saltis. He was in jail at the time of the peace talks in 1926, and died of pneumonia in 1932.

McFALL, Daniel. Chicago gunman. He was involved with four others in a shooting with Spike O'Donnell's gang in 1923. Jerry O'Connor was killed, and McFall was charged with murder, but acquitted due to a convenient mixup in the identification of the murder bullets.

McGINTY, Thomas J. Cleveland gangster and gambler who was named in the Kefauver Report.

McGOVERN, Hughey (Stubby). Chicago gangster. He was a small-time bootlegger. He followed Al Capone's lead and bought a house in Miami in 1929.

McGURN, Jack (Machine-gun) (James de Mora) Sicilian. Chicago gangster. His father, a sugar importer, was shot dead in front of him, in 1923. He was a professional boxer, but after seeing his father killed, he became one of Chicago's toughest gangsters. He was one of Capone's henchmen, and was implicated in the St. Valentine's Day massacre in 1929, but was acquitted of all charges concerning those killings after a long trial. He was one of the first gangsters to use a machine gun in mobster raids, and was credited with 22 murders. In 1930 he was jailed in Miami on gun charges. In 1936 he was shot dead in a bowling alley in Milwaukee.

MEEGHAN, George. Chicago bootlegger. He was a member of one of the O'Donnell gangs, and was killed in 1923.

MERCALDO, Joe. Brooklyn gangster and member of Murder, Inc.

MERLO, Mike, Sicilian. He was an influential gang leader in Illinois. He founded the Chicago Unione Siciliano in 1923, and was its president. Until his death from natural causes in 1924, he used his influence on many occasions to bring conflicts in the Chicago beer wars to more peaceful conclusions than when settled by guns.

MILANO, Jerry. Cleveland gangster. He was named in the Kefauver Report.

MILLER, Davy. Chicago gangster and gambler. He was a bootlegging associate of Torrio's and O'Bannion's, but he annoyed O'Bannion, who took a shot at him one night outside a theatre. Luckily the bullet hit his belt buckle and he was only wounded.

MILLER, Samuel (Gameboy). He was a member of the Cleveland gambling syndicate, and was named in the Kefauver Report.

MINEO, Alfred. New York gangster. He was one of Joe the Boss Masseria's lieutenants and was killed in an ambush by Joe Valachi and his mob in 1930.

MIRANDA, Mike. New York gangster. He was one of Vito Genovese's successors, in 1969. He was present at the La Stella meeting in 1966.

MONTANA, John. A gang boss of Buffalo. He was taken into custody at the Apalachin meeting of 1957.

MORALE, John. New York gang boss. He was second in command in the Bonanno gang in 1966.

MORAN, George (Bugs). Irish. Chicago gangster. He was a bootlegger, and had a long police record for robbery and other offenses. He was first jailed in 1910. After O'Bannion's death he became leader of the O'Bannion gang, and started hijacking Capone beer trucks. It was to stop this presumption that Capone ordered the extermination of Moran and his gang, which ended in the St. Valentine's Day massacre in 1929, which Moran himself managed to avoid. He died of lung cancer in 1957, while in prison.

MORELLO, Pete (Clutching Hand). New York gangster of the old-time "Mustache Pete" type, and Black Hander. He gained much respect from hoods associated with him over a long period of time. He was named by Masseria as boss at the beginning of the Castellammarese War in 1929. He was shot dead in his office in 1930 by a Maranzano hired gunman.

MORESCI, Joseph. Chicago gangster. He was a brother-in-law of big Jim Colosimo, and gunman for O'Bannion.

MORETTI, William (Willie Moore). A New Jersey racketeer and gambler who testified before the Kefauver Committee in 1951, but denied all knowledge of the Mafia. Nevertheless he was shot on Genovese's orders shortly thereafter because paresis was making him talk and act foolishly and heedlessly.

MORTON, Nails. Chicago gangster. He was a gunman and gambler who worked for O'Bannion. He was charged with the murder of two policemen. He set up a Jewish defense league. He was killed in 1923 in a fall from a horse. He was given a really impressive funeral, and gangster friends killed the horse "in revenge."

MURPHY, Tim (Big Tim). He was a pioneer labor union racketeer in Chicago, and a politician. He escaped most charges, but finally was convicted of robbery and jailed for three years in 1921. In 1928 he was gunned down in front of his home.

NANI, Sebastiano. Brooklyn Mafia hoodlum who became a large-scale narcotics operator.

NERONE, Joseph (Spano, The Cavalier). Chicago gangster. At one time he operated with the Genna gang, but in 1925 he killed Tony Genna. He was killed in revenge in 1926.

NEWBERRY, Ted. Chicago gangster. He was chief bootlegging salesman in Bugs Moran's gang.

NIEMOTH, William. Chicago gangster. He was on the 1923 list of public enemies.

NITTI, Frank (The Enforcer). Chicago gangster. He was a cousin of Al Capone, and operated as a Capone aide and collector. He was charged with fraud in connection with money donated for a Mayor Thompson charity. In 1930 he was given a three-year sentence for tax evasion, but fled. He was indicted by a grand jury on charges of racketeering in 1943, but was found dead. The official verdict was suicide.

NOTARO, Joseph. New York gangster. He was one of Bonanno's lieutenants. He died of a heart attack in 1966.

O'BANNION, Dion. Born in 1892. Irish. He was a Chicago bootlegger, and a member of Johnny Torrio's gang, though he tried to operate independently as much as possible. He started his career as altar boy, then became a choirboy. After a road accident when he was ten, he limped badly. From the choir he graduated to singing waiter, and then florist. He always carried three guns, and learned to shoot with deadly accuracy with either hand. He gained considerable political influence, and although he was accused of 25 murders, he was never convicted. He was shot dead by members of the Genna gang in his flower shop in 1924, and his death started the beer wars. He was given a typically impressive funeral.

DION O'BANNION

O'CONNOR, Jerry. Chicago racketeer. He was a gunman for the South Side O'Donnell gang during the beer wars. He was killed in a gang fight during a tour of enforcement around speakeasies in 1923.

O'DONNELL, Steve, Walter, Thomas and Spike. They were Chicago gangsters, and formed the gang known as the South Side O'Donnells. They were bootleggers and operated in opposition to Johnny Torrio. Walter was shot dead in 1925.

O'DONNELL, William (Klondike), Miles and Barnard. Chicago gangsters. They formed the gang known as the West Side O'Donnells. They were bootleggers allied with Torrio and Capone.

ORGEN, Jacob (Li'l Augie). New York gangster, he was leader of a labor enforcement gang in 1925 in association with Lepke Buchalter and Jake Shapiro. He became overambitious and was killed in a car ambush in 1927 by his two bosses.

OSADCHEY, Edward P. (Eddie Spitz). Kansas City gangster and gambler. He gave evidence before the Kefauver Committee in 1950.

PAGANO, Joseph and Pat. New York hoods. They were members of Vito Genovese's mob and used by Joe Valachi in the killing of Eugenio Giannini and Steve Franse.

PARIANO, Giuseppe. New York gangster. He was bodyguard for Peter Morello, and was killed at the same time as his boss in 1930.

PARISI, Dandy Jack. Gangster and gunman, he was associated with Louis Capone and Murder, Inc. in the 1940s.

PATTON, John (Boy Mayor). He was a member of Capone's booze and vice syndicates, and became mayor of Burnham. Later he was an associate of Frank Erickson and Frank Costello in racetrack interests. He joined Abe Allenberg in operating the Wofford Hotel in Miami in 1941.

JOE PROFACI

PERRONE, Santo (Sam). New York labor racketeer and a lieutenant of Joseph Bonanno. The DiGregorio mob was suspected of his murder in 1966.

PERSICO, Carmine (The Snake). New York gangster and aide in the Gallo gang. He later switched to Profaci.

PETRILLI, Dominick (The Gap). New York gangster. He started in petty crime with Joe Valachi, and served various terms of imprisonment. He saw the benefit of joining the organized gangs and later introduced Joe to the Mafia. He was deported to Italy, and turned informer. He sneaked into the United States in 1953, and was promptly shot dead.

PISANO, Little Augie. *See* Carfano, Anthony.

POLIZZI, Alfred (Big Al). Sicilian. Cleveland gang boss and bootlegger. He was associated with gangs in Chicago and Detroit. In 1920, he was convicted on charges of contravening the liquor laws. He "retired" in 1941 to undertake legal estate business, but in 1944, he was again convicted of illegal whiskey deals. He served four months of his sentence and then retired again to Miami.

PROFACI, Joseph. Born 1897 in Sicily. He was head of a large olive oil importing business, and also boss of Brooklyn gang organizations. He was associated closely with Joseph Bonanno. He died of cancer in 1962.

RAGEN, Frank and Mike. Irish. They were schoolboy star baseball players in Chicago, and founded Ragen's Athletic and Benevolent Association in 1902. It was known as Ragen's Colts, and Frank was president. The Colts was founded largely as a philanthropic organization, but it had strong gangster undertones, and accrued considerable political influence. The members used strong-arm tactics at elections, mixed in racial riots, and were implicated in many gangster murders. It was largely an Irish membership.

RAGEN, James, Sr. In 1942 he took over the Continental News

Service. He refused to be muscled by any of Capone's henchmen, who had long hankered after the news service's profits. He kept up his resistance, until he was shot in an ambush in 1950.

RAO, Joey. New York gangster. He was one of Dutch Schultz's aides.

RAPPAPORT, Jack. Chicago gangster and bootlegger. He was killed in 1925, presumably in revenge for the wounding of John Foley.

RASTELLI, Philip. New York gangster. He became boss of the former Bonanno gang on Joseph's death in 1972.

RAY, Earl. St. Louis gangster. He was said to have been one of the gunmen who wore police uniforms in the St. Valentine's Day massacre in 1929. He disappeared afterwards.

RAYMOND, Tony. Chicago bootlegger. He was killed in 1923.

REINA, Gaetano. New York gangster. He led one of the factions in the Castellammarese War under Maranzano, and was killed in 1930.

RELES, Abe (Kid Twist). New York gangster. He was a gunman for Murder, Inc. and turned informer. While being "guarded" by six policemen he fell to his death from a Coney Island hotel window in 1940.

RICCA, Paul (The Waiter). Chicago gangster. He was head of labor rackets, and operated with Al Capone. He was jailed for tax evasion. In 1943 he was sentenced to ten years for extortion from Hollywood movie industry, but was paroled in 1947 with others on the same charges. He was denaturalized and deported to Italy in 1959.

RIO, Frank (Slippery). Chicago gangster. He was Al Capone's bodyguard, and he was implicated in the murder of Assistant District Attorney McSwiggin in 1926. Later that year, when the Weiss gang launched a ten-car-machine-gun attack on Al Capone in a restaurant, Rio saved Capone's life. He was with Capone in Philadelphia in 1929, and they were both arrested. He was jailed for a year on charges of carrying a gun.

ROBILOTTO, John (Johnny Roberts). Gangster, gunman. He had a checkered career with allegiance to various leaders. He was thought to have been implicated in Willie Moretti's death, and many others. After Anastasia's murder he was killed in 1958, probably to prevent him from getting the mob to avenge Anastasia.

ROMERO, Tony. Gangster associated with Lepke Buchalter.

ROSENBAUM, Edward (Lucky Eddie). He was founder-partner in 1944 of the S&G bookmaking syndicate in Miami, and was subpoenaed to testify before the Kefauver Committee in Washington in 1950.

ROSENTHAL, Herman. New York gambler killed in 1912 by assassins hired by Charles Becker.

ROTHKOPF, Louis (alias Rhody or Zarumba). He was a member of the Cleveland gambling syndicate, and was named in the Kefauver Report.

ROTHSTEIN, Arnold. New York gambler, operator of loan-shark rackets. He got involved in importing narcotics in New York, and was exterminated by rivals in 1928.

RUBIN, Max. New Jersey gangster and racketeer. He turned state's evidence when arrested in 1940 after he had been wounded in an assassination attempt.

RUDNICK, George (Whitey). Small-time loan operator in Brooklyn. He was murdered with exceptional brutality in 1940. Happy Maione, Dasher Abbandando and Pittsburgh Phil were accused of killing him in a trial which received a great deal of publicity. Happy and Dasher were convicted and executed.

RUDOLPH, Harry. Hoodlum who was convicted of theft in 1940.

ARNOLD ROTHSTEIN

While in jail he volunteered information about gang crime which led to the arrests of several gangsters, including Kid Twist Reles, whose further disclosures became famous.

RULLO, Jerry. New Jersey gangster who was associated with Willie Moretti. He was present at the gang meeting in Tiny Rosario's house in 1939.

RUPOLO, Ernest (The Hawk). New York gangster and gunman. He was hired by Vito Genovese to kill Walter Gallo, but he missed. Gallo testified against him and he was jailed in 1934. He in turn talked when arrested again in 1944. Soon after his release from jail he was washed ashore, bullet-filled, in 1964.

RUSSO, Anthony. St. Louis gangster. He and his pal Vincent Spicuzza went to Chicago in 1927 to kill Al Capone and collect the fee offered by the Aiello gang. He was machine-gunned to death the day after he reached Chicago.

RUSSO, James. He was an independent alky maker in Chicago, and was killed in 1925.

RYAN, Frank (Chew Tobacco). He was a Chicago gangster.

RYAN, Tommy. *See* Eboli, Thomas.

SAGE, Walter. Brooklyn gangster, member of the Reles-Maione mob. He was given a small slot-machine concession, and when suspected of keeping too much profit he was taken for a ride by Pittsburgh Phil and gang in 1933, stabbed to death, and dumped in a lake.

SAIETTA, Ignazio, *See* Lupo, Joseph.

SALTIS, Joseph (Polack Joe). He was a Chicago gang leader of the Saltis-McErlane gang, a bootlegger who operated in opposition to Capone's gang. In 1926 he was charged with the murder of Mitters Foley. There were five eyewitnesses to the killing, but he was acquitted.

DUTCH SCHULTZ

SALVEY, Harold. Racketeer, bookie and financier, who acquired considerable useful political influence. In 1944 he became a founder-partner of the S&G bookmaking syndicate in Miami. Senator Kefauver called this syndicate "public enemy No. 1 of Miami." In 1950 he was subpoenaed to testify before the Kefauver Committee in Washington.

SAMMONS, James (Fur). Chicago gangster. He was active in the beer wars, and was listed as a public enemy by the Chicago Crime Commission in 1923.

SANTUCCI, Girolamo (Bobby Doyle). New York gangster. He operated with the mob on Maranzano's side in the Castellammarese War.

SAUPP, John. Forger, not connected with the Mafia. He was doing a term of imprisonment in 1962 in the same jail as Joe Valachi in Atlanta and Joe killed him, mistaking him for a Mafia man.

SCALICE, Frank (Don Cheech), and Joseph. New York gangsters and lieutenants of Albert Anastasia. Frank was killed in a gang vendetta in 1957, principally because he had been selling Mafia memberships for as much as $50,000. Joseph talked foolishly of revenge from undercover. Anastasia assured him all would be forgotten, but when Joseph reappeared he was quickly eliminated.

SCALISE, John. Born in Sicily. He had a long prison record in Italy before entering the United States illegally. He was a gangster operating in Chicago, and with Albert Anselmi, was used as triggerman. They were involved in a fray in which two policemen were killed and another wounded in 1925. At the first trial Scalise was sentenced to 14 years for manslaughter, but at a rigged retrial he was acquitted. After the St. Valentine's Day massacre in 1929, he was charged with being one of the executioners, but he was released on bond. He gained promotion in the Unione Siciliano and became overconfident. Capone ordered his death. This was carried out with proper ritual after a dinner party, in 1929.

The other two dinner guests, Albert Anselmi and Joseph Giunta, were also killed.

SCALISH, John. Cleveland gang boss. He was taken into custody at the Apalachin meeting in 1957.

SCHLITTEN, Moishe and Samuel. New York numbers racketeers associated with Vito Genovese.

SCHULTZ, Dutch (born Arthur Flegenheimer). One of New York's most notorious gunmen. He became known as Dutch Schultz after a prizefighter of exceptional ferocity whose opponents in the ring were invariably kayoed. He eliminated many of his enemies with great cruelty. He was the first to see the full potential in the numbers rackets and by taking over all smaller Harlem operators, he made himself "king" in the 1930s. He was a bootlegger, and specialized in restaurant protection rackets, which he operated with his customary brutality. He was one of the few non-Sicilian/Italians involved in the Castellammarese War. He probably arranged the deaths of Legs Diamond, Arnold Rothstein and many other New York competitors. He went into hiding in 1934 to avoid tax charges, and while away most of his operations were taken over by Sicilian-oriented gang leaders, who finally arranged his death when he reappeared in 1935.

SCHWARTZ, Charles. Philadelphia gang leader. He attended the Mafia meeting in Atlantic City in 1929.

SCIACCA, Paul. New York gangster. He was a member of Joseph Bonanno's gang until 1964, then joined DiGregorio, who nominated him to succeed him as boss of the family. This was not approved by others, and he was not strong enough to impose his own leadership.

SCIMONE, John. New York gangster. He was one of the Gallo gang, but switched to Profaci's side during the two-gang feud.

SHAPIRO, Irving, Meyer and Willie. Gang bosses in East New

York in 1920s. Meyer was the oldest, toughest, meanest and most cruel (Irving was a little less so, and Willie didn't count for much). They operated very successfully in alcohol, slot machines and prostitution. Meyer boasted he had 15 houses going for himself alone. They were finally overthrown by some of their own recruits, led by Kid Twist Reles and Buggsy Goldstein. The takeover battle was fought for a year, but by 1931, after 18 encounters and misfires at Meyer, he was finally killed. Irving was also killed and Willie was buried alive.

SHAPIRO, Jake (Gurrah). Gangster and enforcement man for Lepke Buchalter. He was one of the most feared men in the gangs of his day; his pet phrase, "Get out of here" could sound like "Gurrah"—hence his nickname. He was active in labor rackets, and his name appeared as a specialist in extortion at the time of the Cosa Nostra peace talks in 1934.

SHEA, Willie. Gambler, former ward leader, he was Arnold Rothstein's partner in early 1900, but the partnership was dissolved after a dispute over division of swag.

SHELDON, Ralph. He was a Chicago gang leader and bootlegger in the days of Prohibition. His interests were allied with those of Al Capone.

SIANO, Fiore (Fury). New York hood and gunman. He was Joe Valachi's nephew and was implicated in the deaths of Eugenio Giannini and Steve Franse. He then disappeared.

SILVER, Len. He was first elected governor of Illinois in 1921, and held office as a pawn of Mayor Thompson. On taking office he granted pardons to 1,000 killers and hoods. He was defeated in the 1927 election.

SOLOMON, Charles (King). Gang leader in Boston in 1920s.

SPICUZZA, Vincent. St. Louis gangster. He and his pal Anthony Russo went to Chicago to kill Al Capone for the fee of $50,000 offered by the Aiello gang, but he was machine-gunned to death the day after he arrived.

BUGSY SIEGEL

SPINGOLA, Henry. He was a member of a wealthy Italian family and had business interests in Chicago. Angelo Genna was his brother-in-law. He refused to contribute to the Scalise-Anselmi gang funds and was therefore killed in 1926.

STANTON, Danny. Chicago gangster who had graduated from Ragen's Colts. He aligned himself with Al Capone. His name was on the list of public enemies in 1923. In 1924 he was charged with murder, but the case was dropped.

STEVENS, Walter. Gang leader in Chicago in the early 1900s. He was an associate of Mossy Enright, and specialized in labor racket enforcement. He was jailed for the murder of a policeman but promptly paroled by Governor Len Small. He was a small, quiet man who lived by severe, even prim, standards, yet was known to be a ruthless gunman with many deaths to his credit. Capone trusted him to keep order in the Torrio-Capone empire while they concentrated on starting things in Cicero. He retired in 1924 at the age of 57.

STRACI, Joseph (Joe Stretch). New York gangster. He started the Castellammarese War on Masseria's side but later went over to Mangano, and was thought to have been one of the gunmen in Masseria's killing.

STRAUSS, Harry (Pittsburgh Phil). Brooklyn gangster. He was a great dandy and liked to be thought of as the Beau Brummel of the underworld, but was also a skillful and sadistic killer, who enjoyed handling contracts. He was credited with more than 30 deaths. He was such a zealous operator that he took on assignments in Boston, Chicago, Philadelphia, Miami and Detroit. He was executed in 1941 for the murder of Puggy Feinstein.

STROLLO, Anthony (Tony Bender). New York gangster. He was a lieutenant in Genovese's family. He was killed in 1962, probably on orders from Genovese in jail, who suspected that he was double-dealing.

SULLIVAN, Big Tim. New York gambler, boss of Tammany in early 1900s.

JOHNNY TORRIO

SULLIVAN, Manley. Chicago bootlegger. His trial for tax evasion in 1927 established the federal ruling that illegal income should be taxable. This precedent gave the government a very powerful weapon against gangsters, as it could prosecute for tax evasion if no other charges would stick.

TANCL, Eddie. A saloon owner in Chicago, and a former prizefighter. He became known locally as a philanthropist. Although he was associated with Klondike O'Donnell, he tried to say independent in the beer wars. This did not please Capone, who in 1924 sent Miles O'Donnell and James Doherty to shoot him in his own saloon. Although there were witnesses no convictions followed. Capone took over the saloon.

TANNENBAUM, Allie. New York gangster associated with Lepke Buchalter. He was charged with taking part in killing Harry Greenberg in 1938 but got off. He talked when in jail in 1940, and after his release he went straight.

TELLERI, Frank. New York gangster. He was a DiGregorio aide and was shot dead in 1967 during the Banana War. He had defected from the Bonanno side.

TENNES, Monte. Gangster in Chicago. He became a powerful racetrack news king. His home was bombed three times in 1907 by rival gangsters, but he was unhurt. He retired in 1928.

TERRANOVA, Ciro. Sicilian. He was a Brooklyn gangster and racketeer, known as the "artichoke king," because he had a virtual monopoly of artichokes in New York. He was related to Lupo the Wolf. In the Castellammarese War he was on Masseria's side until that side began losing. Then he helped to kill Masseria for Maranzano in 1931.

THOMPSON, William Hale (Big Bill). He was elected mayor of Chicago three times during the twenties. He was known to have criminal connections, and during his terms of office payoffs at City Hall were accepted. He ignored Chicago

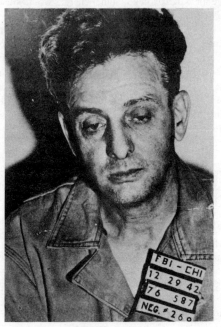

ROGER TOUHY

crime while in office. He died of natural causes, aged 75, in 1944, and when Treasury officials searched his home, they found boxes tightly packed with banknotes and certificates, amounting in all to $1,750,000. During his lifetime his salary had never been high, but he had launched many fund-raising drives for charity, and on many occasions there had been surprise at the small amounts actually handed over to the charities.

TOLIZOTTE, Pasquale. Chicago gangster. He was a bootlegger in the O'Donnell gang, and was killed in 1926.

TORCHIO, Antonio. New York gangster. He was a gunman for Lucky Luciano. He volunteered to kill Al Capone for the fee of $50,000 offered by the Aiellos in 1927, but was machine-gunned to death as he stepped from the train at Chicago.

TORRIO, John. Born 1877 in Italy. He started as a gangster in New York, but he was Big Jim Colosimo's nephew and protege, and his uncle sent for him to come to Chicago in 1910. He succeeded Colosimo as boss in 1920, and took on Al Capone as his lieutenant. By 1923 he was boss of Cicero, a Chicago suburb, operating prostitution and beer rackets, and had also gained considerable political influence. He retired in 1925 to escape possible murder charges, but returned to New York later. In 1939 he was jailed for a short term. He died of a heart attack in 1957 at the age of 75.

TOUHY, Roger (Terrible). Chicago gang leader. His father was a Chicago policeman. He started working as a telegraphist, with a sideline in betting. In 1926 he graduated to a bootlegging business with two trucks in partnership with Matt Kolb, and soon controlled a large area from nearby Des Plaines with profits from booze and slot-machine dealing in the million-dollar bracket. Al Capone tried to make him conform to the Capone syndicate line in 1931. He was not cooperative in spite of pressure. His partner Kolb was kidnaped and later shot dead by Capone's men, but Touhy still resisted. Capone framed him on a charge of kidnaping, for

FRANK YALE

which he served a 25-year sentence. He wrote a book called *The Stolen Years,* which was published on his release from jail. Within three weeks he was killed, probably by the Mafia who feared he might become competitive again.

TRAFFICANTE, Santa. He was a Mafia boss in Tampa, and fled from the Kefauver Committee investigations in 1950. He was present at the Mafia meeting at La Stella Restaurant in 1966.

TRAMUNTI, Carmine. New York gang boss who took over the Lucchese gang in 1972. He was present at the Mafia meeting held in Long Island in 1965, as Lucchese's lieutenant.

TREMONT, Peter. Chicago gangster. He was a numbers racketeer who ran the Roman Silver Wheel game with the Mannos. He was named in the Kefauver Report.

TROPEA, Orassio (The Scourge). Chicago gangster. He was a collector for the Genna brothers, and was shot dead in a revenge killing in 1925.

TUCCELLO, John. Chicago gangster. He was a bootlegger operating with the Sheldon gang, and was killed by the McErlane gang in 1926.

TUCKER, Samuel. He was a member of the Cleveland gambling syndicate and was named in the Kefauver Report.

TUMINARO, Angelo (Little Angie). Brooklyn gangster.

TURNIO, Joe. New York longshoreman murdered in 1925. Albert Anastasia and Jimmy Florio were convicted of his murder, but released after a retrial.

UALE or YALE, Frank. New York gangster. He was a bootlegger and gang chief, and also a philanthropist and politician. He founded the Unione Siciliano in 1925 and was the national president. He was said to have killed Big Jim Colosimo and Dion O'Bannion, and was himself shot dead in 1928. He was given a funeral with full gangster honors.

JOE VALACHI

VALACHI, Joseph. New York gangster. He was a soldier in the Castellammarese War, and was hired by Maranzano as an assassin. After the war he joined Vito Genovese's family. He was involved in many gangland affairs, and while serving a jail term he thought Genovese was plotting his death. He killed Joseph Saupp, another quite uninvolved prisoner, in a brawl, which put him under sentence of death, so he forgot about the Mafia rule of silence and told all he knew. He wrote a history of the Castellammarese War, he testified before a Senate committee in 1963 and he appeared on television. He died of natural causes.

VALENTE, Samuel. Cleveland gangster. He tried to win the $50,000 reward offered by the Aiello gang for killing Al Capone in 1927, but was machine-gunned to death the day after he arrived in Chicago.

VALENTI, Umberto. New York gangster. He disputed Joe Masseria's action in becoming boss of Italian rackets, and in 1922 one of his men took four shots at the Boss in a shop, all of which Masseria dodged. Later Masseria invited him to lunch for peace talks. After lunch he was shot dead by Masseria's men.

VANILLI, Roxie. New York gangster. He became a gunman for Johnny Torrio, and in 1914 was charged with killing a policeman but no indictment followed. He was wounded in the battle.

VARIO, Paul. New York gangster. He was a captain in Lucchese's mob. It was his trailer, parked in a Brooklyn junk yard, which the police bugged in 1972. The trailer proved to be a Mafia headquarters.

VITALE, John. Narcotics racketeer who operated with the Mafia in St. Louis.

VOGEL, Eddie (Big Ed). Chicago racketeer. He operated slot-machine rackets, and was in league with Johnny Torrio. He also gained political influence. In the 1926 peace treaty he was given a small territory.

HYMAN WEISSMAN

VOLLERO, Alessandro. A hoodlum sentenced to life imprisonment for murder in 1919. Joe Valachi later joined him in jail for a while, and from him Joe learned for the first time about the Mafia and some of its ramifications.

VOLPE, Tony (Mops). Chicago gangster and gambler. At one time he was Al Capone's bodyguard, and later became manager of Capone gambling dives. He was acquitted of murder in 1920. He was listed as a public enemy in 1923.

WEINBERG, Abe (Bo). Gangster who managed Dutch Schultz's business affairs. When Dutch went into hiding to avoid a tax inquiry in 1933 he was left in charge of the Schultz operations, but as he didn't expect to see Dutch again, he agreed to hand the operation over to Lepke Buchalter and Lucky Luciano. Dutch did return in 1935, summoned Bo, and Bo was never seen again. Rumor put him on the bottom of the East River wrapped in cement.

WEINSHANK, Albert R. Chicago gangster. He ran a speakeasy for Bugs Moran and was killed in the St. Valentine's Day massacre in 1929.

WEISS, Earl (Hymie). Chicago gangster and safecracker. He was at one time a lieutenant for O'Bannion and on Dion's death led the O'Bannion gang. He was killed in the beer wars in 1926.

WEISS, Mendy. Brooklyn gangster. He was associated with Lepke Buchalter and the rackets of the 1930s and '40s. He was convicted of the murder of Joseph Rosen in 1941, but escaped the chair through various appeals until 1944.

WERTHEIMER, Mert. Detroit gambler.

WEXLER, Mushy. Cleveland gambler.

WHITE, William (Three-Fingered Jack). Chicago gangster and labor racketeer. He was listed as a public enemy in 1923. In 1929 he was charged with murder.

WOLINSKY, Moey (Dimples). Gangster and henchman of Lepke Buchalter. He was manager of the Lepke gambling rackets in New York. In 1939 he lied to Lepke, telling him that a deal had been made with the judiciary for Lepke to get a light sentence. He was shot dead in 1942.

LONGY ZWILLMAN

WORKMAN, Charlie (The Bug). New York gangster. He was a gunman of exceptional ferocity on Lepke Buchalter's personal staff. He liked to work alone, and shot Dutch Schultz and three bodyguards singlehandedly. He was sentenced to life imprisonment for these killings in 1941.

YALE, Frank. *See* Uale, Frank.

ZERILLI, Joseph. Detroit gangster boss. He was related by marriage to both the Bonanno and Profaci families. He was a member of the National Commission in 1962.

ZION, Eddie. Chicago hoodlum. He was associated with Sam Amatuna and killed shortly after Sam in 1925, probably by the same killers who might have expected vengeance.

ZUMO, Thomas. New York gangster and gunman for Di-Gregorio. In 1969 he was killed while at the house of a girlfriend. His was the last death in the Banana War.

ZUTA, Jack. Chicago racketeer. In 1928 he sided with the Aiello brothers against Capone.

ZWILLMAN, Abner (Longy). New Jersey gangster. He was associated with Lucky Luciano with whom he arranged the Cleveland meeting of organized criminals in 1929. He became one of New York's Big Six in 1930. Some years later he was found hanging in the basement of his New Jersey home. Although it was ruled a suicide, there was nothing nearby from which he could have jumped.

CHRONOLOGY

1880

Mass migration of southern Italians and Sicilians brings with it the Black Hand, a centuries-old tradition of intimidating wealthy merchants and property owners to pay. The Black Hand is merely a technique used by the Mafia and not the organization itself. During the next 10 years, Italians and Sicilians settle mainly in poor sections of New York and Chicago. Transplanted Mafia types immediately begin preying on Italian and Sicilian immigrants who know and fear them from the old country.

1900

Johnny Torrio, born in Naples, becomes head of New York's Five Points Gang, a band of toughs, mostly youngsters from immigrant families of all nationalities. Five Points turf is Manhattan's Lower East Side. Gang handles petty robberies, small shakedown rackets and some gambling. Makes itself useful to crooked politicians at election time by coercing voters, guarding polls and terrorizing opposing candidates. An associate of Torrio's is Frank Uale, known as Frank Yale, a Sicilian hoodlum who operates in Brooklyn. Large-scale New York crime run by gangs dominated by Irish, Jewish and Polish gangsters, crimes chiefly gambling, robberies and extortion. Some prostitution.

1905

Chicago rackets dominated by Maurice "Mossy" Enright, pioneer labor gangster, using "paper" unions, emplover shakedowns, theft of union funds. Sicilians concentrate on operating Black Hand, bossed by Sicilian Sunny Jim Cosmano. Various gangs involved in widespread gambling and prostitution enterprises.

1907

Law-abiding Chicago Italians and Sicilians found the White Hand, a society dedicated to good deeds, charity and to offsetting the onus of the Black Hand.

1908

The Unione Siciliano, founded in New York for the same reasons as the White Hand is started in Chicago. Black Handers in Chicago demand money from fast-rising rackets figure Big Jim Colosimo, who operates the city's biggest gambling joint and whorehouse. Big Jim makes several payments. Finally, as three Black Handers attempt to pick up another bag of Colosimo money, all three are killed by shotguns.

1909

The Black Hand again makes demands on Colosimo, who sends for his nephew, Johnny Torrio, in New York. Torrio quickly arranges the deaths of three more Black Handers. The Black Hand's boss, Sunny Jim Cosmano, unable to believe he's being defied, again threatens Colosimo. Torrio and Colosimo meanwhile go into the protection racket themselves, and begin building a chain of Chicago whorehouses. Federal investigators of Chicago crime find former Chicago whore in New York willing to testify against Torrio and Colosimo. She's found dead in Bridgeport, Conn. Torrio's old New York gang and/or Frank Yale are suspected. Sunny Jim Cosmano, Black Hand boss, is shot in stomach, but lives.

Chicago gangsters on scene at this time: Monte Tennes, bookie; Mike (De Pike) Heitler, whoremonger; Joey D'Andrea, racketeer head of Sewer Diggers and Tunnel Miners Union; Izzy the Rat Buchalsky, labor hoodlum; Vincenzo Cosmano, who run Black Hand protection racket; Dion O'Bannion, leader of Chicago's strongest mob. Gunmen: Joe Moresco, Billy Leathers, Joe Grabiner. Gang leaders: Hymie Weiss, who invents the phrase, "Take 'em for a ride." Safecracker and gunman, George "Bugs" Moran; Irish gangsters William, Miles and Bernard O'Donnell; Sicilians, Sam, Vincenzo, Jim, Pete, Angelo, Antonio and Mike Genna; Irish hoods Terry Druggan and Frankie Lake, whose gang

dates from the 1890s. Irish gang leader Frank Ragen. Irish hoodlums. Ed, Steve, Walker and Tommy O'Donnell (no relation to
the other O'Donnells). Jake "Greasy Thumb" Guzik, bookkeeper
for Torrio. Saltis-McErlane gang run by Joe Saltis and Frank
McErlane, a homicidal maniac.

1910

Between 1910 and 1914, the Chicago Vice Commission uncov-
ers 77 known cases of white slavery, women forced into prostitution. The commission estimates that Chicago has 1,020 brothels,
employing some 5,000 prostitutes, all controlled by one gangster
mob or another.

Black Hand hoodlums in Chicago kill a total of 25 people.

1911

Sullivan Law passed in New York, making it illegal to carry
concealed weapons without a license.

Black Hand hoodlums in Chicago kill a total of 40 people.

1912

New York police lieutenant Charles Becker recruits Gyp the
Blood and Lefty Louie to kill gambler Herman Rosenthal, who was
going to expose Becker for taking graft.

Reform wave closes Chicago's red-light district. Torrio and
Colosimo open their first brothel in Chicago's suburbs. Of 1,013
brothels closed in Chicago during the vice blitz, 712 reopen.

Black Hand hoodlums in Chicago kill a total of 31 people.

1913

Chicago's White Hand members decide that offsetting Black
Hand's bad publicity for Italians everywhere is hopeless and they
disband.

1914

Police in Chicago red-light district increase payoff demands.
Threats by both sides. Police have gun battle with Torrio's men,
Roxie Vanilli (a New York hoodlum) and triggerman Mac Fitzpatrick. One policeman is killed, and three are wounded. Also
wounded is Vanilli. Colosimo and others arrested, but charges
dropped for lack of evidence. Colosimo henchman, Duffy the

Goat, kills police stool pigeon, Isaac Hengow Tried and convicted, he wins new trial. This time Duffy is acquitted on grounds of self-defense, although witnesses testify that Hengow never even saw Duffy coming.

New U.S. immigration laws slow the arrival of Italians and Sicilians.

Tony D'Andrea, lawyer, union official and president of Chicago Unione Siciliano, runs for Cook County Commissioner. A brother of Joey D'Andrea, a racketeer killed during a labor dispute, Tony D'Andrea is exposed as a defrocked priest, a convicted bank robber and a counterfeiter. He loses the election.

1915

Al Capone, a teen-ager, joins the Five Points Gang in New York. Another member is Lucky Luciano, a Sicilian. Capone, born in New York, is of Neapolitan parentage.

Big Bill Thompson is elected as Republican reform mayor of Chicago. Thompson makes a few token arrests and then turns a blind eye to crime and vice.

1916

Tony D'Andrea runs for Democratic alderman in Chicago. One of opponent's aides is slain. Police suspect Genna brothers. D'Andrea loses election again.

1917

Frank Yale, the Brooklyn gangster, becomes president of the Unione Siciliano, later called the Italo-American National Union. Founded as a fraternal organization to do charitable work, its membership includes judges, professional men, businessmen and politicians. Critics claim the Unione is nothing but a front for Italian hoods. The Unione expands to include other major cities. Chicago has 38 Unione lodges and 40,000 members.

Capone goes to work as bartender and bouncer in Frank Yale's nightclub. During this time, Capone is suspected of two New York murders and arrested once for disorderly conduct.

1918

New York's old Five Points Gang now run by Paolo Antonini Vaccarelli, known as Paul Kelly, an Italian, and James ''Biff''

Ellison, an Irishman. Brooklyn rackets run by Ciro Terranova, a Sicilian. He helps his relative Ignazio Saietta, known as Lupo the Wolf, recruit more gangsters into the Unione Siciliano.

1919

Torrio sends for his pal Al Capone, who goes to work in Chicago as one of Torrio's flunkies.

1920

Prohibition becomes law.

Chicago labor racketeer Mossy Enright rubbed out by Black Hander Sunny Jim Cosmano as a favor to Big Tim Murphy, a rival of Enright's in the labor rackets.

Torrio, anxious to take over Colosimo mob and exploit Prohibition, has Colosimo shot and killed in his own restaurant. Torrio gives Capone, his lieutenant, 25 percent of the existing Chicago brothel business, and 50 percent of the expected bootleg profits. Al Capone's brother, Ralph, and the Fischetti brothers, Capone's first cousins, all come from New York to join his command.

Torrio, with the Druggan-Lake gang, takes control of five legitimate Chicago breweries, supposedly producing near-beer, with alcohol content only one-half percent. Torrio sells beer to other Chicago gangs at $50 a barrel. O'Bannion smuggles in real whiskey from Canada. The Genna brothers set up hundreds of small stills in tenements to make moonshine. Everyone does what he pleases and there is peace among Chicago gangs. Torrio and Capone open more suburban brothels and speakeasies, virtually take over Chicago suburbs such as Cicero, Illinois.

One of the kingpins of the Cleveland bootlegging operation is Alfred (Big Al) Polizzi, a Sicilian immigrant. Gets help from associates in Chicago and Detroit. Rumrunning and gambling proved against him. He is friendly with Pete Licavoli, the notorious Detroit gang leader.

Sicilian and Italian hoods begin rising to the top in leading crime networks. Young hoods on New York scene: Sicilians Joseph Profaci, Joseph Magliocco, Stefano Magaddino, Frank Labruzzo, Frank Garofalo, and Italians Joe Masseria, Vito Genovese, Frank Costello.

Antonio Spano, gunman known as *Il Cavalieri,* imported from Sicily by the Gennas in Chicago.

1921

Bill Thompson wins second term. Governor Small elected for first term.

Governor Len Small, pawn of Chicago's Mayor Thompson, takes office and pardons as many as 1,000 killers and hoods. Tony D'Andrea runs for alderman. Bombs explode at rallies of both sides. Hoodlums from New York and Buffalo imported for "poll watching." D'Andrea loses. Following the election Genna brothers murder two associates of D'Andrea's opponent, John Powers. Powers's forces strike back. In all 30 people killed in "The Chicago Alderman's War," among them D'Andrea himself.

1922

Capone arrested by Chicago police for drunken driving, assault with an automobile and carrying a gun. Case never comes to trial, as Capone is a Cook County deputy sheriff at the time.

1923

Spike O'Donnell, the O'Donnell gang leader, released from prison. Chicago's South Side O'Donnell gang, with help from New York hoods such as Harry Hasmiller, begins hijacking Torrio beer trucks. O'Donnell gang orders Saltis-McErlane gang's speakeasy clients to take beer from O'Donnell. O'Donnell gang smashes up six Torrio speakeasies. Later, at one of their own joints, the McErlane gang, in league with Torrio men, catches up with the O'Donnells. One O'Donnell man killed. Ten days later, two O'Donnell beer truck drivers killed. The McErlanes are suspected. Two months later, another O'Donnell man killed, all with shotguns. The first Chicago beer war is on.

Torrio expands to Cicero, Illinois, sets up brothels. Eddie Vogel, political boss, gets slot-machine concession. The O'Donnell brothers allowed a few saloons and gambling dens, Torrio gets the rest. Cicero bar owner, Eddie Tancl, ignores "treaty," and says he'll buy beer where he wants to. Due to adverse publicity and a "clean up" movement, Mayor Big Bill Thompson withdraws from the next election.

April. Chicago Crime Commission publishes list of 28 Chicagoans "constantly in conflict with the law." Public Enemies: Alphonse Capone (alias Scarface Capone, alias Al Brown). Tony (Mops) Volpe, Ralph Capone, Frank Rio (alias Frank Kline, alias Frank Gline), Jack (Machine-gun) McGurn, James Belcastro, Rocco Fanelli, Lawrence (Dago Lawrence) Mangano, Jack Zuta, Jake (Greasy Thumb) Guzik, Frank Diamond, George (Bugs) Moran, Joe Aiella, Edward (Spike) O'Donnell, Joe (Polack Joe) Saltis, Frank McErlane, Vincent McErlane, William Niemoth, Danny Stanton, Miles O'Donnell, Frank Lake, Terry Druggan, William (Klondike) O'Donnell, George (Red) Baker, William (Three-Fingered Jack) White, Joseph (Peppy) Genero, Leo Mongoven, James (Fur) Sammons.

1924

Joseph Bonnano, future New York Mafia leader, is smuggled into country in Florida. Mobs at that time: Dutch Schultz controls the numbers rackets in Harlem and the distribution of illegal beer. Lepke Buchalter and Jake Shapiro are labor racketeers. They also run trucks with stolen or bathtub booze around the country. Lepke and Shapiro enforcement gangs are under Bugsy Siegel and Meyer Lansky. Other well-known racketeers are Arnold Rothstein in New York (the gambler and loan racket king), Charles (King) Solomon in Boston, and Frank Erickson, who runs booze and gambling in Florida. Erickson works closely with Frank Costello, one of the first Italo-American gangsters to make a fortune during Prohibition. Costello, who immigrated to the United States from southern Italy at the age of four with his parents, is a prominent rumrunner with Bill Dwyer, who commands a fleet of 12 steel-plated speedboats, armed with machine guns, that carry whiskey from Canada to the eastern seaboard and for Capone in Chicago.

January. Another O'Donnell driver killed. Walter O'Donnell and New York henchman, Harry Hasmiller, killed in gunfight with Saltis-McErlane men.

Capone and Torrio, fearful that reform fever might reach to suburban Cicero, attempt to insure an election victory for their "owned" politicians. More than 200 gunmen are "borrowed" from downtown Chicago. Four people slain on election day. On election night Frank Capone is killed in a gunfight with police. Torrio-Capone puppets win the election. Unione Siciliano Chicago president Mike Merlo dies. In the next five years, 25 men die in the power struggle to succeed him.

In a gunfight at independent Eddie Tancl's saloon, Tancl himself is killed and Miles O'Donnell, his assailant, is wounded. Tancl bartender killed.

May 8. Dion O'Bannion begins underselling Capone-Torrio beer and hijacking Genna beer trucks.

May 19. O'Bannion sells Torrio-Capone his share of their jointly owned brewery; he knows it's about to be raided. O'Bannion shot dead in his florist shop by parties unknown. Hymie Weiss, O'Bannion lieutenant, vows vengeance.

1925

Severe penalties for using the mails to defraud are enforced and the Black Hand stops sending threatening letters and instead uses the telephone.

McErlane gang first to use the Thompson submachine gun for a mob killing. Gun soon becomes so popular it's known as a "Chicago typewriter."

McErlane machine-guns O'Donnell family car. Wounds Tommy O'Donnell. Spike O'Donnell leaves Chicago. McErlane is charged with murder of Jerry O'Connor, an O'Donnell man. McErlane skips town.

January 12. Hymie Weiss, Schemer Drucci and Bugs Moran, all O'Bannion avengers, machine-gun Al Capone's car, but miss Capone. O'Bannion mourners torture and kill another Capone chauffeur, having wounded the first one.

January 24. Johnny Torrio and chauffeur wounded. Bugs Moran is identified as one of their assailants. Recovered Torrio is sentenced to nine months for operating an illegal brewery and announces that he is retiring from Chicago rackets.

May 26. In Chicago Angelo Genna is rubbed out by Hymie Weiss, Bugs Moran and Vincent Drucci to avenge O'Bannion killing. Three weeks later, on **June 13,** Moran and Drucci are wounded in a gunfight with Mike Genna, Samoots Amatuna, John Scalise and Albert Anselmi. After the fight the Genna gang is stopped by police. One policeman is wounded, two killed. Mike Genna also killed.

July 8. Tony Genna killed by ex-henchman Antonio Spano, known as Il Cavaliere. Soon afterwards, *Il Cavaliere* shot and killed in barbershop. The surviving Genna brothers flee Chicago.

October. Johnny Torrio released from jail, retires to Italy. Former Genna mobster Samoots Amatuna claims the presidency of

Chicago's Unione Siciliano. In October he's murdered in a barber-shop by the combined O'Donnell gangs, still avenging O'Bannion. Several more rubouts follow, on both sides. Capone man, Tony Lombardo, succeeds to presidency of Unione. On Christmas Day, Capone and men have shoot-out with Irish gangs in saloon, leaving three dead and several wounded.

1926

The gang war, begun when O'Bannion was killed, heats up. The Irish, German, Polish and Jewish mobsters form behind Weiss, O'Bannion's successor. The Italians and Sicilians—with the exception of remaining Black Handers—join behind Capone.

January. Several hoodlums killed in "fund-raising drive" for Genna's men Scalise and Anselmi, on trial for cop-killing.

April 22. Capone mob ambushes South Side O'Donnell gang and Assistant District Attorney William H. McSwiggen who, for some reason, is riding around in their car. McSwiggen and O'Donnell man Jim Doherty both filled full of holes. O'Donnell gang leaders and Capone vanish until excitement dies down. They're eventually arrested, but no charges are pressed.

May. Al Capone increases his bodyguard to 18, many of whom are hired in New York. Capone is convinced that it's either him or Weiss, O'Bannion's fanatical avenger.

August 10. Weiss and Drucci shot at in broad daylight in front of Standard Oil Building in downtown Chicago. Capone bodyguard seen nearby. Much shooting, but no casualties on either side.

August 15. Second battle of the Standard Oil Building. Same result.

September 20. Weiss commands armada of eleven cars that cruise past Capone headquarters in daylight raid, raking buildings with machine-gun fire. Only victim: an innocent bystander.

October 11. Hymie Weiss walks up steps to his headquarters and is machine-gunned to death by ambushers set up in apartment house across street.

October 21. Al Capone meets with other gang leaders at Chicago's Hotel Sherman and they agree on peaceful division of Chicago and its environs.

October 21-December 30. Chicago enjoys unprecedented 70 days without a single gang slaughter. Hood who spoils the record is Hilary Clements, one of Ralph Sheldon's men, who was presumably killed by Saltis gang. Capone has two Saltis gang members killed to teach Saltis a lesson.

December 24. Genna triggermen Anselmi and Scalise, previously sentenced to 14 years for manslaughter of policemen, are granted retrial. An indication of why justice in Chicago is often lax is suggested by the fact that judges are frequently honorary pallbearers at gangsters' funerals. Total gang killings in Chicago for the year: 64.

1927

The U.S. Supreme Court finds that illegal income is taxable. Appeal brought by bootlegger Manley Sullivan, whose lawyers claimed that for Sullivan to declare his illegal income would be tantamount to asking him to testify against himself, thereby contravening the meaning of the Fifth Amendment. *This ruling gives the federal government a new and powerful weapon against gangsters.*

January. Saltis-McErlane gang kills a rumrunner who's invaded their territory. The O'Bannion avengers, unable to ambush Capone, kill his favorite restaurant owner. Capone cries.

March. Vincent (The Schemer) Drucci takes potshot at Capone at Hot Springs, Arkansas, but misses.

March 21. Diamond Joe Esposito, a Chicago labor racketeer and boss since 1910, runs for Republican ward committeeman against Capone's wishes. Esposito is rubbed out.

April 4. On election eve, Drucci is arrested and shot to death in police car. They say he resisted.

April 5. Big Bill Thompson elected Chicago mayor again. This is his third term, after being elected twice and skipping one election.

June 10. Capone sends James De Amato to New York to see if Frank Yale is hijacking booze trucks after selling contents to Capone. De Amato is gunned to death shortly thereafter.

June 22. Anselmi and Scalise found not guilty of killing policemen.

During the summer, the "War of the Sicilian Succession" is fought over the presidency of Chicago's Unione Siciliano. Joseph Aiello, former Genna triggerman, loses a bullet- and bomb-filled election to Tony Lombardo, Capone's choice. Aiello imports triggermen from New York, Buffalo, St. Louis and Cleveland to kill Capone. The latter hires New York triggerman Louis Campagna. Capone's man, Machine-gun Jack McGurn, blasts all four of

Aiello's hired killers within days of their arrival in Chicago. For good measure, four local Aiello henchmen are killed too. Aiello and two brothers flee to Trenton, New Jersey, continue to offer $50,000 to anyone who will kill Capone.

November 10. Comedian Joe E. Lewis, who had refused to work in a joint partly owned by Machine Gun Jack McGurn has his throat slashed. He recovers, but is out of work for years. Capone forges his own syndicate to run most of Chicago and Cicero. Among his top men: Jake Guzik, Frank Nitti, Tony Accardo, Fellice de Lucia (also known as Paul the Waiter Ricca) Sam Mooney Giancana and James de Mora, also known as Machine-gun Jack McGurn. All of top brass either Sicilians or Italians.

December 5. Capone announces that he may retire to Florida. Chicago Mayor Bill Thompson tries to run for President on the America First ticket, but gains almost no support. Governor Small, who pardoned so many killers and hoodlums, is defeated.

1928

January. Newly elected President Herbert Hoover instructs Treasury Secretary Andrew Mellon to get Al Capone into jail, one way or another. Internal Revenue Service discovers that Capone has never filed a tax return in his life.

In New York Joe the Boss Masseria demands larger split from Brooklyn-based Castellammarese mob. The latter mob so named because most of its members come from the same village, Castellammare del Golfo, in Sicily. Joe the Boss says Brooklyn is his territory.

In Chicago Al Capone moves his headquarters from Metropole Hotel to Lexington Hotel, occupying entire fourth floor, part of third floor and scattered rooms throughout the hotel. Has secret escape hatch to office building next door which is discovered years later. Capone's mistress is found to have syphilis and undergoes treatment. Capone, afraid of hypodermic needles, refuses treatment.

July 1. Capone is reluctant to move against Frank Yale, the New York gangster and national Unione Siciliano president, even though Yale is killing his New York representatives and hijacking Capone beer vans. Capone once worked for Yale, who was imported to Chicago to kill both Colosimo and Dion O'Bannion. Yale is finally killed for refusing to endorse Capone's candidate for Chicago

Unione president and for interfering with Capone's plans for a national bootlegging conspiracy. Aiello brothers return to Chicago.

September 8. Aiello men kill local Unione President Lombardo, who is Capone's man. Capone gang retaliates, kills four Aiello men. New Unione president is Pasquale Lolordo. His opponent is killed. (Lolordo himself is killed five months later, and Joe Aiello is finally elected president of Chicago Unione.)

November 6. Gambler Arnold Rothstein shot and killed in New York by persons unknown. Rothstein was loan shark and also known to be financing narcotics imports.

December 1. Illinois State's Attorney's office says 91 Chicago unions are mob-controlled. The Capone syndicate's annual gross is estimated at $105 million. Capone extends his business interests, taking over a chain of dry-cleaning shops and opening several illegal dog tracks. Capone's plans are constantly disrupted by Bugs Moran, who helps Aiello brothers attack Capone and who hijacks Capone beer and whiskey trucks. Capone leaves for Miami again at Christmas.

December 5. *The national crime syndicate is formed at the Statler Hotel in Cleveland when 23 Sicilians from Chicago, New York, Detroit, Buffalo, St. Louis, Newark and Tampa gather to discuss mutual problems.* The biggest group of delegates is from Chicago. Capone, not being Sicilian, is barred, but his representatives are there. For Capone there is Pasquale Lolordo, the Chicago Unione chief, and Joe Giunta. For New York there is Joe Profaci, Joe Magliocco, Vincent Mangano, Lucky Luciano and several others. Those named all eventually head Mafia families in New York.

1929

Pasquale Lolordo, Capone man and head of Chicago Unione Siciliano, killed, presumably by Aiello brothers.

February 14. Al Capone is questioned about his income by Dade County Solicitor in Miami. On the same day in Chicago, seven members of the Bugs Moran gang are machine-gunned to death. Moran himself misses walking into the trap by minutes. Moran accuses Capone of having it done. Capone says it must have been Moran, wiping out traitors. Because gunners were wearing police uniforms, even the police department is briefly suspected. Police prove that one of the guns in the Chicago massacre is one used in killing Frank Yale in New York.

May 8. Back from Miami, Capone invites Joe Giunta, Scalise and Anselmi to dinner so that they can talk over their opinions on the Unione. All three men are killed after dinner.

May 13-16. Five months after the first national organization meeting in Cleveland *there is another Mafia organizational meeting, this time in Atlantic City, New Jersey.* The Sicilians agree to work with a few non-Sicilian partners. About 30 gang leaders from around the country attend. From Philadelphia: Max Hoff, Sam Lazar and Charles Schwartz. From New York: Frank Costello, Lucky Luciano, Arthur Flegenheimer (also known as Dutch Schultz). From Chicago: Al Capone. From Atlantic City itself: Enoch J. (Nucky) Johnson, the numbers king. The nation is divided into spheres of influence. *Territorial disputes and arguments between gangs are to be taken to a nine-member national "commission."* Bugs Moran and remnants of the Aiello gang do not attend this conclave.

May 16. Al Capone purposely gets himself arrested in Philadelphia for carrying a gun, thereby putting himself out of harm's way during a difficult period in Chicago. Instead of the easy 90-day sentence he expected, he draws one year. He makes the best of it, with a private prison suite, use of a telephone and "open house" visitors' privileges.

Eliot Ness and his squad of "Untouchables" raid 19 Capone distilleries and six breweries, destroying almost $1,000,000 worth of equipment, trucks and liquor. Frank (The Enforcer) Nitti sentenced to 18 months for tax evasion.

October 24. Stock market crashes. Gambling, booze and vice gross in Chicago and New York drop by 50 percent.

November 18. Jake Guzik sentenced to five years for tax fraud. Nicolo Impostato, Chicago hood, goes to Kansas City to work for crime czar John Lazia, later killed.

During 1929, 115 bombs explode for various reasons in Chicago. No convictions.

1930

February. Joe the Boss Masseria, head of main gang of Sicilian hoods in New York, acknowledges Peter Morello as "the boss of bosses" of all gangs in city. He orders the Castellammarese Sicilians to kick back more profits. Salvatore Maranzano, Castellammarese head, refuses. Masseria has Maranzano lieutenant Tom Reina killed and sends Joseph Pinzola to Maranzano as a replacement. Maranzo kills Pinzola and Morello, the boss of bosses. These are the opening shots of the Castellammarese War of New York.

Joseph Valachi, later to gain fame as a squealer, is signed on as Maranzano triggerman. Joseph Bonnano swears Valachi to allegiance.

March. New York Sicilians take sides in Castellammarese War. Luciano, Genovese and Costello line up with Masseria, the new boss of bosses. Meyer Lansky and Dutch Schultz, though not Sicilians, say they are with Masseria. Ciro Terranova also with Masseria. Al Capone and other hoodlums around the country begin sending money to one side or another. Capone sends $5,000 per week to Masseria, for hiring guns, cars, etc. Maranzano forces include gangs of Joseph Profaci, Joseph Bonnano. Plans to take disputes of this sort to a national commission are briefly suspended.

May 16. Al Capone is released from Philadelphia jail after serving 10 months on gun-carrying charge and returns to Chicago.

Ralph Capone is sentenced to three years on tax charges.

June 9. Newspaper reporter Jake Lingle is killed in Chicago street by unidentified gunman. Lingle's death exposes him as highly paid payoff man for hoodlum fixes at City Hall. Immediately thereafter several other Chicago newsmen are revealed as go-betweens.

August 6. Judge Joseph F. Crater, New York Supreme Court Justice, disappears without a trace and is never seen again. Some say he had questionable hoodlum connections and either double-crossed someone or just knew too much and couldn't be bought.

Capone men finally kill Joseph Aiello of Chicago, who has been sending $5,000 a week to Maranzano forces in New York. In the ten years since 1920, records show that there have been 500 gangland slayings in Chicago alone.

There are 64 unsolved gang killings in the St. Louis area between 1930 and 1950. During this time the following gangs were formed, the survivors of some still operating today (1974): the Hogan gang, the Egan Rats, the Cuckoo gang, the so-called Green Dagoes and the Italian-American gang. The Cuckoos were mostly Syrians, the Hogans and Egans were Irish, Poles and Germans, the Green Dagoes were Sicilians, many transplanted from Chicago.

Kansas City gangs and St. Louis gangs often work together. A branch gang to the Green Dagoes was the Pillow gang, so called because its leader, one Carmelo Fresina, was once shot in the buttocks and ever after carried a pillow with him on which he sat. He eventually was shot in the head and died.

In central and southern Illinois, two gangs, the Birgers and the Sheltons, are powerful.

1931

April 1. The Castellammarese War in New York begins to go against Masseria, with Maranzano picking up support from gangs of Tommy (Three-Finger Brown) Lucchese, Joseph Magliocco and Gaetano Gagliano. Another important ally of Maranzano is the Buffalo don, Stefano Magaddino, who sends Marazano $5,000 per week, plus guns and cars.

April 10. Maranzano now commands some 600 armed men and Masseria forces are being killed like flies. Luciano, Costello and Terranova, among others, decide Maranzano will win and try to switch to his side. In exchange for their own safety, they promise to exterminate Masseria.

April 15. Luciano takes Masseria to dinner on Coney Island, where Masseria is killed.

April 16. Maranzano says that now he is the "boss of bosses." This does not go over well with other New York gang leaders and they object. Maranzano attempts to arrange the executions of, among others, Dutch Schultz, Costello, Genovese, Vincent Mangano, Joe Adonis.

September 11. Meyer Lansky and contract killers eliminate Maranzano. Forty other Maranzano thugs in New York killed in the next two days. In all, some 60 New York hoods have been cut down in the Castellammarese War.

September 15. *Lucky Luciano moves to set up nationwide syndicate along the lines discussed at the previous Cleveland and Atlantic City meetings.* He resurrects the "Commission" idea and states that there should be no "boss of bosses." New York is to be divided among five equal bosses. There are to be twenty-four bosses around the country, of which nine will be on the commission, to arbitrate disputes.

October 24. Al Capone draws 11 years in combined sentences on tax charges.

November. Luciano and Dutch Schultz from New York visit Al

Capone in jail. The New Yorkers are arguing over territory in New York. Schultz claims that most of New York should be his. Capone and Luciano are infuriated. Schultz's days are numbered.

1932

In Chicago Terry Druggan and Frank Lake sentenced to 18 months and two years, respectively, for failing to file tax returns.

September 1. An investigation of corruption in New York City government, led by Samuel Seabury, who was appointed by Governor Roosevelt, leads to the resignation of New York's playboy mayor, Jimmy Walker.

Washington, D.C. gambling club operator Jimmy La Fontaine is kidnaped by Philadelphia hoods and held for $100,000 ransom. It's paid and he is released.

1933

February 15. Chicago Mayor Anton Cermak, who has promised great reforms, is assassinated in Miami by Giuseppe Zangara, said to be an irrational person bent on killing President Roosevelt, but hitting Cermak instead. On his deathbed, however, Zangara says that the Capone gang simply wanted him to shoot the mayor.

Prohibition Amendment repealed.

Internal Revenue Agent Alvin E. Giesey quits IRS to set up own tax advice office. Cleveland gambler Morris Kleiman, whom Giesey had sent up on tax charges, offers him a job and certain other Cleveland clients, among them Big Al Polizzi, John Angersika, Chuck Polozzi, Moe Dalitz, Lou Rothkopf, Sam Tucker, Jerry Milano, Mushy Wexler.

1934

Two separate meetings in New York and Kansas City lead to the formation of the national crime syndicate.

1935

Jake Guzik released from Leavenworth, resumes leadership duties with Ralph Capone, also released. Tony Accardo and Paul the Waiter Ricca, onetime Capone underlings, approach head status in old Capone mob.

October 23. Dutch Schultz murdered in New Jersey.

462

1936

February 13. Machine-gun Jack McGurn killed by two men (with machine guns) in Chicago. Police suspect Bugs Moran loyalists who believed McGurn participated in St. Valentine's Day massacre.

Lester (Benny) Binion, run out of Dallas numbers rackets by other hoods, moves into Las Vegas's legal gaming. Keeps hand in Dallas rackets from afar.

Lucky Luciano sentenced to 30 to 50 years on white slavery charges. Prosecutor is Thomas E. Dewey.

1937

Genovese flees country because of murder charge.

1938

Nicolo Gentile arrested in New York on narcotics charge involving 88 persons in United States and Europe. Book found on Gentile in a *Who's Who* of national and international Mafia, for whom he was agent. Gentile jumps bail and returns to Sicily.

Bugsy Siegel sent to organize California.

Joseph De Luca in command narcotics branch of Mafia in Kansas City, Nicolo Impostato, formerly of Chicago, second in command. All members of Mafia or Black Hand in this narcotics traffic group financed by Mafia. Set up on very businesslike lines, legal adviser, supervisor, general manager, traveling representatives, bookkeeper and sales force. Developed contacts with narcotics sources at various ports, supplied Kansas City and Illinois. St. Louis, Missouri branch under direction of John Vitale, who was under Thomas Buffa and Tony Lapiparo, both chiefs of St. Louis Mafia.

1939

Johnny Torrio is sentenced to 30 months for tax evasion.

January 6. Al Capone released from Alcatraz. His mind is gone, due to advanced case of syphilis.

November 8. O'Hare, undercover agent for the government in Chicago for 15 years, is killed by men with shotguns. M.L. (Moe) Annenberg, racing news publisher, about to be jailed for income tax fraud, disbands his news service—the most important racing news distributor working with bookies nationwide. Arthur B. (Mickey) McBride, one of Annenberg's assistants, takes over. McBride is multimillionaire, owns extensive real estate holdings, a taxi fleet, football club, the Cleveland Browns, and has associated previously with many Cleveland hoodlums. His service is now called Continental Press.

1940

Big Al Polizzi, Cleveland Mafia leader, decides to go straight, invests in real estate with Arthur (Mickey) McBride, the founder of Continental Press.

Abe (Kid Twist) Reles tells all to Brooklyn D.A.

Chicago crime expert Virgil Peterson testifies that Meyer Lansky, Lucky Luciano and Bugsy Siegel once comprised enforcement branch of Costello organization—a group known as the Bug-Meyer mob of executioners. Lansky, Luciano and Siegel were called "The Homicide Squad" by other mobsters.

New Orleans dominated by Sicilian-born Mafia don Caloreo Minicari, known as Carlos Marcello. New Orleans becomes a provincial capital of the Costello-Lansky-Adonis mobs of New York and Miami. Costello's man in New Orleans is Philip (Dandy Phil) Kastel, who oversees Costello's slot machine and gambling interests. New Orleans becomes important point for narcotics imports.

1941

Frank Erickson, associate of New York's Frank Costello, and John (Boy Mayor) Patton, Capone's friend, sell their racetrack interests and finance Abe Allenberg, a New York attorney, in operation of Wofford Hotel, Miami. Partners include John Angersola (alias King) of Cleveland, and Anthony Carfano (alias Little Augie Pisano) of New York. The Wofford becomes meeting place for racketeers and headquarters for Erickson's extensive bookmaking operations in Florida, including concessions at the Roney Plaza, Boca Raton, and Hollywood Beach hotels and illegal bookmaking based on Florida racetracks.

November 12. Reles "falls" from sixth-story window, despite six-man police bodyguard.

1942

Police establish that one source of supply of Kansas City narcotics is the Mafia in Tampa, which receives supplies from

Marseilles via Cuba. Also Sebastiano Nani, onetime Brooklyn Mafia hoodlum, gets large shipments from New York for sale in Kansas City.

McBride, unwilling to run Continental himself, asks James M. Ragen to take over. Ragen has tax trouble, so his son James, Jr. takes over.

Costello, Joe Adonis, and Meyer Lansky move into Las Vegas and establish the Flamingo Hotel, the plushest on the Strip at that time. Bugsy Siegel is put in Vegas to oversee the Flamingo and to supervise sales and collections for the wire service. Siegel muscles in on Vegas bookmaking operations.

Government makes deal with Luciano, who's still in prison, to help fight wartime sabotage on New York docks.

1943

Three Chicago syndicate gangsters, Paul Ricca, Louis Campagna and Charles (Cherry Nose) Gioe and other members of mob are sent to penitentiary for 10 years on conviction of conspiracy to extort money from California movie industry by threatening to call strikes. George Browne, President of International Association of Theatrical Stage Employees, and gangster Willie Bioff are central figures in the case. Great efforts are made to get three leading gangsters' sentences commuted.

Kansas City investigation of two alleged Mafiosi, Carl Carramusa, and Tony Lapiparo's associate, Tom Buffa, of St. Louis. Buffa testifies for government only in a collateral matter involving perjury of fellow Mafia member's mistress. His assassination is unsuccessfully attempted on his return to St. Louis but he is eventually killed by gunfire in 1946 in Lodi, California.

Frank Nitti, faced with another prison term for racketeering, kills himself.

U.S. Army finds itself a partner in Italy with Genovese, exiled New York hood. The Army thinks he is a kindly Italian gentleman of some influence who is helping the Army to restore government and control black-marketing.

1944

Genovese returned to United States to stand trial for ten-year-old murder. Case dropped.

Frank Costello is boss of New York's main gang during Genovese's exile and Luciano's imprisonment.

465

Lepke Buchalter executed.

Big Al Polizzi of Cleveland, the "retired" gang leader, convicted of dealing in black-market whiskey. He serves four months and retires again to Miami.

S&G bookmaking service started in Miami Beach by five local boys: Harold Salvey, Jules Levitt, Charles Friedman, Sam Cohen, and Edward (Lucky Eddie) Rosenbaum. S&G syndicate grosses $26 million in 1948, Crime Commission Director Sullivan estimates that annual gross is between $30 and $40 million, with a net profit to operators of $4 to $8 million.

1946

Chicago-Capone mob wants control of Continental Press, the sports wire service. It would provide profits galore and thousands of jobs, and also could be stretched to provide virtual monopoly over illegal bookmaking in United States and would add tremendous power to Chicago crime syndicate. But owner James Ragen, Sr. refuses to be muscled. First approach from mob is a conciliatory and quite dishonest proposition put by Jake Greasy Thumb Guzik, Tony the Enforcer Accardo and Murray the Camel Humphries, who say they do not want to oust Ragen, but become his partners, sharing profits, and increasing business by their participation. However Ragen is afraid that once mob moves in and learns how business works, he'll be found dead in an alley. He is also sure that the Federal Bureau of Investigation would never allow Capone mob to gain control of interstate wire service. At first Capone mob counters Ragen's opposition by setting up its own wire service—Trans-American Publishing and News Service. Because of gang connections Trans-American makes deep inroads into Continental's business.

June. Ragen is shot down in a Chicago street and dies in the hospital.

1947

January 25. Al Capone dies of brain hemorrhage, age 48.

June. Bugsy Siegel, expanding in every direction in Las Vegas, is rubbed out by Chicago and New York hoods for "being too independent" and for forgetting it was them who set him up out there to look after mob interests.

1950

Kefauver Committee hears how Mickey Cohen goes to Los Angeles and manages to work with Jack Dragna, named by the California Crime Commission as the Al Capone of Los Angeles. Cohen eventually falls out with Sicilian-controlled Mafia of Los Angeles and survives five assassination attempts and police harassment. He later serves time in Texas.

Kefauver Committee's "current list" of Cleveland gambling syndicate members: Morris Kleinman, Samuel (Gameboy) Miller, Moe Dalitz (alias Davis), Louis Rothkopf (also known as Rhody and Zarumba), Samuel Tucker and Thomas J. McGinty. Gangsters named include the Polizzis, James Licavoli, Jerry Milano, Joseph DiCarlo.

Kefauver hearings report states that Ralph Capone is on the syndicate's national commission. Chicago itself is controlled by Ralph and Jake Guzik.

Kefauver investigators study testimony of Abe (Kid Twist) Reles, Murder, Inc. informer whose testimony sent Lepke, Buchalter and eight others to chair. Between 1930 and 1940 Murder, Inc. is credited with 130 "for hire" killings.

First Kefauver hearing May 26, in Miami, Florida. Hearings are nationwide and last one year. They establish that the national crime syndicate in the fifties is based on a faction led by Frank Costello, Joe Adonis and Meyer Lansky on the East Coast, and the Chicago mob—the old Capone syndicate. Twenty-five to 30 members of Mafia in Kansas City, including Tony Gizzo, Joe and Frank De-Luca, Pete and Joseph DiGiovanni and Jim Balestrere.

The "Five Iron Men" of Kansas City are Balestrere, Gizzo, Lococo, Charlie Binaggio (later slain) and Charlie Gargotta (murdered henchman of Binaggio). This list is given to Kefauver Committee by Special Assistant U.S. Attorney General Max H. Goldschein.

At Kefauver hearing in Washington, William Moretti, New Jersey gambler and racketeer, testifies that he never heard the word "Mafia" in his life.

At Kefauver hearing in Chicago, Jack Dragna of Los Angeles testifies that he only knows what he reads in the papers about the Mafia. Insists he had never heard of Mafia or Black Hand as a boy in Sicily.

A California police inspector tells Kefauver hearings of murder of Abraham Davidian, who was witness in narcotics case against Joe Sica, a Mafia member. Davidian was fatally shot in mother's home while case pending. Chicago and San Francisco racketeer Nick DeJohn garroted after a meeting in Poodle Dog restaurant, a known Mafia hangout.

Kefauver Committee says in report to Senate that its considered judgment is that Continental Press Service, while professing to be law-abiding and independent, is tool of Chicago-Capone syndicate. The wire service keeps illegal gambling going, which finances a variety of other criminal activities in the United States.

Chicago gang figures: Jake (Greasy Thumb) Guzik, Tony (Joe Batters) Accardo, Murray (the Camel) Humphreys, Anthony (Tough Tony) Capezio, Capone's cousin, Rocco Fischetti. Also lesser fry such as Sam (Golf Bag) Hunt, Frank (Chew Tobacco) Ryan and many others.

Former Chicago Police Lieutenant Drury is killed before he can appear as witness before Kefauver Committee. One witness questioned by committee is Robert (Big Bob) McCullough, an enemy of Drury's.

Joint leaders of Chicago syndicate are Jake Guzik and Tony Accardo, an unlikely partnership, as police records show that in 1945 Accardo was picked up for a gang-style kidnaping of Guzik. Guzik reputedly paid $75,000 for his own release.

Policy-wheel (numbers) operations run in Chicago are very profitable and are investigated by Kefauver Committee. One, called Roman Silver Wheel, is run by Peter Tremont and Patrick Manno. Manno is an important man in policy end of the Chicago syndicate. Three of his brothers are also in Roman Silver Wheel operation —Tom (Mousey), Nick (Jeff) and Fred. A rival setup is Erie-Buffalo Wheel, a family enterprise of Julius Benvenuti. Julius had once done Capone a favor, so had immunity from mob, but when his brothers, Leo and Caesar, take over at his death, that immunity no longer applies.

Kefauver Committee investigates crime in Tampa, well known as important port in nationwide Mafia-backed narcotics ring. Sinister links found between Tampa, Miami, New Orleans, Kansas City, Chicago, Cleveland, New York, Havana, in narcotics, gambling and murder-for-hire. Local law enforcement is corrupt—Cuban gamblers who run bolita racket call Sheriff

Hugh Culbreath "Melon Head." In 19 years there are 14 murders and 6 attempted assassinations in Tampa—and one conviction. Long-standing rivalry between Mafia-backed clique of Sicilian and Italian criminals and a larger group of Cubans, with some local talent as well, and the willingness of the law to go along with underworld, are the main causes of crime in Tampa. One of the fugitives from the committee's process is Santa Trafficante, Sr., reputed Mafia leader in Tampa for more than 20 years.

1951

April. Charles Fischetti, the late Al Capone's cousin and one of his successors to leadership of the Chicago syndicate, dies of a heart attack in Miami Beach after he and his brother Rocco have been taken into custody on a Senate arrest warrant. Fischetti, who liked to pose as "Dr. Charles Fischer, noted art connoisseur," and his brother had evaded a Kefauver Committee subpoena for months by hiding out in Brazil.

Kefauver Committee investigates three notorious gambling joints—Club Boheme, Colonial Inn and Club Greenacres, which have operated for years in Florida. Well-known out-of-state gamblers associated with these clubs, according to testimony of Daniel Sullivan, director of Greater Miami Crime Commission, were: Joe Adonis, Lansky brothers, Meyer and Jake; Vincent (Jimmy Blue Eyes) Alo, and Joe Massei and William G. Bischoff (alias Lefty Clark) from Detroit. Smaller fry from Chicago and Florida also had pieces of Colonial Inn operation.

1952

Willie Moretti has brain damage, talks too much and is killed by Genovese's men.

Vincent Mangano disappears. Anastasia suspected. Mangano rumored to be in concrete foundation of public housing project.

1953

Gaetano Galiano dies of natural causes. Tommy Lucchese takes his place as mob head.

1955

Bill Bonanno joins father's organization after Anastasia makes offer to have him join his own mob.

1956

May. Costello sentenced on tax charges, does year in jail, then released while awaiting appeal.

August 18. Wedding in New York of Bill Bonanno, son of Mafia don Joseph Bonanno, and Rosalie Profaci, niece of Mafia boss Joseph Profaci. Attended by entire hierarchy of Mafia, including Genovese, Costello, Anastasia, Joseph Barbara (whose place was used for the Apalachin meeting) Zerilli, (Detroit), Giancana and Accardo (Chicago), Magaddino (Buffalo). Representatives from everywhere else. The Los Angeles delegation numbers about 80.

1957

May. Vincent (the Chin) Gigante wounds Costello in head in his apartment. Genovese men suspected. Costello retires.

October 25. Albert Anastasia rubbed out in barber shop of New York Sheraton Hotel.

Frank Garofalo visits Sicily just before Apalachin meeting and decides to stay there for good.

Sixty-three Mafia members from all over United States found together in Apalachin, New York.

Johnny Torrio dies at 75 after a heart attack.

Bugs Moran, serving ten-year term for bank robbery, dies of lung cancer.

1959

Genovese takes drugs fall.

New Orleans don is Carlos Marcello.

1960

Gallo brothers in Brooklyn revolt against Profaci organization. National Commission says Profaci should handle it himself. Bonanno and Profaci object. Gallo and Profaci mobs start shooting. Gallo mob kidnaps Joseph Magliocco, three other Profaci men. Profaci flees to Florida, and is forced to make concessions on sharing income with Gallos. Much loss of prestige for Profaci. Many Gallo men killed, but eventual peace, or armed truce. Profaci and Bonanno suspect National Commission members Carlo Gambino and Thomas Lucchese of inspiring Gallo revolt. Son of New York's Lucchese married to daughter of Gambino. Magliocco's sister is Joe Profaci's wife. Joseph Bonanno is on run during Gallo war, but wouldn't have helped Profaci anyway, because it might have started nationwide mob war.

Between 1919 and 1960, Chicago's Police Superintendent Orlando W. Wilson estimates that 976 gangland killings had taken place in Chicago alone.

1962

Joseph Profaci dies of cancer. Joe Magliocco takes over mob. Tony (Bender) Strollo killed, possibly by Tommy Eboli on Genovese's orders. Strollo in dope business against family rules and holding out money on Genovese. National Commission members after Profaci's death: Genovese (in jail), Bonanno, Gambino, Lucchese, all of New York, Magaddino of Buffalo, Giancana of Chicago, Zerilli of Detroit, Angelo Bruno of Philadelphia.

1963

Stefano Magaddino, boss of Buffalo and the Ohio Valley, is brother-in-law of Gaspar Di Gregorio, one of New York City's Joe Bonanno's captains. In 1963 Magaddino decides he doesn't like Bonanno's individuality or his refusal to come to National Commission meetings. He urges Di Gregorio to branch out on his own and take Bonanno's gang with him.

Joseph Valachi, minor Mafia triggerman, spills all he knows to Senate committee. Valachi becomes famous during TV hearings. Ensuing publicity and public outcry causes Justice Department and local police to attack Mafia on all fronts. Use of wiretapping under Attorney General Robert Kennedy drives Mafia to distraction.

July 25. Magliocco, who has taken over Profaci mob, sends men to kill Gambino and Lucchese, believing they inspired Gallo revolt. The killers fail. Gambino and Lucchese think younger Bonanno involved, and trying to unite Profaci and Bonanno organizations.

December 28. Magliocco dies of heart attack. Joe Colombo takes over Profaci mob.

1964

July. Elder Bonanno expelled from Canada. National Commission still trying to reach him for talks.

In famous "French Connection" case, New York police and feds intercept heroin shipment of 116 pounds, largest ever confiscated. Patsy Fuca and other Brooklyn henchmen of Little Angie Tuminaro charged and convicted, along with three Frenchmen.

French mastermind Jean Jehan escapes police net and returns to France.

1965

Meeting at restaurant in Cedarhurst, Long Island to discuss Joseph Bonanno's hiding out. Attending: Sam Giancana, Thomas Eboli (Genovese gang's temporary leader), and Carmine Tramunti, a Lucchese lieutenant.

March 11. Gaspar Di Gregorio, former trusted lieutenant of Joe Bonanno, defects, forming his own mob. Enlists other Bonanno men and tries to take over Bonanno empire, on ground that Bonanno is never around, Bonanno is giving too much authority to son, Salvatore (Bill), who's considered too green, and that Bonanno is out of favor with National Commission because he was too independent.

The New York Times estimates that the Genovese organization has 27 millionaires among its members.

FBI crackdown leads to 400 arrests in New York and other arrests in Columbus, St. Paul, Denver, St. Louis, Nashville and Chester, West Virginia.

New York District Attorney Robert Morgenthau has three grand juries look into organized crime.

November 14. FBI photographs wedding of Di Gregorio's daughter in Long Island.

1966

January 28. Di Gregorio forces, pretending to want peace meeting with Bonanno forces, ambush young Bonanno and others on Troutman Street in Brooklyn. Lots of shooting but no injuries.

May 17. Joseph Bonanno turns up at New York Court House after being missing from October 1964.

May 17. Joseph Notaro, Bonanno lieutenant, dies of heart attack.

La Stella restaurant Mafia meeting in Queens, New York. Present: Santo Trafficante, Miami; Carlos Marcello, New Orleans; Gambino, Colombo, Eboli and Mike Miranda, all of New York.

1967

January. Bill Bonanno and five other men are convicted in Canada of carrying guns. They are fined and deported.

October. Two Bonanno men wounded in Brooklyn. Three Di Gregorio men are killed by machine-gun fire at Cypress Gardens restaurant in Queens, New York.

1968

March. Sam Perrone, a Bonanno lieutenant, is killed at Brooklyn warehouse.

April. Mike Consolo, a Di Gregorio man, shot and killed, presumably for interfering in the Banana War.

Summer. Bonanno home in Tucson, Arizona, is bombed.

September. Frank Mari, Di Gregorio triggerman, and two others disappear, presumed dead.

1969

February 6. Thomas Zummo, Di Gregorio man, killed as he enters his girlfriend's apartment house. The Banana War ends with ten dead.

February 11. Vito Genovese dies in prison of a heart ailment. His successors are Tommy Eboli, Jerry Catena, Mike Miranda. Philip Rastelli in cahoots with Di Gregorio gang and Paul Sciacca, his heir apparent.

President Nixon asks for $61 million to combat organized crime, the narcotics business in particular. United States agents begin to exert pressure on dope racket from New York to Turkey. French and Mexican governments, along with Iran and Italy, begin to feel pressure from United States to help out on their end.

1970

Joseph Colombo charged with tax evasion and contempt. Joseph Colombo, Jr. charged with conspiring to melt down silver coins for silver content.

Summer. Joseph Colombo organizes pickets in front of FBI Building, Manhattan, to protest slurs on Italian-Americans. Objects to insinuations in *The Godfather* book and movie that there is a Mafia. Colombo says the words "Mafia" and "Cosa Nostra" are offensive to Italian-Americans. Colombo appears on Dick Cavett TV show. Campaign actually gets support in some liberal quarters.

1971

May. Rumor has it that Carlo Gambino, New York don, is not pleased at attention Colombo is drawing to the "organization."

Colombo heads old Profaci family. Gallo, once a rebel Profaci member, now a rebel Colombo member, recruits black hoods to replace depleted Mafia ranks. Gallo feels that Colombo is publicity-mad and is neglecting business.

June 28. Joseph Colombo shot three times and crippled by black gunman at Italian-American Unity Day parade at Columbus Circle. His assailant is killed immediately by unidentified gunman. Assassination attempt may have been arranged by National Commission, annoyed over Colombo's public antics, or by Carlo Gambino, for the same reason, or by Gallo in a take-over move.

1972

April 7. Joey Gallo assassinated in Little Italy, New York. Perhaps another Gambino victim, or Colombo avengers. War between Gallo mob and Colombo mob.

July. Tommy Eboli shot five times in head as Carlo Gambino reportedly continues drive to be the "boss of bosses" of New York. Gambino is 73 years old.

August. Carmine Tramunti acknowledges Gambino as "boss of bosses" in New York. Tramunti heads former Tommy Lucchese mob. Phil Rastelli, at this writing still alive, heads old Bonanno gang and does not recognize Gambino as his superior. Some 20 gang killings in New York in 1971-72.

October. Brooklyn DA's office reveals it has tapped phones and overheard conversations in trailer headquarters of New York mob. Trailer parked in Brooklyn junk yard, is visited by members of all five New York families. Brooklyn DA issues subpoenas for 677 people, most of them known hoods. The 1,600,000 feet of FBI tapes show that Mafia controls 200 legitimate businesses in New York City, and has politicians, businessmen and judges for friends. Rackets exposed include prostitution, bookmaking, counterfeiting, hijacking, insurance frauds, smuggling (mostly cigarettes), labor rackets and dope pushing. Trailer was base for Paul Vario, captain in former Lucchese mob.

New York police admit that the dope confiscated in the "French Connection" case of 1963-65 has been stolen from police property room, along with 500 pounds of heroin from other cases. On the street, heroin in this amount could be worth $100 million.

November. Police corruption exposed in New York. One policeman testifies that some entire precincts, from captains on down, are on the take from petty hoodlums and major crime figures.

Meyer Lansky was arrested in Miami by FBI agents after being expelled from Israel as an undesirable. Lansky was under indictment by grand juries in New York, Las Vegas and Miami for gambling and income tax evasion.

December. The Knapp Commission, in an investigation of the New York City Police Department, found that "a majority" of the city's police were involved in some sort of wrongdoing as of October 1971. This included hiring out as killers, some in the pay of organized crime, and involvement in narcotics traffic.

1973

February. Francis Waters, the principal federal narcotics agent in the "French Connection" case, was indicted on charges of dealing in heroin and cocaine from 1968 on.

October. Representative Frank J. Brasco of Brooklyn, was indicted by a New York federal grand jury on charges of conspiring to receive illegal payoffs in 1968 from a Bronx trucking firm headed by an alleged Mafia member.

1974

Summer. There have been over a dozen gangland-style slayings in New York City in the past two months. The police believe that several Mafia families are involved, but as yet have not solved any of the cases.

BIBLIOGRAPHY

Adams, S. *The Incredible Era*. Boston: n.p., 1939.

Allen, Edward J. *Merchants of Menace: The Mafia*. Springfield, Ill.: Charles C. Thomas, 1962.

Allsop, Kenneth. *The Bootleggers*. London: n.p., 1961.

American Bar Association. Report on Organized Crime and Law Enforcement. n.p., 1952.

Asbury, Herbert. *The Gangs of New York*. Garden City, N.Y.: Garden City Publishing Co., 1928.

Bazelow, David T. *The Paper Economy*. New York: Random House, 1963.

Bennett, James O'Donnell: *Chicago Gangland*. Chicago: Chicago Tribune, 1929.

Berger, Meyer. *The Eight Million*. New York: Simon & Schuster, 1942.

Bristow, Joseph L. *Fraud and Politics at the Turn of the Century*. Jericho, N.Y.: Exposition Press, 1952.

Cressey, Donald R. *Theft of the Nation*. New York: Blue Ribbon Books, 1935.

Cumming, Homer. *Selected Papers*. New York: Charles Scribner's Sons, 1939.

Dedmon, Emmett. *Fabulous Chicago*. New York: Random House, 1963.

Demaris, Ovid. *Captive City*. New York: Lyle Stuart, 1969.

FBI Law Enforcement Bulletin. Washington, D.C.: Government Printing Office, 1938.

Feder, Sid and Joesten, Joachim. *The Luciano Story*. New York: David McKay, 1938.

Goodman, Walter. *All Honorable Men*. London: n.p., 1964.

Hearing Before the Permanent Subcommittee on Investigations, Organized Crime and Illicit Traffic in Narcotics. Washington, D.C.: U.S. Senate, 1963.

Held, Virginia. *The Bewildered Age*. New York: Clarkson N. Potter, 1962.

Jennings, Dean. *We Only Kill Each Other, The Life and Bad Times of Bugsy Siegel.* Englewood Cliffs, N.J.: Prentice-Hall, Inc., 1968.

Kefauver, Estes. *Crime in America.* New York: Doubleday & Co., 1951.

Kennedy, Robert F. *The Enemy Within.* New York: n.p., 1960.

Kobler, John. *Capone.* New York: G. P. Putnam's Sons, 1971.

Landesco, John. *Organized Crime in Chicago; Part III of the Illinois Crime Survey.* Chicago: Illinois Association for Criminal Justice, 1929.

Lewis, Norman. *The Honored Society, The Mafia.* London: n.p., 1964.

Lynch, Denis Tilden. *Criminals and Politicians.* New York: Macmillan, 1932.

Maas, Peter. *The Valachi Papers.* New York: G.P. Putnam's Sons, 1968.

McClellan, John L. *Crime Without Punishment.* New York: Macmillan, 1967.

Merz, Charles. *The Dry Decade.* New York: Doubleday, Doran and Co., 1931.

Messick, Hank. *The Silent Syndicate.* New York: Macmillan, 1967.

Pasley, F.D. *Al Capone.* London: n.p., 1966 (reprint).

Reid, Ed. *Mafia.* New York: Random House, 1952.

Salerno, Ralph and Tompkins, John. *The Crime Confederation.* New York: Doubleday & Co., 1969.

Senate Special Committee to Investigate Organized Crime in Interstate Commerce (Kefauver Committee), 1951-1952.

Smith, A. *On the Way to Repeal.* New York: New Outlook, 1933.

Sondern, Frederic, Jr. *Brotherhood of Evil: The Mafia.* New York: Farrar, Straus & Cudahy, 1959.

Stead, W.T. *If Christ Came to Chicago.* London: n.p., 1893.

Talese, Gay. *Honor Thy Father.* New York: World Publishing, 1972.

Tannenbaum, Frank. *Crime and the Community.* Lexington, Mass.: Ginn & Co., 1938.

Task Force Report: The Police, U.S. President's Commission on Law Enforcement and Administration of Justice. Washington, D.C.: Government Printing Office, 1967.

Thompson, Craig and Raymond, Allen. *Gang Rule in New York.* New York: Dial Press, 1940.

Turkus, Burton B. and Feder, Sid. *Murder, Inc.* New York: Farrar, Straus & Young, 1951.

Velie, L. *Labor, U.S.A.* New York: n.p., 1959.

Wilson, C. and Pickett, D. *The Case for Prohibition.* New York: n.p., 1923.

Wilson, E. *The Lexicon of Prohibition: The American Earthquake.* New York: n.p., 1958.

Wilson, H.H. *Congress: Corruption and Compromise*. New York: Rinehart, 1951.

Ziegler, Edward. *Men Who Make Us Rich*. New York: Macmillan, 1962.